絶対『英語の耳』になる!
ビジネス英語リスニング
難関トレーニング50

長尾和夫＋トーマス・マーティン◉著

三修社

Preface
はじめに

　『絶対「英語の耳」になる！ビジネス英語リスニング 難関トレーニング 50』は、好評をいただいている同シリーズの第 6 作目の書籍として企画されました。前作ニューズ・リスニングに続きテーマ別のリスニング・ドリル・ブックとしては 2 作目となります。

　本書では、特にネイティヴとの国際ビジネスの場面で頻繁に遭遇するボキャブラリーの学習や、音声変化に焦点を絞ったリスニング学習が行えるように、アメリカ企業と中国の下請け企業が進めるプロジェクトがリアルに展開していく様子を、ユニットの進行とともに追跡していきます。

　臨場感溢れる国際ビジネスの起承転結が本書の中に丸ごと収まっているため、最終ページまでを読み終え、聴き終える頃には、リスニング力や語彙力の大きな向上が見込めるだけではなく、国際ビジネスの一連の流れまでもが、みなさんの身につくような仕掛けになっています。

　日本人学習者がビジネス英語のリスニングを難しいと感じるのは、おもに次の 2 点の障害が立ちはだかっているからです。

❶ ビジネス英会話のボキャブラリーには、学校英語で学習しなかった特殊なものが多くあり、耳慣れない専門用語やフレーズが頻出する点。また、専門用語や使用フレーズが日本国内で使用されているものや日本人が想像しているものと異なっている場合も多々あること。

❷ ビジネス英会話でのネイティヴの会話速度が、場合によって非常に速くなり、独特の音声変化が生じる点。音の脱落や連結、同化などが数多くまた重なり合って登場すること。特に電話での会話など音質の悪い状態でのコミュニケーションでは、音声の脱落などが通常よりも激しくなる場合もある。

　つまり、「専門的な語彙」＋「独特の音声変化」というふたつ壁が混じり合って同時に存在することで、ビジネス英語の聴き取りは、日本人にとってかなりハードルの高いものになっているのです。

　本書は、これらの問題点を克服していただくために、ネイティヴ・ビジネス・パーソンの音声変化に慣れるとともに、国際ビジネスで頻出する多様なボキャブラリーも身につけられる構成となっています。ビジネスの開始から、見積依頼、価格交渉、スケジュールの決定、契約、生産、進捗報告、トラブル、出張、国際展示会など、多岐にわたる代表的なビジネス・シーンを 50 ユニットの中にバランスよく組み込んでおきました。50 の各シーンそれぞれでは、次の 5 つのステージをこなしながら学習を進めていく仕組みです。

Stage 01	穴埋めビジネス・リスニング
Stage 02	ビジネス・ボキャビル
Stage 03	日本語トランスレーション
Stage 04	英文トランスクリプション
Stage 05	音声変化をチェック

　本書で特徴的な学習法は、シーンごとのダイアローグ（モノローグ）音声を、5つのステージで繰り返し聴き直すことです。Stage 01 では予備知識なしで聴き取りを行い穴埋め問題を解く、Stage 02 では、ボキャブラリーをチェックしてから再度の聴き取り、Stage 03 では日本語で意味を確認してからの聴き取り、Stage 04 では英文を確認してからの聴き取り、最後の Stage 05 では、音声変化のルールを確認してからの聴き取りと、様々なトレーニングを提供しています。

　このように 5 つのステージで重層的なリスニング学習を繰り返すことで、ビジネス英会話の聴き取りに慣れ親しんでいただくことが本書の主眼なのです。

　音声 CD には、
　　（1）ナチュラルスピードのビジネス・ダイアローグ（英語音声）
　　（2）ボキャブラリー（英語／日本語音声）
　　（3）音声変化スロー／ナチュラル（英語音声）
　の 3 種類の音を収録しておきました。

　また、本書の 50 のユニットの内容は典型的な国際ビジネスを再現するために書き起こしたフィクション・ストーリーとなっており、登場する人物名・組織名などはすべて、実在の事物とは一切関係がありません。

　本書の 50 のビジネス・シーンでのドリルをクリアすれば、1000 を超える国際ビジネスの必須ボキャブラリーが身につきます。また、エクササイズに登場する 800 フレーズ超の音声変化に耳慣らしすることで、国際ビジネスの中での英語の多様な音声変化にも十分に対応できる耳づくりが可能です。

　本書が、読者のみなさんの「ビジネス英語の耳」を徹底的に鍛え上げ、国際ビジネスにおけるリスニング力の大きな向上のお役に立てたとすれば著者としてこれ以上のよろこびはありません。

　最後になりますが、本書の実現にご尽力いただいた三修社のスタッフのみなさんへの感謝の気持ちをここにお伝えしておきます。

A+Café 代表 長尾和夫
2012 年 5 月 25 日

Contents — ビジネス英語リスニング◆難関トレーニング50

はじめに 2
本書の使い方 6
本書に登場するルールの用語 8

Unit 01 新規顧客からの問い合わせ
Service Inquiry from Potential Customer 10

Unit 02 見積依頼のフォローアップ
Follow up on Quotation Request 14

Unit 03 プロジェクト詳細の連絡 ①
Detailed Communication About the Project 1 18

Unit 04 プロジェクト詳細の連絡 ②
Detailed Communication About the Project 2 22

Unit 05 価格の交渉 ①
Pricing Negotiation 1 26

Unit 06 価格の交渉 ②
Pricing Negotiation 2 30

Unit 07 エンドユーザーからの受注確定
Business from End User Awarded 34

Unit 08 中国工場での監査依頼
Customer Request for Business Visit/Plant Audit 38

Unit 09 出張の手配
Making Travel Arrangements for Trip 42

Unit 10 出張の詳細について
Confirmation of Business Trip Details 46

Unit 11 空港での待ち合わせ
Pickup at the Airport 50

Unit 12 工場を案内する
Plant Tour 54

Unit 13 上司への紹介
Introduction to Management 58

Unit 14 ランチ・ミーティング
Lunch Meeting 62

Unit 15 製品コンセプトのプレゼン ①
Product Concept Presentation 1 66

Unit 16 製品コンセプトのプレゼン ②
Product Concept Presentation 2 70

Unit 17 ビジネス・ミーティング ①
Business Meeting 1 74

Unit 18 ビジネス・ミーティング ②
Business Meeting 2 78

Unit 19 ビジネス・ミーティング ③
Business Meeting 3 82

Unit 20 価格の交渉 ③
Pricing Negotiation 3 86

Unit 21 ミーティングのまとめ
Meeting Summary 90

Unit 22 出張中のお世話へのお礼
Expression of Appreciation for Business Trip 94

Unit 23 契約書の草案
Drafting the Contract 98

Unit 24 契約書の修正について
Contract Revision 102

Unit 25	契約内容への同意 Contract Detail Agreement 106
Unit 26	試作品発注の訂正依頼 Requesting Correction of Sample Purchase Order 110
Unit 27	進捗の報告 Progress Report 114
Unit 28	計画の大幅な見直し依頼① Major Plan Revision Request 1 118
Unit 29	計画の大幅な見直し依頼② Major Plan Revision Request 2 122
Unit 30	注文数の緊急増加 Sudden Order Increase 126
Unit 31	新スケジュールでの進捗報告 New Schedule Progress Report 130
Unit 32	製品の完成 Product Completion 134
Unit 33	プロトタイプでトラブル発生 Trouble with the Prototype 138
Unit 34	アメリカへの出張依頼 Request for Overseas Business Trip 142
Unit 35	緊急の海外出張 Urgent Overseas Business Trip 146
Unit 36	アメリカ行きのフライト Flight to America 150
Unit 37	入国審査 Clearing Immigration 154
Unit 38	ホテルへのチェックイン Checking Into the Hotel 158
Unit 39	顧客のオフィスを訪問する Visit to the Customer Office 162
Unit 40	製品の問題箇所を検証する Determining the Product Issue 166
Unit 41	製品のトラブルシューティング Troubleshooting the Product 170
Unit 42	不具合についての打ち合わせ Meeting About the Defective Parts 174
Unit 43	ホテルのチェックアウト Checking Out of the Hotel 178
Unit 44	問題解決に関する連絡 Confirmation of the Problem Resolution 182
Unit 45	代替品の検査合格の連絡 Replacement Parts Pass Inspection 186
Unit 46	エキスポにて At the Expo Booth 190
Unit 47	エキスポでの成果 Success Report on the Expo 194
Unit 48	新しい販路 Expansion of Market/New End Users 198
Unit 49	パーティーでの祝杯 Celebration Party 202
Unit 50	メイへのお礼 Thank You Call to May 206

How to Use
本書の使い方

A: ユニット番号とユニット見出し

　ユニットの番号と見出しを掲載してあります。見出しから大まかな内容を推測して、リスニングを開始しましょう。

B: Stage 01: 穴埋めビジネス・リスニング

　まず最初のステージでは、CD を聴きながら空欄部分を穴埋めしてみましょう。空欄部分には音声変化を含む英単語や英語のフレーズが入っています。
　一度で聴き取れなかった場合は、もう一度、聴き直してみてもいいでしょう。

C: 空欄付きダイアローグ原稿

　① 〜 ⑮ の番号の後ろの空欄を穴埋めしてみましょう。

D: Stage 02: ビジネス・ボキャビル

　ここでは、Stage 01 のダイアローグに登場した語句をチェックしましょう。ビジネスに頻出する英単語とその日本語訳を簡潔にまとめてあります。CD にも英語と日本語の両方の音声が入っていますので、書籍を持ち歩かずに学習を行うことも可能です。
　単語学習を終えたら、もう一度 Stage 01 に立ち戻って音声を聴き直してみましょう。聴解力が単語を知っている場合と知らない場合にどのように異なるか実感できると思います。

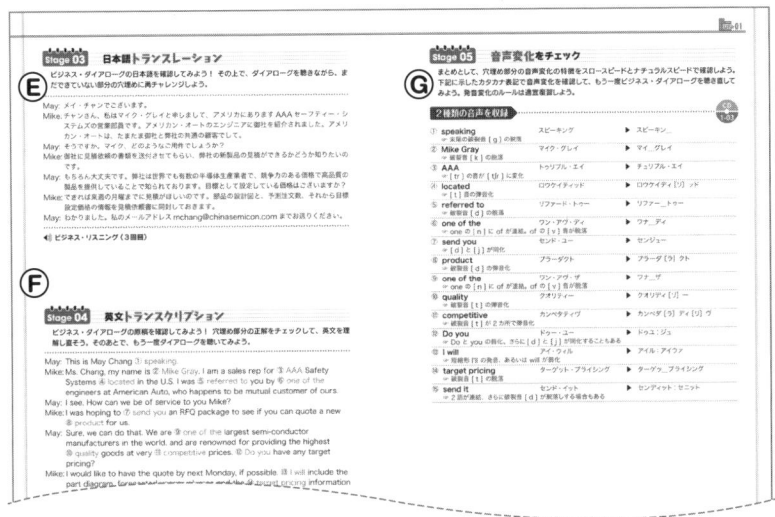

E: Stage 03: 日本語トランスレーション

このステージでは、ビジネス・ダイアローグの日本語訳を頭に入れてみましょう。ダイアローグの内容を理解した上で、もう一度聴き直すことで、余裕をもって音声に集中できるようになり、一段と聴き取りがしやすくなります。

F: Stage 04: 英文トランスクリプション

Stage 04 はビジネス・ダイアローグをすべて文字にして書き出してあります。穴埋めできていなかったところも文字でチェックしてみてから、もう一度ダイアローグ音声を聴き取ってみましょう。さらに格段に英文がよく聴き取れると感じると思います。

G: Stage 05 音声変化をチェック

Stage 05 は、ビジネス・リスニングのまとめとして、空欄部分の音声を、変化していないスロー・スピードの音声と変化語のナチュラル・スピードの音声の両方で収録してあります。

テキストでは、左から順に

【英語の語句】－【変化前の音声のカタカナ】－【変化後の音声のカタカナ】

の順で示してあります。また、次の行では ☞ マークのあとに【音声変化のルール】を簡潔に解説しておきました。

このステージで、音声変化にさらに耳慣らししてから、最後にもう一度ダイアローグの聴き取りにチャレンジしてみましょう。

学習の順番はみなさんの考えで変更していただいてもいいでしょう。本書の狙いはあくまでもボキャブラリーと音声変化の法則を身につけながらビジネス英会話に耳慣らししていくことなのです。その点をしっかり頭に入れて学習を進めてください。

本書に登場するルールの用語

本書では発音のルールを説明するために、次の5つの用語をおもに用いています。本文のCD音声を聴きながら、以下の用語を実地で確認していきましょう。

❶ **脱落**：英語の音の一部が消えてなくなる場合に「脱落」という言葉で説明しています。例えば、good boy の good では [d] の音が脱落してなくなり、「グッ＿ボーイ」のように発話される傾向にあります。

❷ **連結**：英語の音声の中で子音と母音が連続する場面では、音の連結が頻繁に生じます。リエゾンとも呼ばれます。例えば、on it「オン・イット」では、on の [n] の音に it の [ɪ] の音が連なって「オニット」といった発音に変化しますが、これを連結として説明しています。

❸ **弾音化**：英語の破裂音 [t] や [d] などに母音が連なっているところで、よくこの弾音化が起こります。例えば、get away では、get の [t] に away の先頭の母音 [ə] が連なっていますが、この [tə] の部分が [タ] ではなく [ダ] や [ラ] に近い弾くような音に変化してしまいます。「ゲッタウェイ」ではなく「ゲッダ [ラ] ウェイ」のように聴こえるとき、これを弾音化していると言います。

❹ **同化**：同化とは、2つの音が混じり合って、元の音とは別の音になってしまうことです。例えば、meet you では、meet 末尾の [t] の音と you の頭の [j] が混じり合って別の「チュ」といった音に変化します。

❺ **声門閉鎖音化**：声門閉鎖音化とは、button のような単語で [tn] が連続する場面などで生じます。この場合、[t] の音が変化して「バトゥン」ではなく、「バンン」のように聴こえる発音になります。このとき、喉の声門が咳払いをする直前のような状態で閉じられているため、この音声変化を声門閉鎖音化と呼んでいます。

Your New English Ears
–*Business*–

絶対『英語の耳』になる！
ビジネス英語リスニング ◆ 難関トレーニング 50

◎ **本書のおもな登場人物** ◎

● AAA Safety Systems（トゥリプル・エー・セーフティー・システムズ社）
アメリカのエアバッグ・メーカー。新型エアバッグを開発中。
エキスポ出展を目指している。
    Mike Gray ········ Sales Rep（営業部員）
    Tom Smith ······· Production Manager（製造部長）
    Steve Jones ··· Quality Control Manager（品質管理部長）

● China Semicon（チャイナ・セミコン社）
中国の半導体メーカー、AAA Safety Systems の下請け業者。
    May Chan ········ Sales Rep（国際営業部員）
    Mr. Chen ········· Vice President of Operations（業務管理部長）
    Mr. Chan ········· Production Manager and Quality Engineer（製造部長兼、品質管理技術者）

● American Auto（アメリカン・オート社）
アメリカの自動車メーカー、AAA Safety Systems の有望な顧客。
    Jack ················· General Manager（部長）

Unit 01

新規顧客からの問い合わせ
Service Inquiry from Potential Customer

Stage 01 穴埋めビジネス・リスニング

音声変化に注意してCDでビジネスのダイアローグを聴きながら、空欄部分を埋めてみよう。

ダイアローグ音声収録

May: This is May Chang ① _____.

Mike: Ms. Chang, my name is ② _____ _____. I am a sales rep for ③ _____ Safety Systems ④ _____ in the U.S. I was ⑤ _____ _____ you by ⑥ _____ _____ _____ engineers at American Auto, who happens to be mutual customer of ours.

May: I see. How can we be of service to you Mike?

Mike: I was hoping to ⑦ _____ _____ an RFQ package to see if you can quote a new ⑧ _____ for us.

May: Sure, we can do that. We are ⑨ _____ _____ _____ largest semi-conductor manufacturers in the world, and are renowned for providing the highest ⑩ _____ goods at very ⑪ _____ prices. ⑫ _____ _____ have any target pricing?

Mike: I would like to have the quote by next Monday, if possible. ⑬ _____ _____ include the part diagram, forecasted usage volumes and the ⑭ _____ _____ information in my RFQ.

May: Great. Please ⑮ _____ _____ to my email address, mchang@chinasemicon.com.

ビジネス・リスニング（1回目）

Stage 02　ビジネス・ボキャビル

ビジネスのボキャブラリーを CD で確認しよう。そのあとでもう一度、ビジネス・リスニングにチャレンジ。Stage 01 でできなかったところをもう一度聴き取って、穴埋めを完成させよう。

英日 音声収録

1	sales rep	営業部員
2	safety	安全
3	located in ...	…にある
4	be referred to ...	…に紹介される
5	engineer	エンジニア；技術者
6	happen to ...	たまたま…する
7	mutual	相互の
8	customer	顧客
9	RFQ package	見積依頼の書類（Request for Quotation の略）
10	product	製品
11	semi-conductor	半導体
12	manufacturer	製造業者
13	be renowned for ...	…で有名だ
14	provide	提供する
15	high quality goods	高品質の製品
16	competitive price	競争力のある価格
17	target pricing	目標価格
18	quote	見積
19	part diagram	部品の図面；設計図
20	forecasted	予想される
21	usage	使用；用途
22	volume	量；分量

🔊 ビジネス・リスニング（2回目）

Stage 03　日本語トランスレーション

ビジネス・ダイアログの日本語を確認してみよう！　その上で、ダイアローグを聴きながら、まだできていない部分の穴埋めに再チャレンジしよう。

May: メイ・チャンでございます。
Mike: チャンさん、私はマイク・グレイと申しまして、アメリカにありますAAAセーフティー・システムズの営業部員です。アメリカン・オートのエンジニアに御社を紹介されました。アメリカン・オートは、たまたま御社と弊社の共通の顧客でして。
May: そうですか。マイク、どのようなご用件でしょうか？
Mike: 御社に見積依頼の書類を送付させてもらい、弊社の新製品の見積ができるかどうか知りたいのです。
May: もちろん大丈夫です。弊社は世界でも有数の半導体メーカーで、競争力のある価格で高品質の製品を提供していることで知られております。目標として設定している価格はございますか？
Mike: できれば来週の月曜までに見積がほしいのです。部品の設計図と、予測注文数、それから目標設定価格の情報を見積依頼書に同封しておきます。
May: わかりました。私のメールアドレス mchang@chinasemicon.com までお送りください。

🔊 ビジネス・リスニング（3回目）

Stage 04　英文トランスクリプション

ビジネス・ダイアログの原稿を確認してみよう！　穴埋め部分の正解をチェックして、英文を理解し直そう。そのあとで、もう一度ダイアローグを聴いてみよう。

May: This is May Chang ① speaking.
Mike: Ms. Chang, my name is ② Mike Gray. I am a sales rep for ③ AAA Safety Systems ④ located in the U.S. I was ⑤ referred to you by ⑥ one of the engineers at American Auto, who happens to be mutual customer of ours.
May: I see. How can we be of service to you Mike?
Mike: I was hoping to ⑦ send you an RFQ package to see if you can quote a new ⑧ product for us.
May: Sure, we can do that. We are ⑨ one of the largest semi-conductor manufacturers in the world, and are renowned for providing the highest ⑩ quality goods at very ⑪ competitive prices. ⑫ Do you have any target pricing?
Mike: I would like to have the quote by next Monday, if possible. ⑬ I will include the part diagram, forecasted usage volumes and the ⑭ target pricing information in my RFQ.
May: Great. Please ⑮ send it to my email address, mchang@chinasemicon.com.

🔊 ビジネス・リスニング（4回目）

Stage 05 音声変化をチェック

まとめとして、穴埋め部分の音声変化の特徴をスロースピードとナチュラルスピードで確認しよう。下記に示したカタカナ表記で音声変化を確認して、もう一度ビジネス・ダイアローグを聴き直してみよう。発音変化のルールは適宜復習しよう。

2種類の音声を収録

① **speaking** ― 末尾の破裂音 [g] の脱落
スピーキング ▶ スピーキン＿

② **Mike Gray** ― 破裂音 [k] の脱落
マイク・グレイ ▶ マイ＿グレイ

③ **AAA** ― [tr] の音が [tʃr] に変化
トゥリプル・エイ ▶ チュリプルエイ

④ **located** ― [t] 音の弾音化
ロウケイティッド ▶ ロウケイディ [リ] ッド

⑤ **referred to** ― 破裂音 [d] の脱落
リファード・トゥー ▶ リファー＿トゥー

⑥ **one of the** ― one の [n] に of が連結。of の [v] 音が脱落
ワン・アヴ・ディ ▶ ワナ＿ディ

⑦ **send you** ― [d] と [j] が同化
センド・ユー ▶ センジュー

⑧ **product** ― 破裂音 [d] の弾音化
プラーダクト ▶ プラーダ [ラ] クト

⑨ **one of the** ― one の [n] に of が連結。of の [v] 音が脱落
ワン・アヴ・ザ ▶ ワナ＿ザ

⑩ **quality** ― 破裂音 [t] の弾音化
クオリティー ▶ クオリディ [リ] ー

⑪ **competitive** ― 破裂音 [t] が 2 カ所で弾音化
カンペタティヴ ▶ カンペダ [ラ] ディ [リ] ヴ

⑫ **Do you** ― Do と you の弱化。さらに [d] と [j] が同化することもある
ドゥー・ユー ▶ ドゥユ；ジュ

⑬ **I will** ― 短縮形 I'll の発音、あるいは will が弱化
アイ・ウィル ▶ アイル；アイウァ

⑭ **target pricing** ― 破裂音 [t] の脱落
ターゲット・プライシング ▶ ターゲッ＿プライシング

⑮ **send it** ― 2 語が連結、さらに破裂音 [d] が脱落しする場合もある
センド・イット ▶ センディット；セニット

🔊 ビジネス・リスニング (5 回目)

Unit 02

見積依頼のフォローアップ
Follow up on Quotation Request

Stage 01 穴埋めビジネス・リスニング

音声変化に注意してCDでビジネスのダイアローグを聴きながら、空欄部分を埋めてみよう。

ダイアローグ音声収録

Mike: ① _____ _____. This is Mike.

May: This is May Chang from China Semicon. ② _____ _____ get my email and our quotation?

Mike: Sure did. I ③ _____ _____ time to go through it yet, but we have a ④ _____ on this ⑤ _____ today. One thing I ⑥ _____ _____ mention, the diagrams are confidential so I ⑦ _____ _____ to return the document ⑧ _____ form I'm sending you now.

May: That's no problem. I'll ⑨ _____ _____ _____ to you by close of business your time.

Mike: Speaking of which, it's ⑩ _____ _____ o'clock pm there, ⑪ _____ _____? I'm surprised you're ⑫ _____ _____ office this late.

May: I am in our ⑬ _____ sales department so I work a ⑭ _____ shift to ⑮ _____ accommodate our customers in ⑯ _____ _____ zones.

Mike: I see. I'd like to ⑰ _____ _____ a conference call with you on Thursday to discuss the details ⑱ _____ _____ project and ask you some questions. Would this time work for you?

May: That ought to be fine. I look forward to talking with you then.

🔊 ビジネス・リスニング（1回目）

14

Stage 02　ビジネス・ボキャビル

ビジネスのボキャブラリーを CD で確認しよう。そのあとでもう一度、ビジネス・リスニングにチャレンジ。Stage 01 でできなかったところをもう一度聴き取って、穴埋めを完成させよう。

英日 音声収録

1	go through ...	…に目を通す
2	later today	本日後ほど
3	mention	言及する
4	confidential	秘密厳守の；機密の
5	document control form	文書の受け取り・管理確認書
6	no problem	問題ない
7	close of business	業務の終了（時間）
8	your time	そちらの（国の）時間で
9	speaking of which, ...	（前文を受けて）そう言えば…
10	pm	午後
11	international sales department	国際営業部
12	work a later shift	遅いシフトで働く
13	accomodate	適応する
14	time zone	時間帯
15	conference call	電話会議
16	discuss	話し合う
17	details	詳細
18	project	プロジェクト；仕事
19	work for ...	…に都合がつく；…にとって問題ない
20	look forward to ...	…を楽しみにしている；期待している

🔊 ビジネス・リスニング（2回目）

Stage 03 日本語トランスレーション

ビジネス・ダイアローグの日本語を確認してみよう！ その上で、ダイアローグを聴きながら、まだできていない部分の穴埋めに再チャレンジしよう。

Mike: おはようございます。マイクです。
May: チャイナ・セミコンのメイ・チャンです。私のメールと弊社の見積をお受け取りになりましたか？
Mike: 確かに、いただきました。まだ読み終える時間が取れないのですが、本日後ほど、この件の打ち合わせがあります。ひとつお伝えし忘れたのですが、設計図は機密情報となっていますので、私がいまからお送りする文書の受け取り・管理確認書を送り返してください。
May: 問題ありません。そちらの営業時間が終わるまでにご返送いたします。
Mike: そう言えば、そちらはだいたい午後10時頃ではありませんか？ これほど遅くまでオフィスにいるなんて驚きです。
May: 私は国際営業部に所属していますので、いろいろなタイムゾーンにいるお客さまにうまく対応するために遅いシフトで勤務しているんですよ。
Mike: そうですか。プロジェクトの詳細についてお話しや質問がしたいので、木曜日にあなたと打ち合わせの電話会議をもちたいと思っていますが、この時間でも大丈夫でしょうか？
May: おそらく大丈夫ですよ。そのときお話しできるのを楽しみにお待ちしてます。

🔊 ビジネス・リスニング（3回目）

Stage 04 英文トランスクリプション

ビジネス・ダイアローグの原稿を確認してみよう！ 穴埋め部分の正解をチェックして、英文を理解し直そう。そのあとで、もう一度ダイアローグを聴いてみよう。

Mike: ① Good morning. This is Mike.
May: This is May Chang from China Semicon. ② Did you get my email and our quotation?
Mike: Sure did. I ③ haven't had time to go through it yet, but we have a ④ meeting on this ⑤ later today. One thing I ⑥ forgot to mention, the diagrams are confidential so I ⑦ need you to return the document ⑧ control form I'm sending you now.
May: That's no problem. I'll ⑨ get it back to you by close of business your time.
Mike: Speaking of which, it's ⑩ about ten o'clock pm there, ⑪ isn't it? I'm surprised you're ⑫ at your office this late.
May: I am in our ⑬ international sales department so I work a ⑭ later shift to ⑮ better accommodate our customers in ⑯ different time zones.
Mike: I see. I'd like to ⑰ set up a conference call with you on Thursday to discuss the details ⑱ of the project and ask you some questions. Would this time work for you?
May: That ought to be fine. I look forward to talking with you then.

🔊 ビジネス・リスニング（4回目）

Stage 05 音声変化をチェック

まとめとして、穴埋め部分の音声変化の特徴をスロースピードとナチュラルスピードで確認しよう。下記に示したカタカナ表記で音声変化を確認して、もう一度ビジネス・ダイアローグを聴き直してみよう。発音変化のルールは適宜復習しよう。

2種類の音声を収録

① **Good morning** グッド・モーニング ▶ グッ＿モーニン＿
　☞ 破裂音 [d] と [g] の脱落

② **Did you** ディッド・ユー ▶ ディッジュー
　☞ [d] 音と [j] 音が同化

③ **haven't had** ハヴント・ハッド ▶ ハヴナッド
　☞ 破裂音 [t] が脱落して、弱化した had [ァド] に連結

④ **meeting** ミーティング ▶ ミーディ [リ] ング
　☞ [t] 音の弾音化

⑤ **later** レイター ▶ レイダ [ラ] ー
　☞ [t] 音の弾音化

⑥ **forgot to** フォーガット・トゥー ▶ フォーガッ＿トゥー
　☞ 破裂音 [t] の脱落

⑦ **need you** ニード・ユー ▶ ニージュー
　☞ [d] 音と [j] 音が同化

⑧ **control** カントロウル ▶ カンチュロウル
　☞ [ntr] の音が [ntʃr] に変化

⑨ **get it back** ゲット・イット・バック ▶ ゲッディ [リ] ッ＿バック
　☞ 破裂音 [t] の弾音化。2番目の [t] の脱落

⑩ **about ten** アバウト・テン ▶ アバウ＿テン
　☞ 破裂音 [t] の脱落

⑪ **isn't it** イズント・イット ▶ イズニット；イズニッ＿
　☞ 破裂音 [t] が1カ所あるいは2カ所で脱落

⑫ **at your** アット・ユア ▶ アッチュア
　☞ [t] 音と [j] 音が同化

⑬ **international** インターナショヌル ▶ イナーナショヌル
　☞ 破裂音 [t] の脱落

⑭ **later** レイター ▶ レイダ [ラ] ー
　☞ [t] 音の弾音化

⑮ **better** ベター ▶ ベダ [ラ] ー
　☞ [t] 音の弾音化

⑯ **different time** ディファラント・タイム ▶ ディファラン＿タイム
　☞ 破裂音 [t] の脱落

⑰ **set up** セット・アップ ▶ セダ [ラ] ップ
　☞ 2語が連結。連結部で [t] 音の弾音化

⑱ **of the** アヴ・ザ ▶ ア＿ザ
　☞ [v] 音の脱落

🔊 ビジネス・リスニング (5回目)

プロジェクト詳細の連絡 ①
Detailed Communication About the Project 1

Stage 01 穴埋めビジネス・リスニング

音声変化に注意して CD でビジネスのダイアローグを聴きながら、空欄部分を埋めてみよう。

ダイアローグ音声収録 CD 1-07

May: May speaking.

Mike: Hi May, this is Mike Gray and I have my associate Tom Smith here with me, is now a ① _____ _____ to go over a few things?

May: Sure.

Mike: ② _____ _____ hear us okay? ③ _____ _____ on speaker phone.

May: Yes, it sounds like you're in the same room.

Mike: Okay, we are still ④ _____ _____ the details of your quote, but ⑤ _____ _____ give you a rough idea of our project ⑥ _____ and schedule. The semiconductor component we are ⑦ _____ will go into a new air-bag sensor unit our company is developing. The sensor goes under the ⑧ _____ _____ seats ⑨ _____ _____ _____ and informs an electronic CPU in the car whether or not to ⑩ _____ _____ the air bags. We already have a potential customer American Auto, but we are hoping to display our product ⑪ _____ _____ upcoming ⑫ _____ Auto Expo this October.

Tom: As you know our current ⑬ _____ monthly usage is about 50,000 units a month when mass production starts early ⑭ _____ _____, but if we do well ⑮ _____ _____ expo, ⑯ _____ _____ see exponential growth in the next few years.

🔊 ビジネス・リスニング (1 回目)

Stage 02 ビジネス・ボキャビル

ビジネスのボキャブラリーを CD で確認しよう。そのあとでもう一度、ビジネス・リスニングにチャレンジ。Stage 01 でできなかったところをもう一度聴き取って、穴埋めを完成させよう。

英日 音声収録

1	... speaking	［電話で］こちらは…でございます
2	associate	同僚（上司にも使用できる語）
3	sound like ...	…のように聞こえる
4	details	詳細
5	quote	見積
6	rough idea	大まかな考え
7	background	背景
8	schedule	スケジュール
9	component	構成部品；構成要素
10	quote	見積を取る
11	air-bag sensor unit	エアバッグのセンサー装置
12	develop	開発する
13	passenger seat	自動車の助手席
14	inform	情報を伝える
15	electronic	電子の；電子工学の
16	CPU	中央演算処理装置
17	turn on	起動する；動かす
18	potential	見込みのある
19	display	展示する
20	upcoming	近づきつつある
21	expo	展示会；博覧会
22	estimated	見積の；おおよその
23	exponential growth	急激な成長；増加

🔊 ビジネス・リスニング（2回目）

Stage 03 日本語トランスレーション

ビジネス・ダイアローグの日本語を確認してみよう！ その上で、ダイアローグを聴きながら、まだできていない部分の穴埋めに再チャレンジしよう。

May: メイでございます。
Mike: こんにちはメイ。マイク・グレイです。弊社のトム・スミスもいっしょです。少し話をしてもかまいませんか？
May: もちろん。
Mike: われわれの声は聞こえていますか？ スピーカー・フォンにしているのですが。
May: ええ、同じ部屋にいるように聞こえていますよ。
Mike: さて、弊社ではまだ御社のお見積の詳細について検討中なのですが、プロジェクトの背景とスケジュールに関する大まかな考えをお話ししておきたかったのです。現在見積中の半導体パーツは、弊社が開発している新しいエアバッグのセンサー部に組み込まれます。センサーは助手席の下に組み込まれ、自動車の中にある CPU に対して、エアバッグを開くかどうかの情報を与えるものです。すでに、アメリカン・オートを見込み客として抱えていますが、この 10 月に開催される国際自動車展示会で弊社の製品を展示したいと思っています。
Tom: ご存じのとおり、大量生産が始まる来年初頭における毎月の予測使用量は、現在約 5 万ユニットですが、エキスポで首尾よく事が進めば、その後数年で急激な成長が見込めるかもしれません。

🔊 ビジネス・リスニング（3回目）

Stage 04 英文トランスクリプション

ビジネス・ダイアローグの原稿を確認してみよう！ 穴埋め部分の正解をチェックして、英文を理解し直そう。そのあとで、もう一度ダイアローグを聴いてみよう。

May: May speaking.
Mike: Hi May, this is Mike Gray and I have my associate Tom Smith here with me, is now a ① good time to go over a few things?
May: Sure.
Mike: ② Can you hear us okay? ③ We are on speaker phone.
May: Yes, it sounds like you're in the same room.
Mike: Okay, we are still ④ going over the details of your quote, but ⑤ wanted to give you a rough idea of our project ⑥ background and schedule. The semiconductor component we are ⑦ quoting will go into a new air-bag sensor unit our company is developing. The sensor goes under the ⑧ front passenger seats ⑨ in an automobile and informs an electronic CPU in the car whether or not to ⑩ turn on the air bags. We already have a potential customer American Auto, but we are hoping to display our product ⑪ at the upcoming ⑫ International Auto Expo this October.
Tom: As you know our current ⑬ estimated monthly usage is about 50,000 units a month when mass production starts early ⑭ next year, but if we do well ⑮ at the expo, ⑯ we could see exponential growth in the next few years.

🔊 ビジネス・リスニング（4回目）

Stage 05 音声変化をチェック

まとめとして、穴埋め部分の音声変化の特徴をスロースピードとナチュラルスピードで確認しよう。下記に示したカタカナ表記で音声変化を確認して、もう一度ビジネス・ダイアローグを聴き直してみよう。発音変化のルールは適宜復習しよう。

2種類の音声を収録

① **good time** グッド・タイム ▶ グッ＿タイム
　☞ 破裂音 [d] の脱落

② **Can you** キャン・ユー ▶ キャニュー
　☞ 2語の連結

③ **We are** ウィ・アー ▶ ウィアー
　☞ 短縮形 We're の発音

④ **going over** ゴウイング・オウヴァー ▶ ゴウイノウヴァー
　☞ 破裂音 [g] の脱落。going の [n] 音に over が連結

⑤ **wanted to** ワンティッド・トゥー ▶ ワニッ＿トゥー
　☞ 破裂音 [t] と [d] の脱落

⑥ **background** バックグラウンド ▶ バッ＿グラウンド
　☞ 破裂音 [k] の脱落

⑦ **quoting** クォーティング ▶ クォーディ [リ] ング
　☞ 破裂音 [t] の弾音化

⑧ **front passenger** フラント・パッセンジャー ▶ フラン＿パッセンジャー
　☞ 破裂音 [t] の脱落

⑨ **in an automobile** イン・アン・オートモウビール ▶ イナノートモウビール
　☞ 3語が連結

⑩ **turn on** ターン・オン ▶ ターノン
　☞ 2語が連結

⑪ **at the** アット・ズィ ▶ アッ＿ズィ
　☞ 破裂音 [t] の脱落

⑫ **International** インターナショヌル ▶ イナーナショヌル
　☞ 破裂音 [t] の脱落

⑬ **estimated** エスティメイティッド ▶ エスティメイディ [リ] ッド
　☞ 破裂音 [t] の弾音化

⑭ **next year** ネクスト・イヤー ▶ ネクスチャー
　☞ [t] 音と [j] 音が同化

⑮ **at the** アット・ズィ ▶ アッ＿ズィ
　☞ [t] 音の脱落

⑯ **we could** ウィ・クッド ▶ ウィクッ＿
　☞ 末尾の破裂音 [d] の脱落

🔊 ビジネス・リスニング (5 回目)

プロジェクト詳細の連絡 ②
Detailed Communication About the Project 2

Stage 01　穴埋めビジネス・リスニング

音声変化に注意してCDでビジネスのダイアローグを聴きながら、空欄部分を埋めてみよう。

ダイアローグ音声収録

May: How many samples ① _____ _____ need for inspection, product approval and ② _____ _____ your deadline for delivery?

Mike: Right now we are ③ _____ _____ 120 days as our drop-dead date to complete the production of the final product. We would ④ _____ _____ parts in 90 days. We would need 50 units for the parts production approval process and another 50 units for use ⑤ _____ _____ expo. Your quote currently involves a ⑥ _____ _____ of ⑦ _____ days, is that something you can guarantee?

May: We guarantee ⑧ _____ days from the date of purchase order receipt. You will need to air-ship the parts, however. Air freight is ⑨ _____ _____ ⑩ _____ _____ pricing.

Tom: Good, we can work ⑪ _____ _____. We are still building our price matrix to submit our quote to our current customer, American Auto. If we are awarded the business we are ⑫ _____ _____ running. We will be ⑬ _____ with our customer tomorrow to submit our quotation. Mike will follow up with you soon afterwards.

May: Okay then, I will wait to hear from you. We ⑭ _____ look forward to be of service to you.

🔊 ビジネス・リスニング（1回目）

Stage 02 ビジネス・ボキャビル

ビジネスのボキャブラリーを CD で確認しよう。そのあとでもう一度、ビジネス・リスニングにチャレンジ。Stage 01 でできなかったところをもう一度聴き取って、穴埋めを完成させよう。

英日 音声収録

1	inspection	検査
2	product approval	製品の承認
3	deadline	締め切り
4	drop-dead date	締め切り日；期限
5	final product	最終製品
6	currently	現在
7	guarantee	保証する
8	purchase order	発注；注文
9	receipt	受領
10	air-ship	空輸する
11	air freight	航空運賃
12	include	含む
13	pricing	価格付け
14	price matrix	価格表
15	submit	提出する
16	be awarded	与えられる
17	quotation	見積
18	be of service to ...	…の役に立つ

🔊 ビジネス・リスニング（2回目）

Stage 03　日本語トランスレーション

ビジネス・ダイアローグの日本語を確認してみよう！　その上で、ダイアローグを聴きながら、まだできていない部分の穴埋めに再チャレンジしよう。

May: 検査と製品承認にはいくつのサンプルが必要でしょうか？　また、配送のデッドラインはいつになりますか？

Mike: 現在、最終製品の生産終了のデッドラインを 120 日と考えています。御社のパーツは 90 日以内に必要になります。パーツ製造の承認作業に 50 ユニット、展示会で使用するために別に 50 ユニット必要です。御社の見積では、現在のところ 75 日の準備期間となっていますね。これは保証いただける日数でしょうか？

May: 注文書受領日から 75 日を保証いたします。しかし、航空便での発送が必要かと存じますが、航空運賃は弊社の料金に含まれておりません。

Tom: 弊社もその条件でかまいません。弊社ではまだ、現在の顧客であるアメリカン・オートに見積を提出するために価格一覧表を作成中です。仕事がもらえたら、すぐに動き出します。明日、見積を提出するために顧客に会う予定になっています。この件に関しては、後ほどマイクからご連絡します。

May: わかりました。では、ご連絡をお待ちしていますね。お役に立てることを、とても楽しみにしております。

🔊 ビジネス・リスニング（3 回目）

Stage 04　英文トランスクリプション

ビジネス・ダイアローグの原稿を確認してみよう！　穴埋め部分の正解をチェックして、英文を理解し直そう。そのあとで、もう一度ダイアローグを聴いてみよう。

May: How many samples ① will you need for inspection, product approval and ② what is your deadline for delivery?

Mike: Right now we are ③ looking at 120 days as our drop-dead date to complete the production of the final product. We would ④ need your parts in 90 days. We would need 50 units for the parts production approval process and another 50 units for use ⑤ at the expo. Your quote currently involves a ⑥ lead time of ⑦ 75 days, is that something you can guarantee?

May: We guarantee ⑧ 75 days from the date of purchase order receipt. You will need to air-ship the parts, however. Air freight is ⑨ not included ⑩ in our pricing.

Tom: Good, we can work ⑪ with that. We are still building our price matrix to submit our quote to our current customer, American Auto. If we are awarded the business we are ⑫ up and running. We will be ⑬ meeting with our customer tomorrow to submit our quotation. Mike will follow up with you soon afterwards.

May: Okay then, I will wait to hear from you. We ⑭ certainly look forward to be of service to you.

🔊 ビジネス・リスニング（4 回目）

Stage 05 音声変化をチェック

まとめとして、穴埋め部分の音声変化の特徴をスロースピードとナチュラルスピードで確認しよう。下記に示したカタカナ表記で音声変化を確認して、もう一度ビジネス・ダイアローグを聴き直してみよう。発音変化のルールは適宜復習しよう。

2種類の音声を収録

① **will you**   ウィル・ユー   ▶ ウィ＿ユー
 ☞ [l] 音の脱落

② **what is**   ワット・イズ   ▶ ワッディ [リ] ズ
 ☞ 2語の連結。連結部で破裂音 [t] の弾音化

③ **looking at**   ルッキング・アット   ▶ ルッキナット
 ☞ 破裂音 [g] の脱落。2語の連結

④ **need your**   ニード・ユア   ▶ ニージュア
 ☞ [d] 音と [j] 音が同化

⑤ **at the**   アット・ズィ   ▶ アッ＿ズィ
 ☞ [t] 音の脱落

⑥ **lead time**   リード・タイム   ▶ リー＿タイム
 ☞ 破裂音 [d] の脱落

⑦ **75**   セヴンティー・ファイヴ   ▶ セヴニーファイヴ
 ☞ 破裂音 [t] の脱落

⑧ **75**   セヴンティー・ファイヴ   ▶ セヴニーファイヴ
 ☞ 破裂音 [t] の脱落

⑨ **not included**   ナット・インクルーディッド   ▶ ナッディ [リ] ンクルーディッド
 ☞ 2語の連結。連結部で破裂音 [t] が弾音化

⑩ **in our**   イン・アウァ   ▶ イナウァ
 ☞ 2語の連結

⑪ **with that**   ウィズ・ザット   ▶ ウィ＿ザット
 ☞ [ð] 音の脱落

⑫ **up and**   アップ・アンド   ▶ アッパン＿
 ☞ 2語の連結。末尾の破裂音 [d] が脱落する場合もある

⑬ **meeting**   ミーティング   ▶ ミーディ [リ] ング
 ☞ 破裂音 [t] の弾音化

⑭ **certainly**   スートゥンリー   ▶ スーンンリー
 ☞ 破裂音 [t] の声門閉鎖音化

🔊 ビジネス・リスニング（5 回目）

価格の交渉 ①
Pricing Negotiation 1

Stage 01 穴埋めビジネス・リスニング

音声変化に注意してCDでビジネスのダイアローグを聴きながら、空欄部分を埋めてみよう。

ダイアローグ音声収録

Mike: ① _____ _____ know, our target pricing to be able to ② _____ _____ project from American Auto was $0.04 per unit. Your pricing is ③ _____ percent higher than that. We really ④ _____ _____ to sharpen your pencil a ⑤ _____ _____ this.

May: Well, Mike, ⑥ _____ _____ may be aware; ⑦ _____ _____ being ⑧ _____ _____ raw material increases ⑨ _____ across the board. On ⑩ _____ _____ that, labor costs have ⑪ _____ _____ considerably over the ⑫ _____ few years. If your order quantities were higher, we ⑬ _____ _____ some room to maneuver by purchasing raw materials in larger quantities, but as it stands now ⑭ _____ _____ see any way to come ⑮ _____ _____ price.

Mike: As I mentioned the other day, if things go well ⑯ _____ _____ expo we are ⑰ _____ _____ _____ potential for 200% growth within the next three years. If we can expand our product line to other major ⑱ _____ manufacturers then the volumes will increase exponentially. Right now your ⑲ _____ _____ for 50,000 units a month. ⑳ _____ _____ pricing for lots of 100,000 and 500,000 by tomorrow.

🔊 ビジネス・リスニング（1回目）

Stage 02 ビジネス・ボキャビル

ビジネスのボキャブラリーを CD で確認しよう。そのあとでもう一度、ビジネス・リスニングにチャレンジ。Stage 01 でできなかったところをもう一度聴き取って、穴埋めを完成させよう。

英日 音声収録

1	as you know, ...	ご存知のとおり…
2	per unit	1 台につき
3	pricing	値付け；価格設定
4	... percent higher	…％高い
5	sharpen one's pencil	（値段などを）削り落とす
6	a bit	少々
7	be aware	気づいている
8	be hit with ...	…で打撃を受ける
9	raw material	原材料
10	increase	増加；高騰
11	across the board	全般にわたって
12	on top of that	その上
13	labor cost	人件費
14	considerably	かなり
15	over the last few years	過去数年にわたって
16	order quantity	発注数
17	have some room to ...	…する余地がある
18	maneuver	うまく操作する；操る
19	purchase	購入する
20	come down on price	値段を下げる
21	mention	言及する
22	potential	可能性
23	expand	（市場や規模などを）拡張する；発展させる
24	product line	製品群

🔊 ビジネス・リスニング（2 回目）

Stage 03　日本語トランスレーション

ビジネス・ダイアーグの日本語を確認してみよう！ その上で、ダイアローグを聴きながら、まだできていない部分の穴埋めに再チャレンジしよう。

Mike: ご存じのとおり、アメリカン・オートからこの仕事がもらえるようにするための弊社の目標価格は1ユニットにつき0.04ドルでした。御社の価格設定はこれよりも20％高くなっています。もう少し値下げをお願いする必要があります。

May: あー、マイク。お気づきかと思いますが、弊社では昨今、全面的な原材料費の高騰に直面しています。加えて、過去数年で、労働コストもかなり上昇いたしました。御社の注文数が多ければ、原料をより多く購入することでなんとかする余地があるかもしれませんが、現在のところ、値下げする方法はなさそうです。

Mike: 先日申し上げましたが、展示会がうまくいけば、3年以内に200％の成長の可能性を見込んでいます。弊社の製品群をほかの大手自動車メーカーにまで拡大できれば、注文数は急激に増大していきます。現在のところ、御社のお見積は月産5万ユニットに対するものです。明日までに、10万と50万ロットの値段をもらえますか？

🔊 ビジネス・リスニング（3回目）

Stage 04　英文トランスクリプション

ビジネス・ダイアローグの原稿を確認してみよう！ 穴埋め部分の正解をチェックして、英文を理解し直そう。そのあとで、もう一度ダイアローグを聴いてみよう。

Mike: ① As you know, our target pricing to be able to ② get this project from American Auto was $0.04 per unit. Your pricing is ③ twenty percent higher than that. We really ④ need you to sharpen your pencil a ⑤ bit on this.

May: Well, Mike, ⑥ as you may be aware, ⑦ we've been being ⑧ hit with raw material increases ⑨ lately across the board. On ⑩ top of that, labor costs have ⑪ gone up considerably over the ⑫ last few years. If your order quantities were higher, we ⑬ might have some room to maneuver by purchasing raw materials in larger quantities, but as it stands now ⑭ I don't see any way to come ⑮ down on price.

Mike: As I mentioned the other day, if things go well ⑯ at the expo we are ⑰ looking at the potential for 200% growth within the next three years. If we can expand our product line to other major ⑱ auto manufacturers then the volumes will increase exponentially. Right now your ⑲ quote is for 50,000 units a month. ⑳ Get me pricing for lots of 100,000 and 500,000 by tomorrow.

🔊 ビジネス・リスニング（4回目）

Stage 05 　音声変化をチェック

まとめとして、穴埋め部分の音声変化の特徴をスロースピードとナチュラルスピードで確認しよう。下記に示したカタカナ表記で音声変化を確認して、もう一度ビジネス・ダイアローグを聴き直してみよう。発音変化のルールは適宜復習しよう。

2種類の音声を収録　　　　　　　　　　　　　　CD 1-15

① **As you**　　　　　　　　アズ・ユー　　　　　▶ アジュー
　☞ [z] と [j] の同化

② **get this**　　　　　　　　ゲット・ズィス　　　　▶ ゲッ＿ズィス
　☞ 破裂音 [t] の脱落

③ **twenty**　　　　　　　　トゥエンティー　　　　▶ トゥエニー
　☞ 破裂音 [t] の脱落

④ **need you**　　　　　　　ニード・ユー　　　　　▶ ニージュー
　☞ [d] と [j] の同化

⑤ **bit on**　　　　　　　　ビット・オン　　　　　▶ ビッド [ロ] ン
　☞ 2語の連結。連結部で破裂音 [t] が弾音化

⑥ **as you**　　　　　　　　アズ・ユー　　　　　▶ アジュー
　☞ [z] と [j] の同化

⑦ **we've been**　　　　　　ウィヴ・ビン　　　　　▶ ウィ＿ビン
　☞ [v] 音の脱落

⑧ **hit with**　　　　　　　ヒット・ウィズ　　　　▶ ヒッ＿ウィズ
　☞ 破裂音 [t] 脱落

⑨ **lately**　　　　　　　　レイトリー　　　　　　▶ レイド [ロ] リー
　☞ 破裂音 [t] の弾音化

⑩ **top of**　　　　　　　　タップ・アヴ　　　　　▶ タッパヴ
　☞ 2語の連結

⑪ **gone up**　　　　　　　ゴウン・アップ　　　　▶ ゴウナップ
　☞ 2語の連結

⑫ **last**　　　　　　　　　ラスト　　　　　　　　▶ ラス＿
　☞ 末尾の破裂音 [t] の脱落

⑬ **might have**　　　　　　マイト・ハヴ　　　　　▶ マイダ [ラ] ヴ
　☞ 2語が連結。have の [h] 音の脱落。連結部の [t] 音が弾音化

⑭ **I don't**　　　　　　　　アイ・ドウント　　　　▶ アイドン；アイ＿オウン＿
　☞ don't が弱化して [ドン] あるいは [ドント] と発音。[d] や [t] が脱落して [アイ＿オウン＿] と発音することもある

⑮ **down on**　　　　　　　ダウン・オン　　　　　▶ ダウノン
　☞ 2語の連結

⑯ **at the**　　　　　　　　アット・ズィ　　　　　▶ アッ＿ズィ
　☞ [t] 音の脱落

⑰ **looking at the**　　　　ルッキング・アット・ザ　▶ ルッキン＿アッ＿ザ
　☞ 破裂音 [g] と [t] の脱落

⑱ **auto**　　　　　　　　　オートウ　　　　　　　▶ オード [ロ] ウ
　☞ 破裂音 [t] の弾音化

⑲ **quote is**　　　　　　　クォート・イズ　　　　▶ クォーディ [リ] ズ
　☞ 2語の連結。連結部で破裂音 [t] が弾音化

⑳ **Get me**　　　　　　　　ゲット・ミー　　　　　▶ ゲッ＿ミー
　☞ 破裂音 [t] の脱落

🔊 ビジネス・リスニング (5 回目)

価格の交渉 ②
Pricing Negotiation 2

Stage 01 — 穴埋めビジネス・リスニング

音声変化に注意してCDでビジネスのダイアローグを聴きながら、空欄部分を埋めてみよう。

ダイアローグ音声収録

May: ① _____ _____ get my email and revised quote for the volume increase?

Mike: Yes, thank you. I was just ② _____ _____ _____ now.

May: ③ _____ _____ can see, increasing the order lots to 100,000 units per month allows us to lower the cost to $0.045, and if we ④ _____ _____ 500,000 units we are looking at $0.04, which is ⑤ _____ _____ target. We can provide 100 pcs of samples within your time-frame for a one-time charge of $1000.

Mike: Well, our initial mass production volume at ⑥ _____ ⑦ _____ _____ 50,000. To ⑧ _____ _____ ⑨ _____ _____, we are looking at purchasing ten months of inventory. ⑩ _____ _____ _____ sure ⑪ _____ _____ something we can do. What is the shelf life for your product?

May: ⑫ _____, we guarantee our product for three years from the ship-date as long as they are stored where they are protected from ⑬ _____ charge and the temperature is ⑭ _____ ⑮ _____ _____ exceed 30 degrees Celsius.

Mike: Okay, I'll go over this with our production control department and ⑯ _____ _____ pricing to management for approval. I think we ⑰ _____ _____ able to make this work.

◀)) ビジネス・リスニング（1回目）

Stage 02 ビジネス・ボキャビル

ビジネスのボキャブラリーを CD で確認しよう。そのあとでもう一度、ビジネス・リスニングにチャレンジ。Stage 01 でできなかったところをもう一度聴き取って、穴埋めを完成させよう。

英日 音声収録

1	revised	改訂された
2	per month	1カ月の
3	lower	下げる
4	provide	提供する
5	time-frame	期間；時間の枠
6	one-time charge	一括払いの料金
7	initial	最初の；初回の
8	at startup	開始時の
9	right price	適正な価格
10	inventory	在庫
11	shelf life	保存可能期間
12	guarantee	保証する
13	ship-date	出荷日
14	as long as ...	…である限り
15	electrostatic charge	静電気（の荷電）
16	exceed	超過する；超える
17	... degrees Celsius	摂氏…度
18	submit	提出する
19	approval	承認

◀)) ビジネス・リスニング（2回目）

Stage 03　日本語トランスレーション

ビジネス・ダイアローグの日本語を確認してみよう！　その上で、ダイアローグを聴きながら、まだできていない部分の穴埋めに再チャレンジしよう。

May:　メールと数量増加時のお見積の改訂版を受け取りましたか？
Mike:　ええ、ありがとうございます。ちょうどいま確認しているところでした。
May:　ご覧のとおりご注文のロットを月10万に増加すれば、コストを0.045ドルまで下げることができます。さらに50万になれば0.04ドルが見えてきますが、これはちょうど目標どおりの価格です。サンプル100ユニットについては、御社の設定期限内に1000ドルの1回払いでご提供可能です。
Mike:　そうですね。弊社の当初の生産量は5万（ユニット）からスタートします。ぴったりの値段にするためには、10カ月分の在庫を購入することになりますね。それができるかどうかわかりません。御社の製品の保管可能期間はどのくらいでしょう？
May:　静電気の荷電から保護され、温度が摂氏30度を超えないように管理されている場所に保管されている限りは、出荷日から3年間保証しています。
Mike:　わかりました。製造管理部と話をして、決裁をもらうために価格を上層部に提出します。うまくいくかもしれません。

🔊 ビジネス・リスニング（3回目）

Stage 04　英文トランスクリプション

ビジネス・ダイアローグの原稿を確認してみよう！　穴埋め部分の正解をチェックして、英文を理解し直そう。そのあとで、もう一度ダイアローグを聴いてみよう。

May:　① Did you get my email and revised quote for the volume increase?
Mike:　Yes, thank you. I was just ② going over it now.
May:　③ As you can see, increasing the order lots to 100,000 units per month allows us to lower the cost to $0.045, and if we ④ get to 500,000 units we are looking at $0.04, which is ⑤ right on target. We can provide 100 pcs of samples within your time-frame for a one-time charge of $1000.
Mike:　Well, our initial mass production volume at ⑥ startup ⑦ will be 50,000. To ⑧ get the ⑨ right price, we are looking at purchasing ten months of inventory. ⑩ I am not sure ⑪ that is something we can do. What is the shelf life for your product?
May:　⑫ Actually, we guarantee our product for three years from the ship-date as long as they are stored where they are protected from ⑬ electrostatic charge and the temperature is ⑭ controlled ⑮ not to exceed 30 degrees Celsius.
Mike:　Okay, I'll go over this with our production control department and ⑯ submit the pricing to management for approval. I think we ⑰ might be able to make this work.

🔊 ビジネス・リスニング（4回目）

Stage 05 音声変化をチェック

まとめとして、穴埋め部分の音声変化の特徴をスロースピードとナチュラルスピードで確認しよう。下記に示したカタカナ表記で音声変化を確認して、もう一度ビジネス・ダイアローグを聴き直してみよう。発音変化のルールは適宜復習しよう。

2種類の音声を収録

① **Did you**   ディッド・ユー   ▶ ディッジュー
 ☞ [d] と [j] の同化

② **going over it**   ゴウイング・オウヴァー・イット   ▶ ゴウイノウヴァリット
 ☞ 破裂音 [g] の脱落。3 語の連結

③ **As you**   アズ・ユー   ▶ アジュー
 ☞ [z] と [j] の同化

④ **get to**   ゲット・トゥー   ▶ ゲッ_トゥー
 ☞ [t] 音の脱落

⑤ **right on**   ライト・オン   ▶ ライド [ロ] ン
 ☞ 2 語の連結。連結部で破裂音 [t] の弾音化

⑥ **startup**   スタートアップ   ▶ スターダ [ラ] ップ
 ☞ 破裂音 [t] の弾音化

⑦ **will be**   ウィル・ビー   ▶ ウィ_ビ
 ☞ [l] 音の脱落

⑧ **get the**   ゲット・ザ   ▶ ゲッ_ザ
 ☞ [t] 音の脱落

⑨ **right price**   ライト・プライス   ▶ ライ_プライス
 ☞ 破裂音 [t] の脱落

⑩ **I am not**   アイ・アム・ナット   ▶ アイムナッ_
 ☞ 短縮形 I'm の発音。not の [t] も脱落する場合がある

⑪ **that is**   ザット・イズ   ▶ ザッディ [リ] ズ
 ☞ 2 語の連結。連結部で破裂音 [t] の弾音化

⑫ **Actually**   アクチュアリー   ▶ アクシュアリー
 ☞ 破裂音 [t] の脱落

⑬ **electrostatic**   イレクトロウスタティック   ▶ イレクトロウスタディ [リ] ック
 ☞ 破裂音の [t] の弾音化

⑭ **controlled**   カントゥロールド   ▶ カンチュロールド
 ☞ [ntr] の音が [ntʃr] に変化

⑮ **not to**   ナット・トゥー   ▶ ナッ_トゥー
 ☞ [t] 音の脱落

⑯ **submit the**   サブミット・ザ   ▶ サブミッ_ザ
 ☞ [t] 音の脱落

⑰ **might be**   マイト・ビ   ▶ マイ_ビ
 ☞ 破裂音 [t] の脱落

◀)) ビジネス・リスニング (5 回目)

Unit 07

エンドユーザーからの受注確定
Business from End User Awarded

Stage 01 穴埋めビジネス・リスニング

音声変化に注意してCDでビジネスのダイアローグを聴きながら、空欄部分を埋めてみよう。

ダイアローグ音声収録

Jack: We ① _____ _____ your proposal, and management has ② _____ _____ award AAA Safety ③ _____ _____ project.

Mike: That's great, I know ④ _____ _____ _____ _____ be very ⑤ _____ with our product quality, service and ⑥ _____ - _____ - _____ delivery.

Jack: There is one thing though. Even though ⑦ _____ _____ _____ sub-suppliers China Semicon is already an existing supplier to us, given the scope of this project and because your product ⑧ _____ _____ a passenger safety related device, our upper management is demanding that ⑨ _____ - _____ audit be conducted.

Mike: We can do that. We have our own internal audit forms. Would those suffice or do you have one formatted of your own ⑩ _____ _____ would prefer us to use?

Jack: I'll have someone from our ⑪ _____ assurance department send the appropriate forms to you by email.

Mike: Thanks. By the way, I've heard rumors that American ⑫ _____ is considering increasing their production volume for this upcoming model year by ⑬ _____%, is that ⑭ _____?

Jack: Well, ⑮ _____ _____ is a ⑯ _____ too far ⑰ _____ _____ see. Would that present any capacity issues for you?

Mike: No, we can handle anything you need.

◀)) ビジネス・リスニング（1回目）

Stage 02 ビジネス・ボキャビル

ビジネスのボキャブラリーを CD で確認しよう。そのあとでもう一度、ビジネス・リスニングにチャレンジ。Stage 01 でできなかったところをもう一度聴き取って、穴埋めを完成させよう。

英日 音声収録

1	proposal	提案 (書)
2	award	与える;授与する
3	satisfied	満足した
4	quality	品質
5	just-in-time	適時の
6	delivery	配送
7	sub-supplier	下請け業者
8	existing	既存の;現存する
9	given ...	…を考慮すると
10	scope of ...	…の範囲;規模
11	passenger safety	顧客の安全
12	... related device	…に関連する装置
13	demand	要求する
14	on-site	現地での
15	audit	査察;監査
16	internal	内部の
17	form	文書
18	suffice	十分である
19	formatted	書式化された
20	quality assurance	品質保証
21	appropriate	適切な

🔊 ビジネス・リスニング（2回目）

Stage 03 日本語トランスレーション

ビジネス・ダイアローグの日本語を確認してみよう！ その上で、ダイアローグを聴きながら、まだできていない部分の穴埋めに再チャレンジしよう。

Jack: 御社のご提案書を拝見しまして、AAA セーフティーさんにプロジェクトをお願いすることに経営陣が決定しました。

Mike: それはすばらしい。弊社の製品の質とサービス、タイムリーな配送に非常にご満足いただけると思います。

Jack: ただし、ひとつだけ申し上げておくことがあります。御社の下請け業者のひとつであるチャイナ・セミコンはすでに弊社にとっても既存の下請け企業でもあるのですが、このプロジェクトの規模を鑑みても、また御社の製品が乗客の安全に関わる機器であるところからも、弊社の上層部では、現地での監査を実行してほしいと要求しております。

Mike: それは可能です。弊社には、独自の内部監査フォームがございますので、そちらでよろしいでしょうか？ あるいは御社のフォーマットを弊社に使ってほしいのでしょうか？

Jack: 品質管理部の人間に適切なフォームをメールで送らせるようにします。

Mike: 助かります。ところで、アメリカン・オートでは、次のモデル年度に20％の増産を検討中という噂を耳にしますが、それはほんとうでしょうか？

Jack: 来年のことは、まだちょっとわかりません。そうなると御社の生産能力に問題でも出てきますか？

Mike: いいえ、弊社では御社の必要とするものならなんでも対処可能です。

🔊 ビジネス・リスニング（3回目）

Stage 04 英文トランスクリプション

ビジネス・ダイアローグの原稿を確認してみよう！ 穴埋め部分の正解をチェックして、英文を理解し直そう。そのあとで、もう一度ダイアローグを聴いてみよう。

Jack: We ① went over your proposal, and management has ② decided to award AAA Safety ③ with the project.

Mike: That's great, I know ④ you are going to be very ⑤ satisfied with our product quality, service and ⑥ just-in-time delivery.

Jack: There is one thing though. Even though ⑦ one of your sub-suppliers China Semicon is already an existing supplier to us, given the scope of this project and because your product ⑧ will be a passenger safety related device, our upper management is demanding that ⑨ an on-site audit be conducted.

Mike: We can do that. We have our own internal audit forms. Would those suffice or do you have one formatted of your own ⑩ that you would prefer us to use?

Jack: I'll have someone from our ⑪ quality assurance department send the appropriate forms to you by email.

Mike: Thanks. By the way, I've heard rumors that American ⑫ Auto is considering increasing their production volume for this upcoming model year by ⑬ 20％, is that ⑭ true?

Jack: Well, ⑮ next year is a ⑯ little too far ⑰ out to see. Would that present any capacity issues for you?

Mike: No, we can handle anything you need.

🔊 ビジネス・リスニング（4回目）

Stage 05 音声変化をチェック

まとめとして、穴埋め部分の音声変化の特徴をスロースピードとナチュラルスピードで確認しよう。下記に示したカタカナ表記で音声変化を確認して、もう一度ビジネス・ダイアローグを聴き直してみよう。発音変化のルールは適宜復習しよう。

2種類の音声を収録　CD 1-21

① **went over**　ウェント・オウヴァー　▶ ウェノウヴァー
　☞ 破裂音 [t] の脱落。2 語の連結

② **decided to**　ディサイディッド・トゥー　▶ ディサイディ [リ] ッ_トゥー
　☞ 2番目の [d] 音の弾音化。decided 末尾の [d] 音の脱落

③ **with the**　ウィズ・ザ　▶ ウィ_ザ
　☞ [ð] の脱落

④ **you are going to**　ユー・アー・ゴウイング・トゥー　▶ ユーゴナ ; ユゴナ
　☞ you are は [ユー] あるいは [ユ] と弱化。going to は [ゴナ] と変化。

⑤ **satisfied**　サティスファイド　▶ サディ [リ] スファイド
　☞ 破裂音 [t] の弾音化

⑥ **just-in-time**　ジャスト・イン・タイム　▶ ジャスティンタイム
　☞ just に in が連結

⑦ **one of your**　ワン・アヴ・ユア　▶ ワナ_ユア
　☞ one の [n] に of が連結。of の [v] 音が脱落

⑧ **will be**　ウィル・ビー　▶ ウィ_ビ
　☞ [l] 音の脱落

⑨ **an on-site**　アン・オンサイト　▶ アノンサイト
　☞ 2語が連結

⑩ **that you**　ザット・ユー　▶ ザッチュウー
　☞ [t] と [j] の同化

⑪ **quality**　クァラティー　▶ クァラディ [リ] ー
　☞ 破裂音 [t] の弾音化

⑫ **Auto**　オートウ　▶ オード [ロ] ウ
　☞ 破裂音 [t] の弾音化

⑬ **20**　トゥエンティー　▶ トゥエニー
　☞ 破裂音の [t] の脱落

⑭ **true**　トゥルー　▶ チュルー
　☞ [tr] の音が [tʃr] に変化

⑮ **next year**　ネクスト・イヤー　▶ ネクスチャー
　☞ [t] と [j] の同化

⑯ **little**　リトゥル　▶ リドゥ [ル] ル
　☞ 破裂の [t] の弾音化

⑰ **out to**　アウト・トゥー　▶ アウ_トゥー
　☞ [t] 音の脱落

🔊 ビジネス・リスニング (5 回目)

Unit 08

中国工場での監査依頼
Customer Request for Business Visit/Plant Audit

Stage 01 穴埋めビジネス・リスニング

音声変化に注意してCDでビジネスのモノローグを聴きながら、空欄部分を埋めてみよう。

モノローグ音声収録

Mike: May, this is Mike Gray from AAA. Sorry I didn't catch you ① _____ _____ desk. Our customer has asked that we ② _____ _____ and do an on-site audit. ③ _____ _____ know this is ④ _____ standard procedure. ⑤ _____ _____ like to make arrangements for my manager and me to ⑥ _____ _____ office and take a tour of your plant and manufacturing ⑦ _____. We'd like to ⑧ _____ _____ management and ⑨ _____ control staff, and also discuss pricing. ⑩ _____ _____ also ⑪ _____ _____ give a presentation ⑫ _____ _____ company, supplier expectations and where we see this project going. I'm thinking that two nights and three days should do. We are ⑬ _____ _____ either the 23rd through the ⑭ _____ of this month or the 30th 'til the 1st of April. Please check your schedules and email me to ⑮ _____ _____ know what ⑯ _____ _____ suitable for you. We will ⑰ _____ _____ make the necessary travel arrangements and visa applications, so please ⑱ _____ _____ to me as soon as possible. Thanks.

🔊 ビジネス・リスニング（1回目）

Stage 02 ビジネス・ボキャビル

ビジネスのボキャブラリーを CD で確認しよう。そのあとでもう一度、ビジネス・リスニングにチャレンジ。Stage 01 でできなかったところをもう一度聴き取って、穴埋めを完成させよう。

英日 音声収録

1	catch	つかまえる（ここでは電話でつかまえる意）
2	customer	顧客
3	on-site audit	現地査察；監査
4	standard	標準的な
5	procedure	手続き；手順
6	arrangement	手配
7	manager	上司；部課長
8	take a tour of ...	…を査察する；見て回る
9	manufacturing facility	生産設備；施設
10	quality control	品質管理
11	pricing	値付け；価格付け
12	give a presentation	プレゼンテーションを行う
13	supplier	下請け業者；供給業者
14	expectation	期待
15	either A or B	A か B のどちらか
16	schedule	スケジュール
17	suitable for ...	…に適する
18	visa	ビザ；入国査証
19	application	申請
20	get back to ...	…に折り返し連絡する

🔊 ビジネス・リスニング（2回目）

Stage 03　日本語トランスレーション

ビジネス・モノローグの日本語を確認してみよう！　その上で、モノローグを聴きながら、まだできていない部分の穴埋めに再チャレンジしよう。

Mike: メイ、AAA のマイク・グレイです。直接お話できずすみません。うちの顧客が、御社を訪問して現地での監査を行ってほしいと、弊社に依頼してきました。ご存知のとおり、これはとても一般的な手順です。私と上司のために、御社のオフィス訪問と工場と生産施設の見学の手配をしたいと思います。御社の経営陣や品質管理スタッフのみなさんにもお会いして、価格に関してもご相談したいと思っています。また、弊社についてや下請けに希望する事柄、このプロジェクトの先行きになど関して、プレゼンテーションを行いたいと思っています。2泊3日で十分だと思います。今月の23日から25日か、30日から4月の1日のどちらかがいいと思っています。御社のスケジュールをチェックしていただき、御社に都合のいいところをメールでお知らせください。旅行の手配やビザの申請をしなければならないので、できるだけ早めにお返事をください。よろしくお願いいたします。

🔊 ビジネス・リスニング（3回目）

Stage 04　英文トランスクリプション

ビジネス・モノローグの原稿を確認してみよう！　穴埋め部分の正解をチェックして、英文を理解し直そう。そのあとで、もう一度モノローグを聴いてみよう。

Mike: May, this is Mike Gray from AAA. Sorry I didn't catch you ① at your desk. Our customer has asked that we ② visit you and do an on-site audit. ③ As you know this is ④ pretty standard procedure. ⑤ I would like to make arrangements for my manager and me to ⑥ visit your office and take a tour of your plant and manufacturing ⑦ facility. We'd like to ⑧ meet your management and ⑨ quality control staff, and also discuss pricing. ⑩ We would also ⑪ like to give a presentation ⑫ on our company, supplier expectations and where we see this project going. I'm thinking that two nights and three days should do. We are ⑬ looking at either the 23rd through the ⑭ 25th of this month or the 30th 'til the 1st of April. Please check your schedules and email me to ⑮ let me know what ⑯ would be suitable for you. We will ⑰ need to make the necessary travel arrangements and visa applications, so please ⑱ get back to me as soon as possible. Thanks.

🔊 ビジネス・リスニング（4回目）

Stage 05 音声変化をチェック

まとめとして、穴埋め部分の音声変化の特徴をスロースピードとナチュラルスピードで確認しよう。下記に示したカタカナ表記で音声変化を確認して、もう一度ビジネス・モノローグを聴き直してみよう。発音変化のルールは適宜復習しよう。

2種類の音声を収録

CD 1-24

	語句	スロー	ナチュラル
①	**at your** ☞ [t] と [j] の同化	アット・ユァ	▶ アッチュァ
②	**visit you** ☞ [t] と [j] の同化	ヴィズィット・ユー	▶ ヴィズィッチュー
③	**As you** ☞ [z] と [j] の同化	アズ・ユー	▶ アジュー
④	**pretty** ☞ 破裂音 [t] の弾音化	プリティー	▶ プリディ [リ] ー
⑤	**I would** ☞ 短縮形 I'd の発音	アイ・ウッド	▶ アイド
⑥	**visit your** ☞ [t] と [j] の同化	ヴィズィット・ユァ	▶ ヴィズィッチュァ
⑦	**facility** ☞ 破裂音 [t] の弾音化	ファシラティー	▶ ファシラディ [リ] ー
⑧	**meet your** ☞ [t] と [j] の同化	ミート・ユァ	▶ ミーチュァ
⑨	**quality** ☞ 破裂音 [t] の弾音化	クァラティー	▶ クァラディ [リ] ー
⑩	**We would** ☞ 短縮形 We'd の発音	ウィ・ウッド	▶ ウィド
⑪	**like to** ☞ 破裂音 [k] の脱落	ライク・トゥー	▶ ライ__トゥ
⑫	**on our** ☞ 2 語の連結	オン・アウァ	▶ オナウァ
⑬	**looking at** ☞ looking の [g] の脱落。2 語の連結	ルッキング・アット	▶ ルッキナット
⑭	**25th** ☞ 破裂音の [t] が脱落	トゥエンティーフィフス	▶ トゥエニーフィフス
⑮	**let me** ☞ 破裂音の [t] が脱落	レット・ミー	▶ レッ__ミ
⑯	**would be** ☞ 破裂音の [d] が脱落	ウッド・ビー	▶ ウッ__ビ
⑰	**need to** ☞ 破裂音の [d] が脱落。破裂音 [t] は弾音化することもある	ニード・トゥー	▶ ニー__トゥー；ニードゥ [ル] ー
⑱	**get back** ☞ 破裂音の [t] が脱落	ゲット・バック	▶ ゲッ__バック

🔊 ビジネス・リスニング（5 回目）

Unit 09

出張の手配
Making Travel Arrangements for Trip

Stage 01　穴埋めビジネス・リスニング

音声変化に注意して CD でビジネスのダイアローグを聴きながら、空欄部分を埋めてみよう。

ダイアローグ音声収録

ABC travel: Thank you for calling ABC travel, how may I help you?

Mike: This is Mike Gray with AAA Safety Systems. I'd like to ① _____ _____ reservation.

ABC travel: We always ② _____ _____ business. Departing Atlanta when?

Mike: Leaving Atlanta on the ③ _____, flying into Shanghai. Returning on the ④ _____.

ABC travel: Are you ⑤ _____ alone?

Mike: No, Mr. Smith ⑥ _____ _____ accompanying me.

ABC travel: Ok, ⑦ _____ _____ see. I have Delta flight 1389 departing at 11am on the 23rd, arriving in Shanghai at 4 pm local time on the ⑧ _____. Flight 1323 leaves Shanghai at 5pm on the 26th, ⑨ _____ _____ _____ Atlanta at 3pm the 26th local time. ⑩ _____ _____ like business class or economy?

Mike: Economy, but please ⑪ _____ _____ our requests for upgrades.

ABC travel: ⑫ _____ _____ need any hotel reservations or ⑬ _____ cars?

Mike: No, thank you.

ABC travel: Okay then, I will send you both ⑭ _____ _____ with your itineraries. Please ⑮ _____ _____ _____ me with confirmation by 5pm today.

Mike: Thank you.

◀)) ビジネス・リスニング（1回目）

Stage 02 ビジネス・ボキャビル

ビジネスのボキャブラリーを CD で確認しよう。そのあとでもう一度、ビジネス・リスニングにチャレンジ。Stage 01 でできなかったところをもう一度聴き取って、穴埋めを完成させよう。

英日 音声収録

CD 1-26

1	call	電話する
2	make a reservation	予約する
3	appreciate	感謝する；ありがたく思う
4	depart	（乗り物などが）出発する
5	leave	出発する
6	fly into ...	…まで飛行する
7	return	戻る
8	alone	ひとりで
9	accompany	同行する；同伴する
10	flight	フライト；飛行
11	arrive in ...	…に到着する
12	local time	現地時間
13	business class	ビジネスクラス
14	economy (class)	エコノミークラス
15	request	要求；リクエスト
16	upgrade	アップグレード
17	reservation	予約
18	rental car	レンタカー
19	itinerary	旅程；旅程表
20	confirmation	確認

🔊 ビジネス・リスニング（2回目）

Stage 03　日本語トランスレーション

ビジネス・ダイアローグの日本語を確認してみよう！　その上で、ダイアローグを聴きながら、まだできていない部分の穴埋めに再チャレンジしよう。

ABC travel: ABCトラベルにお電話ありがとうございます。どのようなご用件でしょうか？
Mike:　　　AAAセーフティー・システムズのマイク・グレイです。予約をお願いしたいのですが。
ABC travel: いつもありがとうございます。いつアトランタをご出発でしょうか？
Mike:　　　アトランタを23日に出て、上海まで。26日に戻ります。
ABC travel: おひとりでのご出張でしょうか？
Mike:　　　いいえ、スミスさんが同行します。
ABC travel: わかりました。お待ちください。23日午前11時出発のデルタ航空の1389便がございます。上海には現地時間の24日の午後4時到着になります。1323便は上海を26日の午後5時に出発して、アトランタに26日の午後3時に戻ります。ビジネスクラスをご所望でしょうか？それともエコノミーシートですか？
Mike:　　　エコノミーでお願いします。ただし、アップグレード依頼を出しておいてください。
ABC travel: ホテルやレンタカーのご予約は必要ですか？
Mike:　　　いいえ、いりません。
ABC travel: では、おふたりに旅程表をメールでお送りしておきます。本日の午後5時までに確認のご連絡をお願いいたします。
Mike:　　　ありがとう。

◀)) ビジネス・リスニング（3回目）

Stage 04　英文トランスクリプション

ビジネス・ダイアローグの原稿を確認してみよう！　穴埋め部分の正解をチェックして、英文を理解し直そう。そのあとで、もう一度ダイアローグを聴いてみよう。

ABC travel: Thank you for calling ABC travel, how may I help you?
Mike:　　　This is Mike Gray with AAA Safety Systems. I'd like to ① make a reservation.
ABC travel: We always ② appreciate your business. Departing Atlanta when?
Mike:　　　Leaving Atlanta on the ③ 23rd, flying into Shanghai. Returning on the ④ 26th.
ABC travel: Are you ⑤ traveling alone?
Mike:　　　No, Mr. Smith ⑥ will be accompanying me.
ABC travel: Ok, ⑦ let me see. I have Delta flight 1389 departing at 11am on the 23rd, arriving in Shanghai at 4 pm local time on the ⑧ 24th. Flight 1323 leaves Shanghai at 5 pm on the 26th, ⑨ arriving back in Atlanta at 3pm the 26th local time. ⑩ Would you like business class or economy?
Mike:　　　Economy, but please ⑪ put in our requests for upgrades.
ABC travel: ⑫ Do you need any hotel reservations or ⑬ rental cars?
Mike:　　　No, thank you.
ABC travel: Okay then, I will send you both ⑭ an email with your itineraries. Please ⑮ get back to me with confirmation by 5pm today.
Mike:　　　Thank you.

◀)) ビジネス・リスニング（4回目）

Stage 05 　音声変化をチェック

まとめとして、穴埋め部分の音声変化の特徴をスロースピードとナチュラルスピードで確認しよう。下記に示したカタカナ表記で音声変化を確認して、もう一度ビジネス・ダイアローグを聴き直してみよう。発音変化のルールは適宜復習しよう。

2種類の音声を収録　　　　　　　　　　　　　　　　　　　　　　　CD 1-27

① **make a**
☞ 2語が連結
　　　メイク・ア　　　　　　　　　▶　メイカ

② **appreciate your**
☞ [t] と [j] の同化
　　　アプリーシェイト・ユア　　　▶　アプリーシェイチュア

③ **23rd**
☞ 破裂音 [t] の脱落
　　　トゥエンティーサード　　　　▶　トゥエニーサード

④ **26th**
☞ 破裂音 [t] の脱落
　　　トゥエンティーシックスス　　▶　トゥエニーシックスス

⑤ **traveling**
☞ [tr] の音が [tʃr] に変化
　　　トゥラヴェリング　　　　　　▶　チュラヴェリング

⑥ **will be**
☞ [l] 音の脱落
　　　ウィル・ビー　　　　　　　　▶　ウィ＿ビ

⑦ **let me**
☞ 破裂音 [t] の脱落
　　　レット・ミー　　　　　　　　▶　レッ＿ミ

⑧ **24th**
☞ 破裂音 [t] の脱落
　　　トゥエンティーフォース　　　▶　トゥエニーフォース

⑨ **arriving back in**
☞ arriving の [g] 音の脱落。back と in が連結
　　　アライヴィング・バック・イン　▶　アライヴィン＿バッキン

⑩ **Would you**
☞ [d] と [j] の同化
　　　ウッド・ユー　　　　　　　　▶　ウッジュー

⑪ **put in**
☞ 2語が連結。連結部で破裂音 [t] が弾音化
　　　プット・イン　　　　　　　　▶　プッディ[リ]ン

⑫ **Do you**
☞ Do の弱化。さらに [d] と [j] が同化することもある
　　　ドゥー・ユー　　　　　　　　▶　ドゥユ；ジュ

⑬ **rental**
☞ 破裂音 [t] の脱落
　　　レントゥル　　　　　　　　　▶　レヌル

⑭ **an email**
☞ 2語が連結
　　　アン・イーメイル　　　　　　▶　アニーメイル

⑮ **get back to**
☞ 破裂音 [t] と [k] の脱落
　　　ゲット・バック・トゥー　　　▶　ゲッ＿バッ＿トゥー

🔊 ビジネス・リスニング（5回目）

Unit 10

出張の詳細について
Confirmation of Business Trip Details

Stage 01　穴埋めビジネス・リスニング

音声変化に注意してCDでビジネスのダイアローグを聴きながら、空欄部分を埋めてみよう。

ダイアローグ音声収録

May: May Chang, how ① _____ _____ help you?

Mike: May, this Mike Gray with AAA Safety Systems. I ② _____ _____ ③ _____ _____ know the details of our ④ _____. We ⑤ _____ _____ ⑥ _____ _____ Shanghai Pudong at 4pm on the ⑦ _____, and we'll be flying out on the ⑧ _____.

May: Have you ⑨ _____ _____ hotel reservations?

Mike: Yes, we took your ⑩ _____ and booked rooms at the Hilton.

May: That's good. It's ⑪ _____ _____ convenient location and not too far from here. I will make arrangements to have you picked up ⑫ _____ _____ airport. The driver will ⑬ _____ _____ at baggage claim.

Mike: Another thing we need ⑭ _____ _____ _____ of recommendation to apply for the visa.

May: I just ⑮ _____ _____ copy of your and Mr. Smith's passport photo page and I'll draft the letter and file the necessary application documents. It ⑯ _____ _____ good to ⑰ _____ _____ detailed copy of your schedule as well.

Mike: Great, thanks. I'll shoot them to you ⑱ _____ _____ _____ ⑲ _____ today.

🔊 ビジネス・リスニング（1回目）

Stage 02 ビジネス・ボキャビル

ビジネスのボキャブラリーをCDで確認しよう。そのあとでもう一度、ビジネス・リスニングにチャレンジ。Stage 01 でできなかったところをもう一度聴き取って、穴埋めを完成させよう。

英日 音声収録

1	let someone know	…に知らせる
2	details	詳細
3	fly out	(出発するために) 飛び立つ
4	suggestion	提案；おすすめ
5	book	予約する
6	convenient	便利な
7	location	立地
8	far from ...	…から遠い
9	pick up	(人を) 拾う
10	baggage claim	手荷物引き渡し所
11	letter of recommendation	推薦状
12	apply for ...	…に申請する；申し込む
13	passport	パスポート
14	draft	書く
15	necessary	必要な
16	application documents	申請書類
17	detailed	詳細な
18	as well	同様に
19	shoot	急いで送る
20	later today	本日後ほど

◀)) ビジネス・リスニング (2回目)

Stage 03　日本語トランスレーション

ビジネス・ダイアローグの日本語を確認してみよう！ その上で、ダイアローグを聴きながら、まだできていない部分の穴埋めに再チャレンジしよう。

May: メイ・チャンでございます。どのようなご用件でしょうか？
Mike: メイ、AAAセーフティー・システムズのマイク・グレイです。出張の詳細をご連絡させてください。上海のプードンに24日の午後4時に到着し、26日の便で帰国します。
May: ホテルの予約はなさいましたか？
Mike: ええ、ご提案に従って、ヒルトンに部屋を予約しました。
May: それはよかったです。便利な立地にあって、弊社からも遠くないですから。みなさんを空港でピックアップできるように手配しておきますね。運転手が手荷物引き渡し所でお迎えいたします。
Mike: もうひとつ、ビザ申請の推薦状をお願いしたいのですが。
May: あなたとスミスさんのパスポートの写真ページのコピーがあれば、私が手紙を書いて、必要な申請書類を提出しますよ。詳細なスケジュールのコピーもあるといいですね。
Mike: ありがとうございます。本日後ほど急いでメールで送りますね。

🔊 ビジネス・リスニング（3回目）

Stage 04　英文トランスクリプション

ビジネス・ダイアローグの原稿を確認してみよう！ 穴埋め部分の正解をチェックして、英文を理解し直そう。そのあとで、もう一度ダイアローグを聴いてみよう。

May: May Chang, how ① can I help you?
Mike: May, this Mike Gray with AAA Safety Systems. I ② wanted to ③ let you know the details of our ④ trip. We ⑤ will be ⑥ arriving at Shanghai Pudong at 4 pm on the ⑦ 24th, and we'll be flying out on the ⑧ 26th.
May: Have you ⑨ made your hotel reservations?
Mike: Yes, we took your ⑩ suggestion and booked rooms at the Hilton.
May: That's good. It's ⑪ in a convenient location and not too far from here. I will make arrangements to have you picked up ⑫ at the airport. The driver will ⑬ meet you at baggage claim.
Mike: Another thing we need ⑭ is a letter of recommendation to apply for the visa.
May: I just ⑮ need a copy of your and Mr. Smith's passport photo page and I'll draft the letter and file the necessary application documents. It ⑯ would be good to ⑰ have a detailed copy of your schedule as well.
Mike: Great, thanks. I'll shoot them to you ⑱ in an email ⑲ later today.

🔊 ビジネス・リスニング（4回目）

Stage 05 音声変化をチェック

まとめとして、穴埋め部分の音声変化の特徴をスロースピードとナチュラルスピードで確認しよう。下記に示したカタカナ表記で音声変化を確認して、もう一度ビジネス・ダイアローグを聴き直してみよう。発音変化のルールは適宜復習しよう。

2種類の音声を収録　　CD 1-30

① **can I** 　　　　　キャン・アイ　　　　▶ キャナイ
　☞ 2語が連結

② **wanted to** 　　　ワンティッド・トゥー　▶ ワニッ＿トゥー
　☞ 破裂音 [t] と [d] の脱落。to の破裂音 [t] が弾音化することもある

③ **let you** 　　　　レット・ユー　　　　▶ レッチュー
　☞ [t] と [j] の同化

④ **trip** 　　　　　　トゥリップ　　　　　▶ チュリップ
　☞ [tr] の音が [tʃr] に変化

⑤ **will be** 　　　　ウィル・ビー　　　　▶ ウィ＿ビー
　☞ [l] 音の脱落

⑥ **arriving at** 　　アライヴィング・アット　▶ アライヴィン＿アッ＿
　☞ 破裂音 [g] と [t] の脱落。2語が連結することもある

⑦ **24th** 　　　　　トゥエンティーフォース　▶ トゥエニーフォース
　☞ 破裂音 [t] の脱落

⑧ **26th** 　　　　　トゥエンティーシックスス　▶ トゥエニーシックスス
　☞ 破裂音 [t] の脱落

⑨ **made your** 　　メイド・ユア　　　　　▶ メイジュア
　☞ [d] と [j] の同化

⑩ **suggestion** 　　サグジェスチョン　　　▶ サ＿ジェスチョン
　☞ [g] 音の脱落

⑪ **in a** 　　　　　イン・ア　　　　　　▶ イナ
　☞ 2語が連結

⑫ **at the** 　　　　アット・ズィ　　　　　▶ アッ＿ズィ
　☞ 破裂音 [t] の脱落

⑬ **meet you** 　　ミート・ユー　　　　　▶ ミーチュー
　☞ [t] と [j] の同化

⑭ **is a letter** 　　イズ・ア・レター　　　▶ イザレダ [ラ] ー
　☞ is と a が連結。letter の破裂音 [t] の弾音化

⑮ **need a** 　　　　ニード・ア　　　　　　▶ ニーダ [ラ]
　☞ 2語が連結。連結部の破裂音の [d] が弾音化することもある

⑯ **would be** 　　ウッド・ビー　　　　　▶ ウッ＿ビー
　☞ 破裂音 [d] の脱落

⑰ **have a** 　　　　ハヴ・ア　　　　　　　▶ ハヴァ
　☞ 2語が連結

⑱ **in an email** 　イン・アン・イーメイル　▶ イナニーメイル
　☞ 3語が連結

⑲ **later** 　　　　　レイター　　　　　　▶ レイダ [ラ] ー
　☞ 破裂音 [t] の弾音化

🔊 ビジネス・リスニング（5回目）

出張の詳細について

Unit 11

空港での待ち合わせ
Pickup at the Airport

Stage 01 穴埋めビジネス・リスニング

音声変化に注意して CD でビジネスのダイアローグを聴きながら、空欄部分を埋めてみよう。

ダイアローグ音声収録

Tom: Which carousel did they say our bags ① _____ _____?

Mike: D, I think. Yep, there's the driver ② _____ _____.

Driver: Mr. Gray and Mr. Smith?

Mike: That's us.

Driver: Welcome to Shanghai. Ms. Chang wanted to ③ _____ _____ in person but something urgent ④ _____ _____. How was your flight?

Mike: ⑤ _____ smooth, all things considered. We were late taking off but ⑥ _____ _____ the time in the air. It's still a long flight though.

Driver: Glad to ⑦ _____ _____. No problems with Customs, I presume?

Mike: ⑧ _____ _____ _____. How long do you think it will take to get to the hotel?

Driver: Well, it's rush hour but ⑨ _____ _____ think ⑩ _____ _____ take more than ⑪ _____ _____. Of course, it always tends to be rush hour in Shanghai. I'll be the one picking you up in the morning tomorrow. The plant is ⑫ _____ _____ ⑬ _____-minute ride from the hotel. Here, ⑭ _____ _____ help you ⑮ _____ _____ luggage. The limo is ⑯ _____ _____.

Mike: Thanks.

◀)) ビジネス・リスニング (1回目)

Stage 02 ビジネス・ボキャビル

ビジネスのボキャブラリーをCDで確認しよう。そのあとでもう一度、ビジネス・リスニングにチャレンジ。Stage 01 でできなかったところをもう一度聴き取って、穴埋めを完成させよう。

英日 音声収録

1	carousel	ベルトコンベアー
2	welcome to ...	…へようこそ
3	greet	迎えにくる；あいさつする
4	in person	直接；直に
5	urgent	緊急の
6	come up	生じる
7	smooth	支障のない；順調な
8	all things considered	結局は；最終的には
9	take off	飛び立つ
10	make up	取り戻す；埋め合わせる；補う
11	in the air	空で；飛行中に
12	customs	税関
13	..., I presume?	…でしょう？
14	not ... at all	まったく…ない
15	tend to ...	…する傾向がある
16	ride	乗車
17	luggage	荷物
18	limo	リムジン
19	outside	外に

🔊 ビジネス・リスニング（2回目）

空港での待ち合わせ

Stage 03　日本語トランスレーション

ビジネス・ダイアローグの日本語を確認してみよう！ その上で、ダイアローグを聴きながら、まだできていない部分の穴埋めに再チャレンジしよう。

Tom:　僕たちのバッグはどのコンベアーだって言ってたっけ？
Mike:　Dだと思いますね。ああ、あそこにドライバーが！
Driver:　グレイさんとスミスさんですか？
Mike:　そうです。
Driver:　上海へようこそ。チャンさんも直接、迎えにきたがっていたのですが、なにか急用ができたそうです。フライトはいかがでしたか？
Mike:　結局はスムーズでしたね。離陸は遅れましたけど、上空で時間を短縮できましたし。しかし、それでも長いフライトではありますけど。
Driver:　よかったです。税関でも問題はなかったご様子ですね。
Mike:　まったくなかったです。ホテルまではどのくらいかかるでしょう？
Driver:　えーと、ラッシュの時間帯ですが1時間はかからないと思います。当然ですが、上海ではいつもラッシュ気味ですしね。明日の朝も私がお迎えに上がりますよ。工場はホテルから車で約40分です。はい、荷物をお手伝いしますよ。リムジンはすぐ外にありますので。
Mike:　ありがとう。

🔊 ビジネス・リスニング（3回目）

Stage 04　英文トランスクリプション

ビジネス・ダイアローグの原稿を確認してみよう！ 穴埋め部分の正解をチェックして、英文を理解し直そう。そのあとで、もう一度ダイアローグを聴いてみよう。

Tom:　Which carousel did they say our bags ① would be?
Mike:　D, I think. Yep, there's the driver ② right there.
Driver:　Mr. Gray and Mr. Smith?
Mike:　That's us.
Driver:　Welcome to Shanghai. Ms. Chang wanted to ③ greet you in person but something urgent ④ came up. How was your flight?
Mike:　⑤ Pretty smooth, all things considered. We were late taking off but ⑥ made up the time in the air. It's still a long flight though.
Driver:　Glad to ⑦ hear it. No problems with Customs, I presume?
Mike:　⑧ Not at all. How long do you think it will take to get to the hotel?
Driver:　Well, it's rush hour but ⑨ I don't think ⑩ it will take more than ⑪ an hour. Of course, it always tends to be rush hour in Shanghai. I'll be the one picking you up in the morning tomorrow. The plant is ⑫ about a ⑬ forty-minute ride from the hotel. Here, ⑭ let me help you ⑮ with that luggage. The limo is ⑯ right outside.
Mike:　Thanks.

🔊 ビジネス・リスニング（4回目）

Stage 05 音声変化をチェック

まとめとして、穴埋め部分の音声変化の特徴をスロースピードとナチュラルスピードで確認しよう。下記に示したカタカナ表記で音声変化を確認して、もう一度ビジネス・ダイアローグを聴き直してみよう。発音変化のルールは適宜復習しよう。

2種類の音声を収録

① **would be** ウッド・ビー ▶ ウッ_ビー
  ☞ 破裂音 [d] の脱落

② **right there** ライト・ゼア ▶ ライ_ゼア
  ☞ [t] 音の脱落

③ **greet you** グリート・ユー ▶ グリーチュー
  ☞ [t] と [j] の同化

④ **came up** ケイム・アップ ▶ ケイマップ
  ☞ 2語の連結

⑤ **Pretty** プリティー ▶ プリディ [リ] ー
  ☞ 破裂音 [t] の弾音化

⑥ **made up** メイド・アップ ▶ メイダ [ラ] ップ
  ☞ 2語の連結。連結部は弾音化することもある

⑦ **hear it** ヒア・イット ▶ ヒアリット
  ☞ 2語の連結

⑧ **Not at all** ナット・アット・オール ▶ ナッダ [ラ] ッド [ロ] ール
  ☞ 3語の連結。2カ所の連結部で破裂音 [t] が弾音化

⑨ **I don't** アイ・ドゥント ▶ アイドン；アイ_オウン_
  ☞ don't が弱化して [ドン] と発音。[d] や [t] が脱落して [アイ_オウン_] と発音することもある

⑩ **it will** イット・ウィル ▶ イドゥル；イッ_ウィル
  ☞ 短縮形 it'll [イットル] の破裂音 [t] が弾音化し [イドゥル] と発音。it will から [t] 音だけが脱落することもある

⑪ **an hour** アン・アウア ▶ アナウァ
  ☞ 2語が連結

⑫ **about a** アバウト・ア ▶ アバウダ [ラ]
  ☞ 2語が連結。連結部の破裂音 [t] が弾音化

⑬ **forty** フォーティー ▶ フォーディ [リ] ー
  ☞ 破裂音 [t] の弾音化

⑭ **let me** レット・ミー ▶ レッ_ミー
  ☞ 破裂音 [t] の脱落

⑮ **with that** ウィズ・ザット ▶ ウィ_ザット
  ☞ [ð] 音の脱落

⑯ **right outside** ライト・アウトサイド ▶ ライダ [ラ] ウ_サイド
  ☞ 2語が連結。連結部の破裂音 [t] が弾音化。out の [t] が脱落することもある

🔊 ビジネス・リスニング（5回目）

Unit 12

工場を案内する
Plant Tour

Stage 01 穴埋めビジネス・リスニング

音声変化に注意してCDでビジネスのダイアローグを聴きながら、空欄部分を埋めてみよう。

ダイアローグ音声収録　　CD 1-34

May: This is our main production ① _____. We ② _____ _____ sister plant ③ _____ ④ _____ _____ hours from here. Our production lines are completely ⑤ _____, and ⑥ _____ most of the production processes are ⑦ _____ _____ clean rooms.

Tom: Are you ISO and TS ⑧ _____?

May: Yes we are certified ISO 9000 and TS 16949. After each stage during manufacture, the parts go through a vigorous inspection method.

Mike: How many ⑨ _____ employees do you have?

May: Including sales, marketing, operations, ⑩ _____ control and management, we have ⑪ _____ staff ⑫ _____ _____ facility and 65 at our sister plant. ⑬ _____ _____ where the final parts are inspected, packaged and warehoused until they are shipped out to the customer. We implement the ⑭ _____ technology in our bar code labels, and can customize labels to suit any of the customer's needs. We are continuously reviewing our production ⑮ _____ and design to improve our efficiency and streamline cost. ⑯ _____ _____ alone we have invested ⑰ _____ _____ one-point two million dollars in equipment upgrades.

🔊 ビジネス・リスニング（1回目）

Stage 02 ビジネス・ボキャビル

ビジネスのボキャブラリーを CD で確認しよう。そのあとでもう一度、ビジネス・リスニングにチャレンジ。Stage 01 でできなかったところをもう一度聴き取って、穴埋めを完成させよう。

英日 音声収録

1. facility — 施設；設備
2. production line — 生産ライン
3. obviously — 言うまでもないことだが
4. be conducted in ... — …で行われる
5. clean room — 無塵室；無菌室
6. ISO — 国際標準化機構（The International Standards Organization の略）
7. TS — TS；ISO 関連の製造品質基準のひとつ（Technical Specification の略）
8. certified — 公認された；認定された
9. manufacture — 製造；生産
10. vigorous — 厳しい；猛烈な
11. inspection method — 検査方法；検査体系
12. operations — 業務管理
13. quality control — 品質管理
14. management — 経営
15. warehouse — 保管する
16. implement — 実行する
17. review — 見直す
18. setup — 仕組み；機構；装備
19. efficiency — 効率
20. streamline — 合理化する；能率化する
21. invest — 投資する
22. equipment upgrade — 設備の更新

🔊 ビジネス・リスニング（2 回目）

Stage 03　日本語トランスレーション

ビジネス・ダイアローグの日本語を確認してみよう！ その上で、ダイアローグを聴きながら、まだできていない部分の穴埋めに再チャレンジしよう。

May: ここが弊社のおもな製造施設になります。ここから2時間のところにも、もうひとつの施設があります。弊社の生産ラインは、完全にオートメーション化していまして、言うまでもなく、ほとんどの製造過程はクリーンルームで行われています。

Tom: ISOやTSの認定はされていますか？

May: ええ、ISO 9000とTS 16949に認定されています。製造の各工程の後に、部品は厳しい検査を通過します。

Mike: 従業員は全部でどのくらいいるのですか？

May: セールス、マーケティング、業務管理、品質管理、経営まで含めますと、この施設に85名、もうひとつの施設に65名がおります。こちらが最終部品の検査、梱包を行い、顧客に発送されるまで保管される場所です。バーコードラベルには、最新のテクノロジーを採用していまして、どんな顧客のニーズにも適応するようにカスタマイズすることができます。弊社では、効率とコストの改善のために、随時、製造システムとデザインを見直しています。今年だけでも、設備更新のために120万ドルを投資しました。

🔊 ビジネス・リスニング（3回目）

Stage 04　英文トランスクリプション

ビジネス・ダイアローグの原稿を確認してみよう！ 穴埋め部分の正解をチェックして、英文を理解し直そう。そのあとで、もう一度ダイアローグを聴いてみよう。

May: This is our main production ① facility. We ② have a sister plant ③ located ④ about two hours from here. Our production lines are completely ⑤ automated, and ⑥ obviously most of the production processes are ⑦ conducted in clean rooms.

Tom: Are you ISO and TS ⑧ certified?

May: Yes we are certified ISO 9000 and TS 16949. After each stage during manufacture, the parts go through a vigorous inspection method.

Mike: How many ⑨ total employees do you have?

May: Including sales, marketing, operations, ⑩ quality control and management, we have ⑪ 85 staff ⑫ at this facility and 65 at our sister plant. ⑬ Here is where the final parts are inspected, packaged and warehoused until they are shipped out to the customer. We implement the ⑭ latest technology in our bar code labels, and can customize labels to suit any of the customer's needs. We are continuously reviewing our production ⑮ setup and design to improve our efficiency and streamline cost. ⑯ This year alone we have invested ⑰ more than one-point two million dollars in equipment upgrades.

🔊 ビジネス・リスニング（4回目）

Stage 05 音声変化をチェック

まとめとして、穴埋め部分の音声変化の特徴をスロースピードとナチュラルスピードで確認しよう。下記に示したカタカナ表記で音声変化を確認して、もう一度ビジネス・ダイアローグを聴き直してみよう。発音変化のルールは適宜復習しよう。

2種類の音声を収録

① **facility** — ファシラティー ▶ ファシラディ [リ] ー
   ☞ 破裂音 [t] の弾音化

② **have a** — ハヴ・ア ▶ ハヴァ
   ☞ 2語の連結

③ **located** — ロウケイティッド ▶ ロウケイディ [リ] ッド
   ☞ 破裂音 [t] の弾音化

④ **about two** — アバウト・トゥー ▶ アバウ__トゥー
   ☞ 破裂の [t] の脱落

⑤ **automated** — オートメイティッド ▶ オード [ロ] メイディ [リ] ッド
   ☞ 2カ所で破裂音 [t] の弾音化

⑥ **obviously** — アブヴィアスリー ▶ ア__ヴィアスリー
   ☞ 破裂音 [b] の脱落

⑦ **conducted in** — カンダクティッド・イン ▶ カンダクティッディ [リ] ン
   ☞ 2語の連結。連結部の破裂音 [d] は弾音化することもある

⑧ **certified** — スータファイド ▶ スーダ [ラ] ファイド
   ☞ 破裂音 [t] の弾音化

⑨ **total** — トウトゥル ▶ トウドゥ [ル] ル
   ☞ -tal の破裂音 [t] の弾音化

⑩ **quality** — クァラティー ▶ クァラディ [リ] ー
   ☞ 破裂音 [t] の弾音化

⑪ **85** — エイティーファイヴ ▶ エイディ [リ] ーファイヴ
   ☞ 破裂音 [t] の弾音化

⑫ **at this** — アット・ズィス ▶ アッ__ズィス
   ☞ [t] 音の脱落

⑬ **Here is** — ヒア・イズ ▶ ヒア__ズ
   ☞ 2語の連結。[r] 音は弱まるか脱落

⑭ **latest** — レイティスト ▶ レイディ [リ] スト
   ☞ 破裂音の [t] の弾音化

⑮ **setup** — セットアップ ▶ セッダ [ラ] ップ
   ☞ 破裂音の [t] の弾音化

⑯ **This year** — ズィス・イヤー ▶ ズィシャー
   ☞ [s] と [j] が同化

⑰ **more than** — モー・ザン ▶ モー__アン
   ☞ [ð] 音の脱落

🔊 ビジネス・リスニング (5回目)

Unit 13

上司への紹介
Introduction to Management

Stage 01 　穴埋めビジネス・リスニング

音声変化に注意してCDでビジネスのダイアローグを聴きながら、空欄部分を埋めてみよう。

ダイアローグ音声収録

May: Mike this is Mr. Chen, our vice president of operations.

Mike: Mr. Chen, nice to ① _____ _____. Here's my card. This is Tom Smith, our production manager.

Mr. Chen: Mr. Smith, pleasure. I trust you were ② _____ ③ _____ _____ tour of our production ④ _____ that May ⑤ _____ _____?

Tom: ⑥ _____ _____ very impressive indeed. This entire plant looks brand new. When ⑦ _____ _____ built?

Mr. Chen: Our company was ⑧ _____ _____ 1996, but we outgrew our previous location and established this plant in 2005 and our other ⑨ _____ in 2007. We are ⑩ _____ in the development stage of opening a brand new plant ⑪ _____ _____ Beijing.

May: Mike, you mentioned that you had a presentation you ⑫ _____ _____ give. Mr. Chang, our production manager and ⑬ _____ engineer ⑭ _____ _____ attending ⑮ _____ _____. I have reserved a meeting room for 1: ⑯ _____. We have any equipment you ⑰ _____ _____ for your presentation. ⑱ _____ _____, if you're hungry ⑲ _____ _____ like to take you both to lunch.

Mike: That sounds great. I'm famished!

🔊 ビジネス・リスニング（1回目）

Stage 02　ビジネス・ボキャビル

ビジネスのボキャブラリーを CD で確認しよう。そのあとでもう一度、ビジネス・リスニングにチャレンジ。Stage 01 でできなかったところをもう一度聴き取って、穴埋めを完成させよう。

英日 音声収録

CD 1-38

1	vice president	部長；副社長
2	card	名刺
3	production manager	製造部長
4	satisfied	満足して
5	tour	ツアー；見学
6	impressive	感銘深い
7	indeed	実に
8	entire	すべての；全部丸ごとの
9	brand new	新品の
10	be founded	創設される
11	outgrow	手狭な施設から移る
12	previous	前の；以前の
13	establish	設立する；設置する
14	currently	現在
15	development stage	開発準備段階
16	attend	出席する
17	equipment	設備
18	sound ...	…に聞こえる
19	famished	とても空腹な

🔊 ビジネス・リスニング（2回目）

Stage 03　日本語トランスレーション

ビジネス・ダイアローグの日本語を確認してみよう！　その上で、ダイアローグを聴きながら、まだできていない部分の穴埋めに再チャレンジしよう。

May: マイク、こちらが業務管理部長のチェンさんです。

Mike: チェンさん、はじめまして。こちらが私の名刺になります。こちらが弊社の製造部長のトム・スミスです。

Mr. Chen: スミスさん、お目にかかれて光栄です。メイが行いました、弊社の生産設備のツアーは、きっとお気に召していただけましたでしょう？

Tom: ほんとうにすばらしかったです。工場全体が最新のようですね。いつ建設されたのですか？

Mr. Chen: 弊社は1996年に創業しましたが、以前の場所は手狭になり、この工場を2005年に、もう1カ所の施設を2007年に立ち上げました。現在、北京郊外にも、新しい工場を開設する準備をしています。

May: マイク、プレゼンテーションを行いたいとおっしゃっていましたね。弊社の製造管理部長兼、品質管理技術者のチャンさんもそのミーティングに出席いたします。1時半にミーティングルームを予約してあります。プレゼンテーションに必要になりそうな機材はなんでも揃っています。いまは、おなかが空いていらっしゃれば、おふたりをランチにお連れしたいと思いますが。

Mike: それはいい。もうおなかぺこぺこなんですよ！

🔊 ビジネス・リスニング（3回目）

Stage 04　英文トランスクリプション

ビジネス・ダイアローグの原稿を確認してみよう！　穴埋め部分の正解をチェックして、英文を理解し直そう。そのあとで、もう一度ダイアローグを聴いてみよう。

May: Mike this is Mr. Chen, our vice president of operations.

Mike: Mr. Chen, nice to ① meet you. Here's my card. This is Tom Smith, our production manager.

Mr. Chen: Mr. Smith, pleasure. I trust you were ② satisfied ③ with the tour of our production ④ facility that May ⑤ gave you?

Tom: ⑥ It was very impressive indeed. This entire plant looks brand new. When ⑦ was it built?

Mr. Chen: Our company was ⑧ founded in 1996, but we outgrew our previous location and established this plant in 2005 and our other ⑨ facility in 2007. We are ⑩ currently in the development stage of opening a brand new plant ⑪ outside of Beijing.

May: Mike, you mentioned that you had a presentation you ⑫ wanted to give. Mr. Chang, our production manager and ⑬ quality engineer ⑭ will be attending ⑮ that meeting. I have reserved a meeting room for 1: ⑯ 30. We have any equipment you ⑰ might need for your presentation. ⑱ Right now, if you're hungry ⑲ we would like to take you both to lunch.

Mike: That sounds great. I'm famished!

🔊 ビジネス・リスニング（4回目）

Stage 05 音声変化をチェック

まとめとして、穴埋め部分の音声変化の特徴をスロースピードとナチュラルスピードで確認しよう。下記に示したカタカナ表記で音声変化を確認して、もう一度ビジネス・ダイアローグを聴き直してみよう。発音変化のルールは適宜復習しよう。

2種類の音声を収録

① **meet you** ミート・ユー ▶ ミーチュー
　☞ [t] と [j] が同化

② **satisfied** サティスファイド ▶ サディ [リ] スファイド
　☞ 破裂音 [t] の弾音化

③ **with the** ウィズ・ザ ▶ ウィ＿ザ
　☞ [ð] 音の脱落

④ **facility** ファシラティー ▶ ファシラディ [リ] ー
　☞ 破裂音 [t] の弾音化

⑤ **gave you** ゲイヴ・ユー ▶ ゲイヴュ
　☞ 2語の連結

⑥ **It was** イット・ワズ ▶ イッ＿ワズ
　☞ 破裂音 [t] の脱落

⑦ **was it** ワズ・イット ▶ ワズィッ＿
　☞ 末尾の破裂音 [t] の脱落

⑧ **founded in** ファウンディッド・イン ▶ ファウンディディン
　☞ 2語の連結。2カ所の破裂音 [d] は弾音化することもある

⑨ **facility** ファシラティー ▶ ファシラディ [リ] ー
　☞ 破裂音 [t] の弾音化

⑩ **currently** カレントゥリー ▶ カレン＿リー
　☞ 破裂音 [t] の脱落

⑪ **outside of** アウトサイド・アヴ ▶ アウトサイダ [ラ] ヴ
　☞ 2語の連結。連結部の破裂音 [d] の弾音化や末尾の [v] の脱落が生じることもある

⑫ **wanted to** ワンティッド・トゥー ▶ ワニッ＿トゥー
　☞ 破裂音 [t] と [d] の脱落。to の破裂音 [t] が弾音化することもある

⑬ **quality** クァラティー ▶ クァラディ [リ] ー
　☞ 破裂音の [t] の弾音化

⑭ **will be** ウィル・ビー ▶ ウィ＿ビ
　☞ [l] 音の脱落

⑮ **that meeting** ザット・ミーティング ▶ ザッ＿ミーディ [リ] ング
　☞ that の破裂音 [t] の脱落。meeting の [t] が弾音化。

⑯ **30** サーティー ▶ サーディ [リ] ー
　☞ 破裂音 [t] の弾音化

⑰ **might need** マイト・ニード ▶ マイ＿ニード
　☞ 破裂音 [t] の脱落

⑱ **Right now** ライト・ナウ ▶ ライ＿ナウ
　☞ 破裂音 [t] の脱落

⑲ **we would** ウィ・ウッド ▶ ウィド
　☞ 短縮形 we'd の発音

🔊 ビジネス・リスニング (5回目)

Unit 14

ランチ・ミーティング
Lunch Meeting

Stage 01 穴埋めビジネス・リスニング

音声変化に注意してCDでビジネスのダイアローグを聴きながら、空欄部分を埋めてみよう。

ダイアローグ音声収録

CD 1-40

May: This is a restaurant that serves a wide ① _____ of local specialties, ② _____ _____ ③ _____ _____ few items ④ _____ _____ American style, in case you would prefer that. Do you like Chinese food?

Mike: I love all ⑤ _____ _____ food.

Mr. Chen: If you like things spicy, I recommend the simmered fish ⑥ _____, ⑦ _____ _____ ⑧ _____ _____ _____ most popular dishes they serve.

Mike: That sounds good to me. I am a huge ⑨ _____ _____ seafood prepared Asian style.

Tom: I've ⑩ _____ _____ be careful with spicy food, I've ⑪ _____ _____ very sensitive stomach.

May: In ⑫ _____ _____ you should try the Drunken Chicken. It is chicken ⑬ _____ overnight with rice wine and special seasonings.

Tom: Sold! That sounds really good.

Mr. Chen: Let's get an order of Lion Head Meatballs to share. May, have you decided ⑭ _____ _____ going to have?

May: ⑮ _____ _____ _____ have the usual, Four Happiness Pork.

Tom: And ⑯ _____ _____ that? Oh, I see. Pork simmered in soy sauce, sherry and seasonings … that sounds really good too. Can we come back here tomorrow?

🔊 ビジネス・リスニング（1回目）

Stage 02 ビジネス・ボキャビル

ビジネスのボキャブラリーを CD で確認しよう。そのあとでもう一度、ビジネス・リスニングにチャレンジ。Stage 01 でできなかったところをもう一度聴き取って、穴埋めを完成させよう。

英日 音声収録

1	serve	食事・料理を出す
2	a wide variety of ...	バラエティー豊かな…
3	in case ...	…の場合に備えて
4	prefer ...	…のほうを好む
5	spicy	スパイス・香辛料の利いた
6	recommend	すすめる
7	simmered	煮込んだ
8	hotpot	鍋
9	prepared	準備・料理された
10	sensitive	敏感な
11	in that case ...	その場合は…
12	marinate	マリネにする
13	overnight	ひと晩
14	rice wine	料理酒
15	seasoning	調味料
16	share	取り分ける
17	the usual	いつも食べるもの；飲むもの
18	soy sauce	醤油
19	sherry	シェリー酒

◆ ビジネス・リスニング（2回目）

ランチ・ミーティング

Stage 03　日本語トランスレーション

ビジネス・ダイアローグの日本語を確認してみよう！　その上で、ダイアローグを聴きながら、まだできていない部分の穴埋めに再チャレンジしよう。

May: このレストランは、いろいろな地元のごちそうを出してくれるんですが、アメリカン・スタイルの料理も少しあります。そちらをお好みになることもあるかと思いまして。中国料理はお好きですか？
Mike: 料理ならなんでも大好きですよ。
Mr. Chen: スパイシーなものがよければ、魚の鍋物がおすすめですよ。ここの人気メニューのひとつですので。
Mike: それがよさそうですね。私はアジア・スタイルで料理したシーフードが大好きなんですよ。
Tom: 私はスパイシーなのはちょっと注意しないと。おなかがかなり過敏なんですよ。
May: それでしたら、ドランクン・チキンを試してはどうですか？　お酒と特別な香料で、鶏肉をひと晩漬け込んだものなんです。
Tom: それにしましょう！　すごくおいしそうですね。
Mr. Chen: 分けて食べられるように、獅子頭ミートボールを注文しましょう。メイ、なにを食べるか決めましたか？
May: 私はいつものフォー・ハッピネス・ポークにします。
Tom: で、それはどんなものですか？　へえ、そうか、醤油とシェリー酒、薬味で煮た豚肉ですね…それもすごくおいしそうですね。明日もここに来られますかね？

🔊 ビジネス・リスニング（3回目）

Stage 04　英文トランスクリプション

ビジネス・ダイアローグの原稿を確認してみよう！　穴埋め部分の正解をチェックして、英文を理解し直そう。そのあとで、もう一度ダイアローグを聴いてみよう。

May: This is a restaurant that serves a wide ① variety of local specialties, ② but also ③ has a few items ④ that are American style, in case you would prefer that. Do you like Chinese food?
Mike: I love all ⑤ kinds of food.
Mr. Chen: If you like things spicy, I recommend the simmered fish ⑥ hotpot, ⑦ it is ⑧ one of the most popular dishes they serve.
Mike: That sounds good to me. I am a huge ⑨ fan of seafood prepared Asian style.
Tom: I've ⑩ got to be careful with spicy food, I've ⑪ got a very sensitive stomach.
May: In ⑫ that case you should try the Drunken Chicken. It is chicken ⑬ marinated overnight with rice wine and special seasonings.
Tom: Sold! That sounds really good.
Mr. Chen: Let's get an order of Lion Head Meatballs to share. May, have you decided ⑭ what you're going to have?
May: ⑮ I'm going to have the usual, Four Happiness Pork.
Tom: And ⑯ what is that? Oh, I see. Pork simmered in soy sauce, sherry and seasonings ... that sounds really good too. Can we come back here tomorrow?

🔊 ビジネス・リスニング（4回目）

Unit 14

Stage 05 音声変化をチェック

まとめとして、穴埋め部分の音声変化の特徴をスロースピードとナチュラルスピードで確認しよう。下記に示したカタカナ表記で音声変化を確認して、もう一度ビジネス・ダイアローグを聴き直してみよう。発音変化のルールは適宜復習しよう。

2種類の音声を収録　　CD 1-42

① **variety**　　ヴァライアティ　▶ ヴァライアディ [リ]
☞ 破裂音 [t] の弾音化

② **but also**　　バット・オールソウ　▶ バッド [ロ] ールソウ
☞ 2語の連結。連結部の破裂音 [t] の弾音化

③ **has a**　　ハズ・ア　▶ ハズァ
☞ 2語の連結

④ **that are**　　ザット・アー　▶ ザッダ [ラ] ー
☞ 2語の連結。連結部の破裂音 [t] の弾音化

⑤ **kinds of**　　カインズ・アヴ　▶ カインザヴ
☞ 2語の連結

⑥ **hotpot**　　ハットパット　▶ ハッ＿パット
☞ 破裂音 [t] の脱落

⑦ **it is**　　イット・イズ　▶ イディ [リ] イズ；イッツ
☞ 2語の連結。連結部の破裂音 [t] の弾音化。短縮形の it's の発音になる場合もある

⑧ **one of the**　　ワン・アヴ・ザ　▶ ワナ＿ザ
☞ one の [n] に of が連結。of の [v] 音が脱落

⑨ **fan of**　　ファン・アヴ　▶ ファナヴ
☞ 2語の連結。ダイアローグでは末尾の [v] 音も脱落している

⑩ **got to**　　ガット・トゥー　▶ ガッ＿ドゥ [ル] ー；ガッ＿トゥー
☞ got の破裂音 [t] が脱落。to の破裂音 [t] が弾音化することもある

⑪ **got a**　　ガット・ア　▶ ガッダ [ラ]
☞ 2語の連結。連結部の破裂音 [t] の弾音化

⑫ **that case**　　ザット・ケイス　▶ ザッ＿ケイス
☞ 破裂音 [t] の脱落

⑬ **marinated**　　マラネイティッド　▶ マラネイディ [リ] ッド
☞ 破裂音 [t] の弾音化

⑭ **what you're**　　ワット・ユア　▶ ワッチュア
☞ [t] と [j] が同化

⑮ **I'm going to**　　アイム・ゴウイング・トゥー　▶ アイムゴナ；アムナ
☞ going to は [ゴナ] と発音。さらに [アムナ] のように短く発音されることもある

⑯ **what is**　　ワット・イズ　▶ ワッディ [リ] ズ
☞ 2語の連結。連結部の破裂音 [t] の弾音化

🔊 ビジネス・リスニング（5回目）

ランチ・ミーティング

Unit 15

製品コンセプトのプレゼン ①
Product Concept Presentation 1

Stage 01 穴埋めビジネス・リスニング

音声変化に注意して CD でビジネスのモノローグを聴きながら、空欄部分を埋めてみよう。

モノローグ音声収録

Mike: Our company, AAA Safety Systems was ① _____ _____ 1993, primarily focused on manufacturing seatbelts and other high- ② _____ safety systems for the ③ _____ industry. We have since acquired several other companies through several ④ _____ _____ acquisitions, ⑤ _____ _____ ⑥ _____ ⑦ _____ _____ employing current and developing technologies to provide our customers with the ⑧ _____ _____ in safety system products. ⑨ _____ _____ ⑩ _____ _____ base of $53,000,000, four production ⑪ _____ and employee base of 300, we have experienced a growth of ten to fifteen percent each year over the last ⑫ _____-_____-_____-half years. We are in the process of launching our newest product, an ⑬ _____ sensor unit that we think will change industry standards for passenger safety. I cannot go into many of the details due to the proprietary technology involved, but ⑭ _____ _____ our sincere belief ⑮ _____, with China Semicon's help ⑯ _____ _____ valued ⑰ _____, we can build a product ⑱ _____ _____ literally save the lives of the ultimate end users, the people who drive the cars in which our products are installed.

🔊 ビジネス・リスニング (1回目)

Stage 02 ビジネス・ボキャビル

ビジネスのボキャブラリーを CD で確認しよう。そのあとでもう一度、ビジネス・リスニングにチャレンジ。Stage 01 でできなかったところをもう一度聴き取って、穴埋めを完成させよう。

英日 音声収録

1	primarily	当初
2	focused on ...	…に焦点を絞って
3	high-quality	高品質の
4	automotive industry	自動車産業
5	since ...	…以来
6	acquire	買収する；獲得する
7	mergers and acquisitions	M&A；吸収合併
8	employ	使用する；利用する；採用する
9	current	現在の
10	technology	技術
11	capital	資本
12	experience	経験する
13	growth	成長
14	be in the process of ...	…の過程にある
15	launch	世に送り出す
16	industry standards	業界標準
17	passenger safety	乗客の安全
18	due to ...	…のため
19	proprietary technology	占有技術；独自技術
20	sincere	誠実な；心からの
21	literally	文字どおり
22	ultimate	究極の
23	install	取り付ける；設置する

🔊 ビジネス・リスニング（2回目）

Stage 03　日本語トランスレーション

ビジネス・モノローグの日本語を確認してみよう！　その上で、モノローグを聴きながら、まだできていない部分の穴埋めに再チャレンジしよう。

Mike: 私ども AAA セーフティー・システムズは 1993 年に設立されました。当初は自動車産業向けのシートベルトやその他の高品質なセーフティー・システムの生産に照準を定めておりました。その後、いくつかの M & A を経て、いくつかの企業を買収しました。現在は、顧客に最新のセーフティー・システム製品を提供するため、現今のそして開発途上のテクノロジーを採用しようとしています。弊社は、現在 5,300 万ドルの資本と、4 つの製造施設、300 名の従業員をもち、過去 6 年半にわたり、毎年 10 〜 15％の成長を経験してきました。弊社は新製品である電子センサーユニットの立ち上げ途上にあり、この製品が乗客の安全のための業界基準を変革してくれるものと考えております。独自技術を含むため、詳細の多くには触れられませんが、すばらしいパートナーとしてのチャイナ・セミコンの助けがあれば、文字どおり究極のエンドユーザーである車のドライバーたちの生命を守る製品を開発できると心から信じております。そしてその車には私たちの製品が組み込まれているのです。

🔊 ビジネス・リスニング（3回目）

Stage 04　英文トランスクリプション

ビジネス・モノローグの原稿を確認してみよう！　穴埋め部分の正解をチェックして、英文を理解し直そう。そのあとで、もう一度モノローグを聴いてみよう。

Mike: Our company, AAA Safety Systems was ① founded in 1993, primarily focused on manufacturing seatbelts and other high- ② quality safety systems for the ③ automotive industry. We have since acquired several other companies through several ④ mergers and acquisitions, ⑤ and are ⑥ currently ⑦ looking toward employing current and developing technologies to provide our customers with the ⑧ cutting edge in safety system products. ⑨ With a ⑩ current capital base of $53,000,000, four production ⑪ facilities and employee base of 300, we have experienced a growth of ten to fifteen percent each year over the last ⑫ six-and-a-half years. We are in the process of launching our newest product, an ⑬ electronic sensor unit that we think will change industry standards for passenger safety. I cannot go into many of the details due to the proprietary technology involved, but ⑭ it is our sincere belief ⑮ that, with China Semicon's help ⑯ as a valued ⑰ partner, we can build a product ⑱ that will literally save the lives of the ultimate end users, the people who drive the cars in which our products are installed.

🔊 ビジネス・リスニング（4回目）

Stage 05 音声変化をチェック

まとめとして、穴埋め部分の音声変化の特徴をスロースピードとナチュラルスピードで確認しよう。下記に示したカタカナ表記で音声変化を確認して、もう一度ビジネス・モノローグを聴き直してみよう。発音変化のルールは適宜復習しよう。

2種類の音声を収録

CD 1-45

① **founded in** ファウンディッド・イン ▶ ファウンディディン
  ☞ 2語の連結。連結部の破裂音 [d] は弾音化する場合もある

② **quality** クァラティー ▶ クァラディ [リ] ー
  ☞ 破裂音 [t] の弾音化

③ **automotive** オートモウティヴ ▶ オード [ロ] モウディ [リ] ヴ
  ☞ 1カ所または 2カ所で破裂音 [t] の弾音化

④ **mergers and** マージャーズ・アンド ▶ マージャーザン＿
  ☞ 2語の連結。末尾の破裂音 [d] が脱落する場合もある

⑤ **and are** アンド・アー ▶ アナー
  ☞ 破裂音 [d] が脱落し、2語が連結

⑥ **currently** カレントゥリー ▶ カレン＿リー
  ☞ 破裂音 [t] の脱落

⑦ **looking toward** ルッキング・トゥワード ▶ ルッキン＿トゥワード
  ☞ 破裂音 [g] の脱落

⑧ **cutting edge** カッティング・エッジ ▶ カッディ [リ] ングエッジ
  ☞ 破裂音 [t] の弾音化

⑨ **With a** ウィズ・ア ▶ ウィザ
  ☞ 2語の連結

⑩ **current capital** カレント・キャパトゥル ▶ カレン＿キャパドゥ [ル] ル
  ☞ current 末尾の破裂音 [t] の脱落。capital の破裂音 [t] の弾音化

⑪ **facilities** ファシラティーズ ▶ ファシラディ [リ] ーズ
  ☞ 破裂音 [t] の弾音化

⑫ **six-and-a** シックス・アンド・ア ▶ シックサナ
  ☞ and の破裂音 [d] の脱落。3語の連結

⑬ **electronic** イレクトラニック ▶ イレクチュラニック
  ☞ [tr] の音が [tʃr] に変化

⑭ **it is** イット・イズ ▶ イディ [リ] イズ；イッツ
  ☞ 2語が連結し、連結部の破裂音 [t] が弾音化。短縮形 it's の発音になることもある

⑮ **that** ザット ▶ ザッ＿
  ☞ 末尾の破裂音の [t] の脱落

⑯ **as a** アズ・ア ▶ アザ
  ☞ 2語の連結

⑰ **partner** パートナー ▶ パーんナー
  ☞ 破裂音 [t] の声門閉鎖音化

⑱ **that will** ザット・ウィル ▶ ザッ＿ウィル；ザドゥ [ル] ル
  ☞ 破裂音 [t] の脱落。また、短縮形 that'll [ザットゥル] の [t] が弾音化する場合もある

🔊 ビジネス・リスニング（5回目）

Unit 16

製品コンセプトのプレゼン ②
Product Concept Presentation 2

Stage 01　穴埋めビジネス・リスニング

音声変化に注意してCDでビジネスのモノローグを聴きながら、空欄部分を埋めてみよう。

モノローグ音声収録

Mike: There are three pillars of business ① _____ _____ ② _____ supplier, ③ _____, cost and delivery. We implement the most stringent of ④ _____ controls to ensure that we are providing our customers ⑤ _____ _____ finest product available. ⑥ _____ _____ to do so, it's ⑦ _____ that our supply chain ⑧ _____ do the same. Our target is zero PPM defects. ⑨ _____ cannot come ⑩ _____ _____ price of delivery. We provide a monthly order release with a two month forecast, and require all of our suppliers to support a manufacture capacity level of plus-or-minus fifteen percent. All product ⑪ _____ _____ packaged per spec, and bar-coded ⑫ _____.
Any projected delays of any kind ⑬ _____ _____ communicated immediately in writing. Lastly, but not least ⑭ _____ is cost. We expect all of our suppliers to ⑮ _____ streamline their manufacture, and implement or provide VA/VE plans to reduce costs whenever possible. Our customers demand a five percent cost reduction each year, and that ⑯ _____ _____ _____ achieved with the cooperation and dedication of our supply base. We rank all of our suppliers based on these three factors, and continued business ⑰ _____ _____ determined by performance in these areas.

🔊 ビジネス・リスニング（1回目）

Stage 02 ビジネス・ボキャビル

ビジネスのボキャブラリーをCDで確認しよう。そのあとでもう一度、ビジネス・リスニングにチャレンジ。Stage 01でできなかったところをもう一度聴き取って、穴埋めを完成させよう。

英日 音声収録

CD 1-47

#	英語	日本語
1	pillar	支柱；中心的存在
2	stringent	厳格な；厳しい
3	ensure	確実にする；確保する
4	provide	提供する
5	available	入手可能な
6	supply chain	供給チェーン
7	zero PPM	100万パーツのうち0（Parts Per Millionの略；ビジネスの決まり文句）
8	defect	欠陥
9	release	公表；発表
10	forecast	予測；予想
11	manufacture capacity	生産能力
12	per spec	仕様どおりに
13	appropriately	適切に
14	delay	遅延
15	communicate	伝達する
16	immediately	直ちに
17	least important	もっとも重要性の低い
18	VA/VE	付加価値／バリュー・エンジニアリング（Value Added/Value Engineeringの略）
19	achieve	達成する
20	dedication	尽力；専心
21	determine	決定する；結論を出す

🔊 ビジネス・リスニング（2回目）

製品コンセプトのプレゼン ②

Stage 03　日本語トランスレーション

ビジネス・モノローグの日本語を確認してみよう！　その上で、モノローグを聴きながら、まだできていない部分の穴埋めに再チャレンジしよう。

Mike: 品質、コスト、配送の3つは、自動車産業のサプライヤーとしてのビジネスの3本柱です。顧客にできうる限り最高品質の製品を確実に提供するために、弊社ではもっとも厳しい品質管理を行っております。そのためには、弊社の下請け企業群のパートナー各社にも同様の取り組みを行ってもらうことが大切です。私たちは「百万分のゼロの欠陥」を目標としています。配送を犠牲にして品質を重視することはできません。弊社では、毎月の注文と同時に2カ月前倒しでの発注予測を公表しており、すべての下請け業者には工場生産能力のレベルを±15％に保つためのサポートをお願いしています。すべての製品は仕様どおりに、また適切にバーコードを施されてパッケージングされなければなりません。予想される遅延があれば、どんなものでも迅速に書面で連絡がなされなければなりません。そして最後になりますが、コスト面も重要性の低いことではありません。弊社ではすべての業者に対して、常に生産の合理化を期待しています。可能な場面で常時コストカットを行えるようにするための、バリューエンジニアリングプランの実施や提供も同様です。弊社の顧客は毎年5％のコストカットを要求してきます。そしてその実現は、提携企業群の協力と尽力なくしてはありえないのです。弊社ではすべての提携企業をこの3つの要素でランク付けしております。これらの要素でのパフォーマンスによって、ビジネスの継続が決定されるのです。

🔊 ビジネス・リスニング（3回目）

Stage 04　英文トランスクリプション

ビジネス・モノローグの原稿を確認してみよう！　穴埋め部分の正解をチェックして、英文を理解し直そう。そのあとで、もう一度モノローグを聴いてみよう。

Mike: There are three pillars of business ① as an ② automotive supplier, ③ quality, cost and delivery. We implement the most stringent of ④ quality controls to ensure that we are providing our customers ⑤ with the finest product available. ⑥ In order to do so, it's ⑦ important that our supply chain ⑧ partners do the same. Our target is zero PPM defects. ⑨ Quality cannot come ⑩ at the price of delivery. We provide a monthly order release with a two month forecast, and require all of our suppliers to support a manufacture capacity level of plus-or-minus fifteen percent. All product ⑪ must be packaged per spec, and bar-coded ⑫ appropriately. Any projected delays of any kind ⑬ must be communicated immediately in writing. Lastly, but not least ⑭ important is cost. We expect all of our suppliers to ⑮ constantly streamline their manufacture, and implement or provide VA/VE plans to reduce costs whenever possible. Our customers demand a five percent cost reduction each year, and that ⑯ can only be achieved with the cooperation and dedication of our supply base. We rank all of our suppliers based on these three factors, and continued business ⑰ will be determined by performance in these areas.

🔊 ビジネス・リスニング（4回目）

Stage 05 音声変化をチェック

まとめとして、穴埋め部分の音声変化の特徴をスロースピードとナチュラルスピードで確認しよう。下記に示したカタカナ表記で音声変化を確認して、もう一度ビジネス・モノローグを聴き直してみよう。発音変化のルールは適宜復習しよう。

2種類の音声を収録

① **as an** アズ・アン ▶ アズァン
☞ 2語の連結

② **automotive** オートモウティヴ ▶ オード[ロ]モウディ[リ]ヴ
☞ 1カ所あるいは2カ所の破裂音 [t] の弾音化

③ **quality** クァラティー ▶ クァラディ[リ]ー
☞ 破裂音 [t] の弾音化

④ **quality** クァラティー ▶ クァラディ[リ]ー
☞ 破裂音 [t] の弾音化

⑤ **with the** ウィズ・ザ ▶ ウィ_ザ
☞ [ð] 音の脱落

⑥ **In order** イン・オーダー ▶ イノーダー
☞ 2語の連結

⑦ **important** イムポータント ▶ イムポーダ[ラ]ント
☞ 破裂音 [t] の弾音化

⑧ **partners** パートナーズ ▶ パーんナーズ
☞ 破裂音 [t] の声門閉鎖音化

⑨ **Quality** クァラティー ▶ クァラディ[リ]ー
☞ 破裂音 [t] の弾音化

⑩ **at the** アット・ザ ▶ アッ_ザ
☞ 破裂音 [t] の脱落

⑪ **must be** マスト・ビー ▶ マス_ビ
☞ 破裂音 [t] の脱落

⑫ **appropriately** アプロウプリアトリー ▶ アプロウプリア_リー
☞ 破裂音 [t] の脱落

⑬ **must be** マスト・ビー ▶ マス_ビ
☞ 破裂音 [t] の脱落

⑭ **important** イムポータント ▶ イムポーダ[ラ]ント
☞ 破裂音の [t] の弾音化

⑮ **constantly** コンスタントゥリー ▶ コンスタン_リー
☞ 破裂音 [t] の脱落

⑯ **can only be** キャン・オウンリ・ビー ▶ キャノウンリビ
☞ can と only の連結。be は弱化

⑰ **will be** ウィル・ビー ▶ ウィ_ビ
☞ [l] 音の脱落

🔊 ビジネス・リスニング（5回目）

Unit 17

ビジネス・ミーティング ①
Business Meeting 1

Stage 01 　穴埋めビジネス・リスニング

音声変化に注意して CD でビジネスのダイアローグを聴きながら、空欄部分を埋めてみよう。

ダイアローグ音声収録

Mr. Chen: Thank you for the presentation, Mr. Gray. ① _____ _____ asked Mr. Chang, our production ② _____ manager and ③ _____ engineer to join us when he can. He is wrapping up another ④ _____ and ⑤ _____ _____ here shortly. I have a few initial questions ⑥ _____ _____ like to ask.

Mike: By all means.

Mr. Chen: Initially, how many samples ⑦ _____ _____ need for the product display ⑧ _____ _____ expo?

Mike: We are ⑨ _____ _____ order one hundred units from you as soon as we can draw up a service contract. Fifty of these ⑩ _____ _____ used for the approval process, and the remainder ⑪ _____ _____ used for products to be displayed ⑫ _____ _____ expo. May has told us ⑬ _____ _____ production ⑭ _____ _____ is ⑮ _____-five days.

Tom: We are ⑯ _____ _____ have a working model ⑰ _____ _____ trade show, which will include the front seat of an actual car in which our product ⑱ _____ _____ installed. Our production time is ten days once we have all of the components on hand.

Mike: We are still in the process of sourcing about five more components, including these semiconductors.

🔊 ビジネス・リスニング（1回目）

Stage 02 ビジネス・ボキャビル

ビジネスのボキャブラリーを CD で確認しよう。そのあとでもう一度、ビジネス・リスニングにチャレンジ。Stage 01 でできなかったところをもう一度聴き取って、穴埋めを完成させよう。

英日 音声収録

CD 1-50

	英語	日本語
1	wrap up	終える
2	shortly	まもなく
3	initial	最初の；手始めの
4	By all means.	是非とも；どうぞどうぞ
5	display	展示
6	draw up	書き上げる
7	service contract	サービス契約
8	approval process	承認過程
9	remainder	残り；残りのもの
10	lead time	準備期間
11	model	模型
12	trade show	貿易見本市
13	include	含む
14	actual	実際の
15	once ...	いったん…すれば
16	component	構成部品；構成要素
17	on hand	手元に
18	be in the process of ...	…の過程にある
19	source	供給先を見つける
20	semiconductor	半導体

🔊 ビジネス・リスニング（2回目）

Stage 03　日本語トランスレーション

ビジネス・ダイアローグの日本語を確認してみよう！　その上で、ダイアローグを聴きながら、まだできていない部分の穴埋めに再チャレンジしよう。

Mr. Chen: プレゼンテーション、ありがとうございます、グレイさん。製造管理部長兼、品質管理技術者のチャン氏にも可能なときに参加するように声をかけています。ほかのミーティングを終えてまもなくこちらに参りますので。最初にいくつか私のほうから質問させてください。

Mike: どうぞどうぞ。

Mr. Chen: まず、エキスポの製品展示用にはいくつのサンプルが必要でしょうか？

Mike: サービス契約を作成できたら、できるだけ早く100台の注文を出そうと考えています。このうち50台を承認プロセスに使用し、残りをエキスポで展示する製品として使用します。メイから聞きましたが、御社の製造準備期間は75日とのことですよね。

Tom: トレードショーでは、実際に動くモデルを使用する予定にしています。これには弊社の製品が組み込まれた実際の自動車のフロント座席が含まれます。すべての部品が手元に届けば、弊社の製造は10日でできます。

Mike: 弊社では現在、半導体を含むあと約5つの部品の供給先を確保している段階なのです。

🔊 ビジネス・リスニング（3回目）

Stage 04　英文トランスクリプション

ビジネス・ダイアローグの原稿を確認してみよう！　穴埋め部分の正解をチェックして、英文を理解し直そう。そのあとで、もう一度ダイアローグを聴いてみよう。

Mr. Chen: Thank you for the presentation, Mr. Gray. ① I have asked Mr. Chang, our production ② control manager and ③ quality engineer to join us when he can. He is wrapping up another ④ meeting and ⑤ should be here shortly. I have a few initial questions ⑥ I would like to ask.

Mike: By all means.

Mr. Chen: Initially, how many samples ⑦ will you need for the product display ⑧ at the expo?

Mike: We are ⑨ planning to order one hundred units from you as soon as we can draw up a service contract. Fifty of these ⑩ will be used for the approval process, and the remainder ⑪ will be used for products to be displayed ⑫ at the expo. May has told us ⑬ that your production ⑭ lead time is ⑮ seventy-five days.

Tom: We are ⑯ planning to have a working model ⑰ at the trade show, which will include the front seat of an actual car in which our product ⑱ will be installed. Our production time is ten days once we have all of the components on hand.

Mike: We are still in the process of sourcing about five more components, including these semiconductors.

🔊 ビジネス・リスニング（4回目）

Stage 05 音声変化をチェック

まとめとして、穴埋め部分の音声変化の特徴をスロースピードとナチュラルスピードで確認しよう。下記に示したカタカナ表記で音声変化を確認して、もう一度ビジネス・ダイアローグを聴き直してみよう。発音変化のルールは適宜復習しよう。

2種類の音声を収録

CD 1-51

① **I have**
☞ 短縮形 I've [アイヴ] の発音
アイ・ハヴ ▶ アイヴ

② **control**
☞ [ntr] の音が [ntʃr] に変化
カントゥロウル ▶ カンチュロウル

③ **quality**
☞ 破裂音 [t] の弾音化
クァラティー ▶ クァラディ [リ] ー

④ **meeting**
☞ 破裂音 [t] の弾音化
ミーティング ▶ ミーディ [リ] ング

⑤ **should be**
☞ 破裂音 [d] の脱落
シュッド・ビー ▶ シュッ_ビー

⑥ **I would**
☞ 短縮形 I'd [アイド] の発音
アイ・ウッド ▶ アイド

⑦ **will you**
☞ [l] 音の脱落
ウィル・ユー ▶ ウィ_ユー

⑧ **at the**
☞ 破裂音 [t] の脱落
アット・ズィ ▶ アッ_ズィ

⑨ **planning to**
☞ 破裂音 [g] の脱落
プラニング・トゥー ▶ プラニン_トゥー

⑩ **will be**
☞ [l] 音の脱落
ウィル・ビー ▶ ウィ_ビー

⑪ **will be**
☞ [l] 音の脱落
ウィル・ビー ▶ ウィ_ビー

⑫ **at the**
☞ 破裂音 [t] の脱落
アット・ズィ ▶ アッ_ズィ

⑬ **that your**
☞ [t] と [j] が同化
ザット・ユア ▶ ザッチュア

⑭ **lead time**
☞ 破裂音の [d] の脱落
リード・タイム ▶ リー_タイム

⑮ **seventy**
☞ 破裂音の [t] の脱落
セヴンティー ▶ セヴニー

⑯ **planning to**
☞ 破裂音の [g] の脱落
プラニング・トゥー ▶ プラニン_トゥー

⑰ **at the**
☞ 破裂音の [t] の脱落
アット・ザ ▶ アッ_ザ

⑱ **will be**
☞ [l] 音の脱落
ウィル・ビー ▶ ウィ_ビー

🔊 ビジネス・リスニング (5回目)

Unit 18

ビジネス・ミーティング ②
Business Meeting 2

Stage 01 穴埋めビジネス・リスニング

音声変化に注意して CD でビジネスのダイアローグを聴きながら、空欄部分を埋めてみよう。

ダイアローグ音声収録

Mr. Chen: Gentlemen this is Mr. Chang, our production manager and top ① _____ engineer. He wants to go over some of the logistical aspects with you.

Mr. Chang: Nice to ② _____ _____ both. The first thing I want to ③ _____ _____ is shipping. Our product has to be specially ④ _____ _____ protect the components from moisture and other ⑤ _____ factors when shipped by ocean freight. I noticed ⑥ _____ _____ quote package mentioned weekly releases. But we would like to arrange to ship mass production parts monthly. Is this doable?

Tom: Given the small size of your part, ⑦ _____ _____ see a problem consolidating shipments to monthly as ⑧ _____ _____ weekly.

Mr. Chang: Another question I have is if you can provide ⑨ _____ _____ a three-month forecasts of future requirements when placing your order each month. Is ⑩ _____ something you can do?

Tom: We can issue a forecast, but our customer only provides us ⑪ _____ _____ five-week forecast, and their numbers ⑫ _____ _____ fluctuate ⑬ _____ _____ _____. We could provide you with a three-month forecast, ⑭ _____ _____ ⑮ _____ _____ for reference only.

🔊 ビジネス・リスニング（1回目）

Stage 02 ビジネス・ボキャビル

ビジネスのボキャブラリーを CD で確認しよう。そのあとでもう一度、ビジネス・リスニングにチャレンジ。Stage 01 でできなかったところをもう一度聴き取って、穴埋めを完成させよう。

英日 音声収録

#	英語	日本語
1	logistical	物流の
2	specially	特別に
3	protect	保護する
4	moisture	湿気；水分
5	environmental	環境の
6	factor	要因；要素
7	by ocean freight	船便で
8	notice	認識する
9	quote	見積
10	mention	言及する
11	Given ...	…を考慮に入れると
12	consolidate	統合する；ひとつにまとめる
13	as opposed to ...	…ではなく
14	at least	少なくとも
15	future requirement	将来の需要
16	place one's order	発注する
17	issue	発する；出す
18	tend to ...	…しがちだ
19	fluctuate	変動する
20	quite a bit	かなり
21	for reference only	参考のためだけの

◀)) ビジネス・リスニング（2回目）

ビジネス・ミーティング ② 79

Stage 03　日本語トランスレーション

ビジネス・ダイアローグの日本語を確認してみよう！　その上で、ダイアローグを聴きながら、まだできていない部分の穴埋めに再チャレンジしよう。

Mr. Chen:	みなさん、こちらが弊社の製造部長でトップの品質管理技術者のチャンさんです。彼のほうでは、いくつか物流面について確認したいと思っています。
Mr. Chang:	みなさん、お会いできてうれしいです。まず私がお伺いしたいのは、発送についてです。弊社の製品は、船便で発送する場合、部品を湿気やその他の環境的な要因から保護するために特別な梱包を行わねばなりません。御社の見積書類に週毎の発送と書いてあったのに気づいたのですが、弊社的には、大量生産の部品を月ごとの発送で準備したいのです。これは可能でしょうか？
Tom:	御社の製品の小ささを考えれば、発送を週単位ではなく、月単位にまとめることも問題なさそうです。
Mr. Chang:	もうひとつ質問ですが、毎月ご注文をいただくときに少なくとも3カ月先までの将来の需要予測をご提供いただけるかということですが。これは可能なことでしょうか？
Tom:	予測は出すことができますが、弊社の顧客は5週間の予測しかくれませんし、数量はかなり変動しがちなんです。3カ月予測は可能ですが、参考のためだけのものになります。

🔊 ビジネス・リスニング（3回目）

Stage 04　英文トランスクリプション

ビジネス・ダイアローグの原稿を確認してみよう！　穴埋め部分の正解をチェックして、英文を理解し直そう。そのあとで、もう一度ダイアローグを聴いてみよう。

Mr. Chen:	Gentlemen this is Mr. Chang, our production manager and top ① quality engineer. He wants to go over some of the logistical aspects with you.
Mr. Chang:	Nice to ② meet you both. The first thing I want to ③ ask about is shipping. Our product has to be specially ④ packed to protect the components from moisture and other ⑤ environmental factors when shipped by ocean freight. I noticed ⑥ that your quote package mentioned weekly releases. But we would like to arrange to ship mass production parts monthly. Is this doable?
Tom:	Given the small size of your part, ⑦ I don't see a problem consolidating shipments to monthly as ⑧ opposed to weekly.
Mr. Chang:	Another question I have is if you can provide ⑨ at least a three-month forecasts of future requirements when placing your order each month. Is ⑩ that something you can do?
Tom:	We can issue a forecast, but our customer only provides us ⑪ with a five-week forecast, and their numbers ⑫ tend to fluctuate ⑬ quite a bit. We could provide you with a three-month forecast, ⑭ but it ⑮ would be for reference only.

🔊 ビジネス・リスニング（4回目）

Stage 05　音声変化をチェック

まとめとして、穴埋め部分の音声変化の特徴をスロースピードとナチュラルスピードで確認しよう。下記に示したカタカナ表記で音声変化を確認して、もう一度ビジネス・ダイアローグを聴き直してみよう。発音変化のルールは適宜復習しよう。

2種類の音声を収録　CD 2-03

① **quality**
☞ 破裂音 [t] の弾音化
クァラティー　▶ クァラディ [リ] ー

② **meet you**
☞ [t] と [j] が同化
ミート・ユー　▶ ミーチュー

③ **ask about**
☞ 2 語の連結
アスク・アバウト　▶ アスカバウト

④ **packed to**
☞ 破裂音 [t] の脱落
パックト・トゥー　▶ パック＿トゥー

⑤ **environmental**
☞ 破裂音 [t] の脱落
エンヴァイアランメントゥル　▶ エンヴァイアランメナル

⑥ **that your**
☞ [t] と [j] が同化
ザット・ユア　▶ ザッチュア

⑦ **I don't**
☞ don't が弱化して [ドン] と発音。[d] や [t] が脱落して [アイ＿オウン＿] と発音することもある
アイ・ドゥント　▶ アイドン；アイ＿オウン＿

⑧ **opposed to**
☞ 破裂音 [d] の脱落
オポウズド・トゥー　▶ オポウズ＿トゥー

⑨ **at least**
☞ 破裂音 [t] の脱落
アット・リースト　▶ アッ＿リースト

⑩ **that**
☞ 破裂音 [t] の脱落
ザット　▶ ザッ＿

⑪ **with a**
☞ 2 語の連結
ウィズ・ア　▶ ウィザ

⑫ **tend to**
☞ 破裂音 [d] の脱落
テンド・トゥー　▶ テン＿トゥー

⑬ **quite a bit**
☞ quite と a が連結。連結部の破裂音の [t] が弾音化。bit の末尾の [t] も脱落することがある
クワイト・ア・ビット　▶ クワイダ [ラ] ビット

⑭ **but it**
☞ 2 語が連結。連結部の破裂音 [t] の弾音化
バット・イット　▶ バッディ [リ] ット

⑮ **would be**
☞ 破裂音 [d] の脱落
ウッド・ビー　▶ ウッ＿ビー

🔊 ビジネス・リスニング (5 回目)

Unit 19

ビジネス・ミーティング ③
Business Meeting 3

Stage 01 穴埋めビジネス・リスニング

音声変化に注意してCDでビジネスのダイアローグを聴きながら、空欄部分を埋めてみよう。

ダイアローグ音声収録　CD 2-04

Mr. Chang: From the production ① _____ _____ things, the last thing we ② _____ _____ go over is the time schedule for samples. Since this ③ _____ _____ the initial production run, we will need time to ④ _____ _____ our lines and to purchase raw materials. How long do you think ⑤ _____ _____ take before we are awarded this business and can begin?

Mike: Once we present the audit results and ⑥ _____ _____ for pricing we ⑦ _____ _____ able to issue a purchase order within the next two weeks.

Tom: With ⑧ _____ _____ pricing, your pricing is more than we had budgeted for, ⑨ _____ _____ was ⑩ _____ than any of your ⑪ _____. As Mike said, we are waiting on approval, but as we ⑫ _____ _____ the presentation, we are ⑬ _____ _____ provide a five percent cost reduction each year to our customer. Your cooperation and participation in helping us do that ⑭ _____ _____ _____ a factor in whether we award you this contract.

Mr. Chen: I am sure you are still ⑮ _____-_____ from your trip. Let's call it a day and we can pick things up again tomorrow morning.

🔊 ビジネス・リスニング（1回目）

Stage 02　ビジネス・ボキャビル

ビジネスのボキャブラリーを CD で確認しよう。そのあとでもう一度、ビジネス・リスニングにチャレンジ。Stage 01 でできなかったところをもう一度聴き取って、穴埋めを完成させよう。

英日 音声収録

1	production side	製造サイド
2	initial production run	初回の生産稼働
3	set up	セットする
4	purchase	購入する
5	raw material	原料
6	award	与える
7	audit result	査察結果
8	approval	承認
9	pricing	価格付け
10	purchase order	発注書
11	with respect to ...	…の面では
12	budget	予算に組む
13	competitor	競合他社
14	indicate	明らかにする
15	be required to ...	…するように求められる
16	reduction	削減
17	cooperation	協力
18	participation	参加
19	contract	契約
20	jet-lagged	時差ぼけした
21	call it a day	（仕事などを）終わりにする

🔊 ビジネス・リスニング（2回目）

Stage 03　日本語トランスレーション

ビジネス・ダイアローグの日本語を確認してみよう！　その上で、ダイアローグを聴きながら、まだできていない部分の穴埋めに再チャレンジしよう。

Mr. Chang: 製造サイドの話になりますが、最後にお話ししなければならないのがサンプルのタイムスケジュールです。これが最初の生産稼働になりますので、生産ラインをセットする時間と原料を仕入れる時間が必要になります。私たちがこの仕事を与えられてスタートできるまでにどのくらいの時間がかかると思われますか？

Mike: 査察の結果を提出し、価格設定に関する承認を得られれば、2週間以内には発注ができるはずです。

Tom: 価格に関しては、御社の値段は弊社の予算を超えていますが、どの競合他社よりもいいものでした。マイクが話しましたようにわれわれは承認を待ってはいます。しかし、プレゼンテーションでも明らかにしたように、われわれは年に5％のコストカットを顧客に提供することが求められています。これを弊社が実行する場面での御社の協力と参画が、弊社が御社にこの契約を差し上げるかどうかの重要なファクターになります。

Mr. Chen: まだご旅行の時差が残っていらっしゃいますよね。今日はこの辺にして、明日の朝また再開いたしましょう。

🔊 ビジネス・リスニング（3回目）

Stage 04　英文トランスクリプション

ビジネス・ダイアローグの原稿を確認してみよう！　穴埋め部分の正解をチェックして、英文を理解し直そう。そのあとで、もう一度ダイアローグを聴いてみよう。

Mr. Chang: From the production ① side of things, the last thing we ② need to go over is the time schedule for samples. Since this ③ will be the initial production run, we will need time to ④ set up our lines and to purchase raw materials. How long do you think ⑤ it will take before we are awarded this business and can begin?

Mike: Once we present the audit results and ⑥ get approval for pricing we ⑦ should be able to issue a purchase order within the next two weeks.

Tom: With ⑧ respect to pricing, your pricing is more than we had budgeted for, ⑨ but it was ⑩ better than any of your ⑪ competitors. As Mike said, we are waiting on approval, but as we ⑫ indicated in the presentation, we are ⑬ required to provide a five percent cost reduction each year to our customer. Your cooperation and participation in helping us do that ⑭ will also be a factor in whether we award you this contract.

Mr. Chen: I am sure you are still ⑮ jet-lagged from your trip. Let's call it a day and we can pick things up again tomorrow morning.

🔊 ビジネス・リスニング（4回目）

Stage 05 音声変化をチェック

まとめとして、穴埋め部分の音声変化の特徴をスロースピードとナチュラルスピードで確認しよう。下記に示したカタカナ表記で音声変化を確認して、もう一度ビジネス・ダイアローグを聴き直してみよう。発音変化のルールは適宜復習しよう。

2種類の音声を収録　　CD 2-06

① **side of**　　サイド・アヴ　　▶ サイダ [ラ] __
　☞ 2語の連結。連結部の破裂音 [d] の弾音化、末尾の [v] 音の脱落が生じることもある

② **need to**　　ニード・トゥー　　▶ ニードゥ [ル] ー；ニー__トゥー
　☞ 破裂音 [d] の脱落。to の破裂音 [t] が弾音化することもある

③ **will be**　　ウィル・ビー　　▶ ウィ__ビ
　☞ [l] 音の脱落

④ **set up**　　セット・アップ　　▶ セダ [ラ] ップ
　☞ 2語の連結。連結部の破裂音 [t] の弾音化

⑤ **it will**　　イット・ウィル　　▶ イドゥル；イッ__ウィル
　☞ 破裂音 [t] の脱落。it'll の破裂音 [t] が弾音化することもある

⑥ **get approval**　　ゲット・アプルーヴル　　▶ ゲッダ [ラ] プルーヴル
　☞ 2語の連結。連結部の破裂音 [t] の弾音化

⑦ **should be**　　シュッド・ビー　　▶ シュッ__ビ
　☞ 破裂音 [d] の脱落

⑧ **respect to**　　リスペクト・トゥー　　▶ リスペク__トゥー
　☞ 破裂音 [t] の脱落

⑨ **but it**　　バット・イット　　▶ バッディ [リ] ット
　☞ 2語の連結。連結部の破裂音 [t] の弾音化

⑩ **better**　　ベター　　▶ ベダ [ラ] ー
　☞ 破裂音 [t] の弾音化

⑪ **competitors**　　カンペティターズ　　▶ カンペディ [リ] ダ [ラ] ーズ
　☞ 破裂の [t] が2カ所で弾音化

⑫ **indicated in**　　インディケイティッド・イン　　▶ インディケイディ [リ] ッディ [リ] ン
　☞ 2語が連結。破裂音 [t] や連結部の破裂音 [d] は弾音化することもある

⑬ **required to**　　リクワイアード・トゥー　　▶ リクワイアー__トゥー
　☞ 破裂音 [d] の脱落

⑭ **will also be**　　ウィル・オールソウ・ビー　　▶ ウィ__オールソウビ
　☞ [l] 音の脱落

⑮ **jet-lagged**　　ジェット・ラグド　　▶ ジェッ__ラグド
　☞ 破裂音 [t] の脱落

🔊 ビジネス・リスニング（5 回目）

Unit 20

価格の交渉 ③
Pricing Negotiation 3

Stage 01 — 穴埋めビジネス・リスニング

音声変化に注意してCDでビジネスのダイアローグを聴きながら、空欄部分を埋めてみよう。

ダイアローグ音声収録

May: Good morning. I ① _____ _____ accommodations ② _____ _____ hotel were satisfactory.

Mike: Yes, the rooms were much larger ③ _____ _____ expected and quite comfortable.

May: Good.

Mr. Chen: We ④ _____ _____ the numbers again last night, and with respect to the cost-down request, ⑤ _____ _____ hard to commit before the project even starts. However, we can propose a two ⑥ _____ _____ ⑦ _____ _____ end of the first full year of production. Under the condition that the discount is in the form of a rebate and ⑧ _____ _____ change to unit cost.

Tom: Can we take that to mean that you will ⑨ _____ _____ two percent discount or rebate each year?

Mr. Chen: There are too many unforeseen issues to ⑩ _____ _____ that yearly. Exchange rate changes, raw material increases, production costs. But ⑪ _____ _____ our policy to work with our customers, so ⑫ _____ _____ certainly do our best to help you achieve your cost-reduction goals as they are determined.

Tom: And you are ⑬ _____ _____ ⑭ _____ _____ initial discount promise in writing?

Mr. Chen: Absolutely.

🔊 ビジネス・リスニング (1回目)

Stage 02 ビジネス・ボキャビル

ビジネスのボキャブラリーを CD で確認しよう。そのあとでもう一度、ビジネス・リスニングにチャレンジ。Stage 01 でできなかったところをもう一度聴き取って、穴埋めを完成させよう。

英日 音声収録
CD 2-08

#	英語	日本語
1	accommodations	ホテルの設備
2	satisfactory	満足のいく
3	comfortable	快適な
4	cost-down request	値下げの要求
5	commit	約束する
6	discount	値下げ；値引き
7	at the end of ...	…の終わりに
8	production	生産
9	condition	条件
10	in the form of ...	…の形で
11	rebate	払い戻し
12	unit cost	ユニット単価
13	unforeseen issues	予測不能な問題
14	exchange rate	貨幣の交換レート
15	increase	高騰；増加
16	production cost	製造コスト
17	policy	方針
18	certainly	確かに；確実に
19	achieve	達成する
20	in writing	書面に

◀)) ビジネス・リスニング（2回目）

Stage 03　日本語トランスレーション

ビジネス・ダイアローグの日本語を確認してみよう！　その上で、ダイアローグを聴きながら、まだできていない部分の穴埋めに再チャレンジしよう。

May: おはようございます。ホテルの設備はご満足いただけましたよね？
Mike: ええ、部屋は予想してたよりも広くて、快適でしたよ。
May: よかったです。
Mr. Chen: 弊社では昨夜、もう一度、数字を確認しました。コストダウンの要求に関しましては、プロジェクトがまだスタートしてもいませんので、確約は難しいものがあります。しかしながら、生産の最初の1年の終わりには、2％のディスカウントをご提案可能です。ユニットの価格を変更するのではなく、払い戻しという形でのディスカウントとするのが条件ではありますが。
Tom: それは、御社が毎年2％のディスカウントか払い戻しを提供してくれるという意味だと考えてよろしいですか？
Mr. Chen: 毎年それをお約束するのには、あまりにも多くの予測不能な点があります。貨幣の交換レートの変動や、原料代の高騰、製造コストなどです。しかし、お客さまと共同で仕事をするのが弊社のポリシーですから、弊社としましては、御社のコスト削減目標を、目標どおりに実現するお手伝いを必ず全力で行います。
Tom: で、その最初の値引きのお約束を書面にしていただけるのでしょうか？
Mr. Chen: もちろんです。

🔊 ビジネス・リスニング（3回目）

Stage 04　英文トランスクリプション

ビジネス・ダイアローグの原稿を確認してみよう！　穴埋め部分の正解をチェックして、英文を理解し直そう。そのあとで、もう一度ダイアローグを聴いてみよう。

May: Good morning. I ① trust your accommodations ② at the hotel were satisfactory.
Mike: Yes, the rooms were much larger ③ than I expected and quite comfortable.
May: Good.
Mr. Chen: We ④ went over the numbers again last night, and with respect to the cost-down request, ⑤ it is hard to commit before the project even starts. However, we can propose a two ⑥ percent discount ⑦ at the end of the first full year of production. Under the condition that the discount is in the form of a rebate and ⑧ not a change to unit cost.
Tom: Can we take that to mean that you will ⑨ provide your two percent discount or rebate each year?
Mr. Chen: There are too many unforeseen issues to ⑩ commit to that yearly. Exchange rate changes, raw material increases, production costs. But ⑪ it is our policy to work with our customers, so ⑫ we will certainly do our best to help you achieve your cost-reduction goals as they are determined.
Tom: And you are ⑬ willing to ⑭ put that initial discount promise in writing?
Mr. Chen: Absolutely.

🔊 ビジネス・リスニング（4回目）

Stage 05 音声変化をチェック

まとめとして、穴埋め部分の音声変化の特徴をスロースピードとナチュラルスピードで確認しよう。下記に示したカタカナ表記で音声変化を確認して、もう一度ビジネス・ダイアローグを聴き直してみよう。発音変化のルールは適宜復習しよう。

2種類の音声を収録

① **trust your** — トゥラスト・ユア ▶ トゥラスチュア
☞ [t] 音と [j] 音の同化

② **at the** — アット・ザ ▶ アッ_ザ
☞ 破裂音 [t] の脱落

③ **than I** — ザン・アイ ▶ ザナイ
☞ 2 語の連結

④ **went over** — ウェント・オウヴァー ▶ ウェノウヴァー
☞ 破裂音 [t] が脱落し、2 語が連結

⑤ **it is** — イット・イズ ▶ イッディ [リ] イズ；イッツ
☞ 2 語が連結し、連結部の破裂音 [t] が弾音化。短縮形の it's [イッツ] の発音になることもある

⑥ **percent discount** — プーセント・ディスカウント ▶ プーセン_ディスカウント
☞ 破裂音 [t] の脱落

⑦ **at the** — アット・ズィ ▶ アッ_ズィ
☞ 破裂音 [t] の脱落

⑧ **not a** — ナット・ア ▶ ナッダ [ラ]
☞ 2 語の連結。連結部の破裂音 [t] の弾音化

⑨ **provide your** — プラヴァイド・ユア ▶ プラヴァイジュア
☞ [d] と [j] が同化

⑩ **commit to** — カミット・トゥー ▶ カミッ_トゥー
☞ 破裂音 [t] の脱落

⑪ **it is** — イット・イズ ▶ イッディ [リ] イズ；イッツ
☞ 2 語が連結し、連結部の破裂音 [t] が弾音化。短縮形の it's [イッツ] の発音になることもある

⑫ **we will** — ウィ・ウィル ▶ ウィル；ウィゥ
☞ 短縮形 we'll [ウィル] の発音。さらに弱化して [ウィゥ] のように発音されることもある

⑬ **willing to** — ウィリング・トゥー ▶ ウィリン_トゥー
☞ 破裂音 [g] の脱落

⑭ **put that** — プット・ザット ▶ プッ_ザット
☞ 破裂音 [t] の脱落

🔊 ビジネス・リスニング（5 回目）

Unit 21

ミーティングのまとめ
Meeting Summary

Stage 01 　穴埋めビジネス・リスニング

音声変化に注意してCDでビジネスのダイアローグを聴きながら、空欄部分を埋めてみよう。

ダイアログ音声収録

Mike: Okay, let's go over things as they stand. We will meet with our customer this week and present the audit findings. ① _____ _____ see any issues ② _____ _____ with that. Once we ③ _____ final approval and maker layout is determined, we will draft a service contract and ④ _____ _____ to you for approval and execution. Once ⑤ _____ _____ concluded, we will issue a purchase order for the samples.

Tom: You will provide the samples within the allotted ⑥ _____ _____. They ⑦ _____ _____ inspected and tested for approval, then we will assemble the components for the products to be displayed ⑧ _____ _____ expo.

Mr. Chen: Are we ⑨ _____ _____ be able to have any representation or advertising ⑩ _____ _____ expo?

Mike: We will have a display ⑪ _____ _____ that lists our supply-chain ⑫ _____. We will also invite two members from each supplier to attend the expo.

Tom: Mass production is ⑬ _____ _____ begin ⑭ _____ _____ of ⑮ _____ _____. We will provide forecasts and initial production orders just after the first of the year.

Mr. Chen: Well, we ⑯ _____ look forward to being a ⑰ _____ _____ this.

🔊 ビジネス・リスニング（1回目）

Stage 02　ビジネス・ボキャビル

ビジネスのボキャブラリーを CD で確認しよう。そのあとでもう一度、ビジネス・リスニングにチャレンジ。Stage 01 でできなかったところをもう一度聴き取って、穴埋めを完成させよう。

英日 音声収録

1	as they stand	いまあるままに；現状の
2	audit findings	査察結果
3	issue	問題（となる点）
4	final approval	最終承認
5	maker layout	メーカーの割り振り
6	execution	（契約の）締結；執行
7	conclude	締結する
8	purchase order	発注
9	allotted	割り当てられた
10	inspect	検査する
11	assemble	組み立てる
12	representation	社名の表示・露出；代表
13	advertising	広告
14	set up	設置された
15	list	一覧表にする；掲載する
16	invite	招待する
17	forecast	予想；予測
18	initial	最初の
19	production orders	生産の発注
20	just after the first of the year	新年早々に

🔊 ビジネス・リスニング（2回目）

Stage 03　日本語トランスレーション

ビジネス・ダイアログの日本語を確認してみよう！　その上で、ダイアローグを聴きながら、まだできていない部分の穴埋めに再チャレンジしよう。

Mike:　さて、ここまでの話を振り返っておきましょう。弊社では今週顧客とミーティングをもち、査察でわかったことを報告します。この点ではなにも問題はなさそうですね。最終的な承認をもらえて、仕入れ先メーカーが決まったら、サービス契約を起草して、承認と締結のために御社にお送りします。締結が終わったら、サンプル向けの発注を行います。

Tom:　決められた準備期間でサンプルをご提供いただきます。サンプルは、承認のための検査とテストを行います。それからエキスポでの展示のために、製品の各部品を組み立てます。

Mr. Chen:　エキスポでは、弊社の社名の表示や広告が可能でしょうか？

Mike:　弊社の提携チェーンのパートナー会社をリストしたディスプレイを設置します。また、提携企業からそれぞれ2名ずつエキスポへの出席をいただけるようご招待します。

Tom:　大量生産は来年の4月に開始の予定です。予測と最初の生産の発注を年明け早々に提供します。

Mr. Chen:　弊社としましては、このプロジェクトに参加できることを心から楽しみにしています。

🔊 ビジネス・リスニング（3回目）

Stage 04　英文トランスクリプション

ビジネス・ダイアログの原稿を確認してみよう！　穴埋め部分の正解をチェックして、英文を理解し直そう。そのあとで、もう一度ダイアローグを聴いてみよう。

Mike:　Okay, let's go over things as they stand. We will meet with our customer this week and present the audit findings. ① I don't see any issues ② at all with that. Once we ③ get final approval and maker layout is determined, we will draft a service contract and ④ send it to you for approval and execution. Once ⑤ that is concluded, we will issue a purchase order for the samples.

Tom:　You will provide the samples within the allotted ⑥ lead time. They ⑦ will be inspected and tested for approval, then we will assemble the components for the products to be displayed ⑧ at the expo.

Mr. Chen:　Are we ⑨ going to be able to have any representation or advertising ⑩ at the expo?

Mike:　We will have a display ⑪ set up that lists our supply-chain ⑫ partners. We will also invite two members from each supplier to attend the expo.

Tom:　Mass production is ⑬ scheduled to begin ⑭ in April of ⑮ next year. We will provide forecasts and initial production orders just after the first of the year.

Mr. Chen:　Well, we ⑯ certainly look forward to being a ⑰ part of this.

🔊 ビジネス・リスニング（4回目）

Stage 05 音声変化をチェック

まとめとして、穴埋め部分の音声変化の特徴をスロースピードとナチュラルスピードで確認しよう。下記に示したカタカナ表記で音声変化を確認して、もう一度ビジネス・ダイアローグを聴き直してみよう。発音変化のルールは適宜復習しよう。

2種類の音声を収録

① **I don't** アイ・ドゥント ▶ アイドン；アイ__オウン__
　☞ don't が弱化して [ドン] と発音。[d] や [t] が脱落して [アイ__オウン__] と発音することもある

② **at all** アット・オール ▶ アッド [ロ] ール
　☞ 2語の連結。連結部の破裂音 [t] の弾音化

③ **get** ゲット ▶ ゲッ__
　☞ 末尾の破裂音 [t] の脱落

④ **send it** センド・イット ▶ センディット；セニット
　☞ 2語の連結。破裂音 [d] が脱落して連結することもある

⑤ **that is** ザット・イズ ▶ ザッディ [リ] ズ
　☞ 2語の連結。連結部の破裂音 [t] の弾音化

⑥ **lead time** リード・タイム ▶ リー__タイム
　☞ 破裂音 [d] の脱落

⑦ **will be** ウィル・ビー ▶ ウィ__ビ
　☞ [l] 音の脱落

⑧ **at the** アット・ズィ ▶ アッ__ズィ
　☞ 破裂音 [t] の脱落

⑨ **going to** ゴウイング・トゥー ▶ ゴウイン__トゥ；ゴウイヌ；ゴナ
　☞ 破裂音 [g] の脱落。さらに to の破裂音 [t] が脱落することもある。また、さらに短く [ゴナ] とも発音

⑩ **at the** アット・ズィ ▶ アッ__ズィ
　☞ 破裂音 [t] の脱落

⑪ **set up** セット・アップ ▶ セダ [ラ] ップ
　☞ 2語の連結。連結部の破裂音 [t] の弾音化

⑫ **partners** パートナーズ ▶ パーんナーズ
　☞ 破裂音 [t] の声門閉鎖音化

⑬ **scheduled to** スケジュールド・トゥー ▶ スケジュール__トゥー
　☞ 破裂音 [d] の脱落

⑭ **in April** イン・エイプリル ▶ イネイプリル
　☞ 2語の連結

⑮ **next year** ネクスト・イヤー ▶ ネクスチャー
　☞ [t] と [j] が同化

⑯ **certainly** スートゥンリー ▶ スーんンリー
　☞ 破裂音 [t] の声門閉鎖音化

⑰ **part of** パート・アヴ ▶ パーダ [ラ] ヴ
　☞ 2語の連結。連結部の破裂音 [t] の弾音化

🔊 ビジネス・リスニング (5 回目)

Unit 22

出張中のお世話へのお礼
Expression of Appreciation for Business Trip

Stage 01 穴埋めビジネス・リスニング

音声変化に注意してCDでビジネスのダイアローグを聴きながら、空欄部分を埋めてみよう。

ダイアローグ音声収録

Mike: May, ① _____ _____. This is Mike with AAA Safety Systems, how are you?

May: Fine thanks. ② _____ _____ have a good trip back?

Mike: Yes. I just wanted to give you a call and thank you for your ③ _____ while we were there. ④ _____ _____ _____ I think ⑤ _____ _____ a very successful trip and hopefully we can formally award this business to you within the next two weeks. We are ⑥ _____ with our customer tomorrow to ⑦ _____ _____ finalize things.

May: Excellent. We ⑧ _____ look ⑨ _____ _____ ⑩ _____ this contract. I think our companies are a ⑪ _____ _____ and I foresee a long and mutually beneficial relationship.

Mike: I agree. Assuming ⑫ _____ _____ no hang-ups, you ⑬ _____ _____ hearing ⑭ _____ _____ soon and we can go ⑮ _____ _____ ⑯ _____ _____ the contract. I will send it via email and follow up with a phone call after you have had time to ⑰ _____ _____ _____.

May: That's fine. Please give my regard to Tom.

Mike: I will, and please thank Mr. Chen for us as well.

May: Will do Mike. ⑱ _____ _____ good weekend.

🔊 ビジネス・リスニング（1回目）

Stage 02 ビジネス・ボキャビル

ビジネスのボキャブラリーを CD で確認しよう。そのあとでもう一度、ビジネス・リスニングにチャレンジ。Stage 01 でできなかったところをもう一度聴き取って、穴埋めを完成させよう。

英日 音声収録

1	hospitality	厚意
2	all in all	全般には
3	successful	成功裏の
4	hopefully	願わくば；できれば
5	formally	正式に
6	business	仕事
7	finalize	仕上げる；決着をつける
8	certainly	ほんとうに
9	perfect fit	最高の相性
10	foresee	予見する；予感する
11	mutually	相互に
12	beneficial	有益な；利益のある
13	relationship	関係
14	Assuming ...	…であれば
15	hang-up	支障
16	via email	E メールで
17	look over	吟味する
18	give one's regard to ...	…によろしくと伝える
19	as well	同様に

◀)) ビジネス・リスニング（2回目）

出張中のお世話へのお礼

Stage 03 日本語トランスレーション

ビジネス・ダイアローグの日本語を確認してみよう！ その上で、ダイアローグを聴きながら、まだできていない部分の穴埋めに再チャレンジしよう。

Mike: おはようございます、メイ。AAA セーフティー・システムズのマイクです。元気ですか？
May: 元気ですよ。帰りの旅はスムーズでしたか？
Mike: ええ。そちらにいたときのあなたのご厚意へのお礼を言いたくて、ちょっと電話しました。全般にすばらしい出張になったと思っています。この仕事を2週間以内に正式に御社に発注できればいいですね。明日が最終的に話を詰めるための顧客とのミーティングになっています。
May: すばらしい。ほんとうにこの契約を獲得できることを楽しみにしています。弊社と御社は最高のコンビネーションだと思いますし、長期にわたって互恵的な関係を築けると思います。
Mike: 私もそう思います。なにも問題がなければ、すぐにもこちらから電話します。そして、契約書の作成を進められるはずです。契約書はメールで送信して、そちらが確認する時間を取ったあとに電話で話をさせてもらいます。
May: わかりました。トムによろしくお伝えください。
Mike: 伝えておきます。チェンさんにもわれわれからの感謝をお伝えください。
May: わかりました、マイク。よい週末を。

🔊 ビジネス・リスニング（3回目）

Stage 04 英文トランスクリプション

ビジネス・ダイアローグの原稿を確認してみよう！ 穴埋め部分の正解をチェックして、英文を理解し直そう。そのあとで、もう一度ダイアローグを聴いてみよう。

Mike: May, ① good morning. This is Mike with AAA Safety Systems, how are you?
May: Fine thanks. ② Did you have a good trip back?
Mike: Yes. I just wanted to give you a call and thank you for your ③ hospitality while we were there. ④ All in all I think ⑤ it was a very successful trip and hopefully we can formally award this business to you within the next two weeks. We are ⑥ meeting with our customer tomorrow to ⑦ try and finalize things.
May: Excellent. We ⑧ certainly look ⑨ forward to ⑩ getting this contract. I think our companies are a ⑪ perfect fit and I foresee a long and mutually beneficial relationship.
Mike: I agree. Assuming ⑫ there are no hang-ups, you ⑬ should be hearing ⑭ from me soon and we can go ⑮ ahead and ⑯ write up the contract. I will send it via email and follow up with a phone call after you have had time to ⑰ look it over.
May: That's fine. Please give my regard to Tom.
Mike: I will, and please thank Mr. Chen for us as well.
May: Will do Mike. ⑱ Have a good weekend.

🔊 ビジネス・リスニング（4回目）

Stage 05 音声変化をチェック

まとめとして、穴埋め部分の音声変化の特徴をスロースピードとナチュラルスピードで確認しよう。下記に示したカタカナ表記で音声変化を確認して、もう一度ビジネス・ダイアローグを聴き直してみよう。発音変化のルールは適宜復習しよう。

2種類の音声を収録　CD 2-15

① **good morning**　　　　グッド・モーニング　　　▶ グッ__モーニング
　☞ 破裂音 [d] の脱落

② **Did you**　　　　　　　ディド・ユー　　　　　　▶ ディッジュー
　☞ [d] と [j] が同化

③ **hospitality**　　　　　ハスパタラティー　　　　▶ ハスパタラディ [リ] ー
　☞ 破裂音 [t] の弾音化

④ **All in all**　　　　　　オール・イン・オール　　▶ オーリノール
　☞ 3 語が連結

⑤ **it was**　　　　　　　イット・ワズ　　　　　　▶ イッ__ワズ
　☞ 破裂音 [t] の脱落

⑥ **meeting**　　　　　　 ミーティング　　　　　　▶ ミーディ [リ] ング
　☞ 破裂音 [t] の弾音化

⑦ **try and**　　　　　　　トゥライ・アンド　　　　▶ トゥライアン__
　☞ 末尾の破裂音 [d] の脱落

⑧ **certainly**　　　　　　サートゥンリー　　　　　▶ サーんンリー
　☞ 破裂音 [t] の声門閉鎖音化

⑨ **forward to**　　　　　フォーワード・トゥー　　▶ フォーワー__トゥー
　☞ 破裂音 [d] の脱落

⑩ **getting**　　　　　　　ゲッティング　　　　　　▶ ゲッディ [リ] ング
　☞ 破裂音 [t] の弾音化

⑪ **perfect fit**　　　　　プーフェクト・フィット　▶ プーフェク__フィット
　☞ 破裂音 [t] の脱落

⑫ **there are**　　　　　　ゼア・アー　　　　　　　▶ ゼアラー
　☞ 短縮形 there're [ゼアラー] の発音

⑬ **should be**　　　　　　シュッド・ビー　　　　　▶ シュッ__ビー
　☞ 破裂音の [d] の脱落

⑭ **from me**　　　　　　 フラム・ミー　　　　　　▶ フラ__ミ
　☞ 重複した [m] 音の片方が脱落

⑮ **ahead and**　　　　　 アヘッド・アンド　　　　▶ アヘッダン__
　☞ 2 語の連結。連結部の破裂音 [d] が弾音化したり、末尾の [d] が脱落することもある

⑯ **write up**　　　　　　ライト・アップ　　　　　▶ ライダ [ラ] ップ
　☞ 2 語の連結。連結部の破裂音 [t] の弾音化

⑰ **look it over**　　　　ルック・イット・オウヴァー ▶ ルッキド [ロ] ウヴァー
　☞ 3 語が連結。it と over の連結部で破裂音 [t] が弾音化

⑱ **Have a**　　　　　　　ハヴ・ア　　　　　　　　▶ ハヴァ
　☞ 2 語が連結

🔊 ビジネス・リスニング (5 回目)

出張中のお世話へのお礼　○○○ **97**

Unit 23

契約書の草案
Drafting the Contract

Stage 01 穴埋めビジネス・リスニング

音声変化に注意してCDでビジネスのダイアローグを聴きながら、空欄部分を埋めてみよう。

ダイアローグ音声収録　CD 2-16

Mike: Good morning May. ① _____ _____ ② _____ _____ chance to review my email?

May: Yes, we received the draft of the contract ③ _____ _____ upper management is reviewing it.

Mike: ④ _____ _____ straight forward, typical of the contracts we enter into with each of our suppliers. If you have any questions or requests for amendments, please ⑤ _____ _____ know and we can discuss any changes. However, please do not edit the original file.

May: ⑥ _____ _____ probably take a day or two to go over it, since we will ⑦ _____ _____ translate it into Chinese for our official records since ⑧ _____ _____ a legal document.

Mike: That is fine. ⑨ _____ _____ aware that as the contract states, the English version will be the ⑩ _____ _____ should there be any discrepancies. We do ⑪ _____ _____ ⑫ _____ _____ contract ⑬ _____ _____ the end of this week so we can go ⑭ _____ _____ issue a purchase order for the samples.

May: Can the contract be signed by any member of executive management, or ⑮ _____ _____ ⑯ _____ _____ be the president?

Mike: Any manager with the authority to sign contracts will do.

🔊 ビジネス・リスニング（1回目）

Stage 02 ビジネス・ボキャビル

ビジネスのボキャブラリーを CD で確認しよう。そのあとでもう一度、ビジネス・リスニングにチャレンジ。Stage 01 でできなかったところをもう一度聴き取って、穴埋めを完成させよう。

英日 音声収録　CD 2-17

#	英語	日本語
1	chance to ...	…する機会；時間
2	review	審査する
3	draft	草案
4	upper management	（会社の）上層部
5	straight forward	簡潔な
6	typical	典型的な
7	enter into	（契約を）締結する
8	amendment	修正
9	discuss	議論する
10	however	しかしながら
11	edit	編集する
12	original file	ファイルの原本
13	translate	翻訳する
14	official record	正式な記録
15	legal document	法的な書類
16	aware	気づいて
17	state	述べる；記載がある
18	binding document	法的拘束力のある書類
19	discrepancy	不一致；食い違い
20	sign	署名する
21	member of executive management	取締役会の一員
22	with the authority to ...	…する職権のある

◀)) ビジネス・リスニング（2回目）

Stage 03　日本語トランスレーション

ビジネス・ダイアローグの日本語を確認してみよう！ その上で、ダイアローグを聴きながら、まだできていない部分の穴埋めに再チャレンジしよう。

Mike: おはようございます、メイ。私のメールをご覧になれましたか？
May: 契約書の草案を受領しました。上層部が確認しているところです。
Mike: かなり簡潔な契約で、弊社が各下請け企業と仕事を始めるときに締結する典型的なものになっています。なにかご質問や変更の要求があればお知らせいただき、こちらで検討いたします。ただし、オリジナルのファイルは編集しないでくださいね。
May: おそらく確認に1日か2日かかると思います。法的な文書なので、正式な記録にするために中国語に翻訳する必要があるのです。
Mike: かまいませんよ。ただし、契約にもあるように、なんらかの見解の相違があった場合には、英語版が拘束力をもつ書類となることにご注意ください。サンプルの発注ができるように、今週の終わりまでにこの契約を締結する必要があります。
May: 契約の署名は、どの取締役でもかまいませんか？ それとも社長である必要がありますか？
Mike: 契約書にサインする資格のある人なら、どの役員でもかまいません。

🔊 ビジネス・リスニング（3回目）

Stage 04　英文トランスクリプション

ビジネス・ダイアローグの原稿を確認してみよう！ 穴埋め部分の正解をチェックして、英文を理解し直そう。そのあとで、もう一度ダイアローグを聴いてみよう。

Mike: Good morning May. ① Did you ② get a chance to review my email?
May: Yes, we received the draft of the contract ③ and our upper management is reviewing it.
Mike: ④ It's pretty straight forward, typical of the contracts we enter into with each of our suppliers. If you have any questions or requests for amendments, please ⑤ let us know and we can discuss any changes. However, please do not edit the original file.
May: ⑥ It will probably take a day or two to go over it, since we will ⑦ need to translate it into Chinese for our official records since ⑧ it is a legal document.
Mike: That is fine. ⑨ Just be aware that as the contract states, the English version will be the ⑩ binding document should there be any discrepancies. We do ⑪ need to ⑫ get this contract ⑬ executed by the end of this week so we can go ⑭ ahead and issue a purchase order for the samples.
May: Can the contract be signed by any member of executive management, or ⑮ does it ⑯ need to be the president?
Mike: Any manager with the authority to sign contracts will do.

🔊 ビジネス・リスニング（4回目）

Stage 05 音声変化をチェック

まとめとして、穴埋め部分の音声変化の特徴をスロースピードとナチュラルスピードで確認しよう。下記に示したカタカナ表記で音声変化を確認して、もう一度ビジネス・ダイアローグを聴き直してみよう。発音変化のルールは適宜復習しよう。

2種類の音声を収録

① **Did you**   ディッド・ユー   ▶ ディッジュー
  ☞ [d]音と[j]音が同化
② **get a**   ゲット・ア   ▶ ゲッダ[ラ]
  ☞ 2語が連結。連結部の破裂音[t]の弾音化
③ **and our**   アンド・アウァ   ▶ アンナウァ
  ☞ 破裂音[d]が脱落し、2語が連結
④ **It's pretty**   イッツ・プリティー   ▶ __スプリデ[リ]ィー
  ☞ it'sは[s]の音だけを残して脱落。prettyの破裂音[t]が弾音化
⑤ **let us**   レット・アス   ▶ レッダ[ラ]ス
  ☞ 2語の連結。連結部の破裂音[t]の弾音化
⑥ **It will**   イット・ウィル   ▶ イッ__ウィル;イドゥル
  ☞ it willから[t]音だけが脱落。短縮形it'll[イットゥル]の破裂音[t]が弾音化し[イドゥル]と発音することもある
⑦ **need to**   ニード・トゥー   ▶ ニードゥ[ル]ー;ニー__トゥー
  ☞ need toの破裂音[d]が脱落。toの破裂音[t]が弾音化することもある
⑧ **it is**   イット・イズ   ▶ イッディ[リ]イズ;イッツ
  ☞ 2語が連結し、連結部の破裂音[t]が弾音化。短縮形のit's[イッツ]の発音になることもある
⑨ **Just be**   ジャスト・ビー   ▶ ジャス__ビー
  ☞ 破裂音[t]の脱落
⑩ **binding document**   バインディング・ドキュメント   ▶ バインディン__ドキュメント
  ☞ 破裂音[g]の脱落
⑪ **need to**   ニード・トゥー   ▶ ニードゥ[ル]ー;ニー__トゥー
  ☞ need toの破裂音[d]が脱落。toの破裂音[t]が弾音化することもある
⑫ **get this**   ゲット・ズィス   ▶ ゲッ__ズィス
  ☞ 破裂音の[t]が脱落
⑬ **executed by**   エクセキューティッド・バイ   ▶ エクセキューディ[リ]ッ__バイ
  ☞ 破裂音[t]の弾音化。破裂音[d]の脱落
⑭ **ahead and**   アヘッド・アンド   ▶ アヘッダン__
  ☞ 2語の連結。and末尾の破裂音[d]の脱落
⑮ **does it**   ダズ・イット   ▶ ダズィッ__
  ☞ it末尾の破裂音[t]の脱落
⑯ **need to**   ニード・トゥー   ▶ ニー__トゥー;ニードゥ[ル]ー
  ☞ need toの破裂音[d]が脱落。toの破裂音[t]が弾音化することもある

🔊 ビジネス・リスニング (5回目)

Unit 24

契約書の修正について
Contract Revision

Stage 01 穴埋めビジネス・リスニング

音声変化に注意してCDでビジネスのダイアローグを聴きながら、空欄部分を埋めてみよう。

ダイアローグ音声収録　CD 2-19

May: Hi Mike. I'm following up on the contract revisions we requested ① _____ _____ sent yesterday. Have you had time to ② _____ _____ over yet?

Mike: Yes. I have ③ _____ them to my manager for review.

May: The biggest issue we had was the condition that you would only be responsible for five weeks' worth of raw material. ④ _____ _____ the long lead times and the need to ship these overseas, we ⑤ _____ _____ purchase raw material in bulk. This is in part how we were able to give you the ⑥ _____ _____.

Mike: I see ⑦ _____ _____ are requesting six-months advance notice if the parts are to be phased-out.

May: Yes, ⑧ _____ _____ allow us to work together to minimize any surplus inventory, whether ⑨ _____ _____ ⑩ _____ _____ or raw material.

Mike: ⑪ _____ _____ my decision, but I don't think that ⑫ _____ _____ a problem. I did see your request that we guarantee a ⑬ _____ amount of units per year. I am sure we ⑭ _____ _____ _____ able to agree to that, since we cannot ⑮ _____ the production volumes of our customers. I'll ⑯ _____ _____ tomorrow with our response.

🔊 ビジネス・リスニング（1回目）

Stage 02 ビジネス・ボキャビル

ビジネスのボキャブラリーをCDで確認しよう。そのあとでもう一度、ビジネス・リスニングにチャレンジ。Stage 01 でできなかったところをもう一度聴き取って、穴埋めを完成させよう。

英日 音声収録

1	contract revisions	契約の変更；改訂
2	submit	提出する
3	issue	問題（点）
4	condition	条件
5	responsible for ...	…に責任のある
6	five weeks' worth of ...	5週間分の…
7	raw material	原材料
8	overseas	海外に
9	in bulk	大量に
10	in part	ある程度
11	reduced pricing	減額した値付け
12	advance notice	事前通知
13	be phased-out	廃止される
14	minimize	最小化する
15	surplus	余剰の
16	inventory	在庫
17	finished product	最終製品
18	decision	決定
19	guarantee	保証する
20	certain amount of units	ある決まった台数
21	per year	1年に
22	production volumes	生産数；生産量
23	response	返答

◀)) ビジネス・リスニング（2回目）

契約書の修正について

Stage 03 　日本語トランスレーション

ビジネス・ダイアローグの日本語を確認してみよう！ その上で、ダイアローグを聴きながら、まだできていない部分の穴埋めに再チャレンジしよう。

May: こんにちは、マイク。昨日お送りした契約変更のお願いについての電話です。もうお読みになれましたか？

Mike: ええ、チェックしてもらうために上司に提出してあります。

May: もっとも大きな問題は、御社が5週間分の原材料にしか責任をもたないという条件ですね。リードタイムが長いことと、海外への出荷が必要ですから、原材料をまとめて購入する必要があるのです。これは、御社に低価格をご提供するための要素でもあるのです。

Mike: パーツの発注が（今後）なくなるのかどうかの通知を、6カ月前にしてほしいと要求されていますね。

May: ええ、そうしていただけると、最終製品であれ原材料であれ、余剰在庫を最小化するための協力が可能です。

Mike: 私が判断できることではありませんが、その点は問題にはならないと思います。毎年一定の数量（の購入）を保証するように求めていらっしゃいましたよね。この点は同意できないことは確実だと思います。弊社は顧客の生産量をコントロールできないからです。明日、ご連絡してお返事をいたしますね。

🔊 ビジネス・リスニング（3回目）

Stage 04 　英文トランスクリプション

ビジネス・ダイアローグの原稿を確認してみよう！ 穴埋め部分の正解をチェックして、英文を理解し直そう。そのあとで、もう一度ダイアローグを聴いてみよう。

May: Hi Mike. I'm following up on the contract revisions we requested ① that I sent yesterday. Have you had time to ② look them over yet?

Mike: Yes. I have ③ submitted them to my manager for review.

May: The biggest issue we had was the condition that you would only be responsible for five weeks' worth of raw material. ④ Due to the long lead times and the need to ship these overseas, we ⑤ need to purchase raw material in bulk. This is in part how we were able to give you the ⑥ reduced pricing.

Mike: I see ⑦ that you are requesting six-months advance notice if the parts are to be phased-out.

May: Yes, ⑧ that will allow us to work together to minimize any surplus inventory, whether ⑨ it be ⑩ finished product or raw material.

Mike: ⑪ It's not my decision, but I don't think that ⑫ will be a problem. I did see your request that we guarantee a ⑬ certain amount of units per year. I am sure we ⑭ will not be able to agree to that, since we cannot ⑮ control the production volumes of our customers. I'll ⑯ contact you tomorrow with our response.

🔊 ビジネス・リスニング（4回目）

Stage 05 音声変化をチェック

まとめとして、穴埋め部分の音声変化の特徴をスロースピードとナチュラルスピードで確認しよう。下記に示したカタカナ表記で音声変化を確認して、もう一度ビジネス・ダイアローグを聴き直してみよう。発音変化のルールは適宜復習しよう。

2種類の音声を収録

CD 2-21

① **that I** — ザット・アイ ▶ ザッダ[ラ]イ
☞ 2語の連結。連結部の破裂音 [t] の弾音化

② **look them** — ルック・ゼム ▶ ルッケム
☞ look が弱化した them [エム] に連結

③ **submitted** — サブミッティッド ▶ サブミッディ[リ]ッド
☞ 破裂音 [t] の弾音化

④ **Due to** — デュー・トゥー ▶ デュードゥ[ル]—
☞ 破裂音 [t] の弾音化

⑤ **need to** — ニード・トゥー ▶ ニードゥ[ル]—；ニー__トゥー
☞ need to の破裂音 [d] が脱落。to の破裂音 [t] が弾音化することもある

⑥ **reduced pricing** — リデュースト・プライシング ▶ リデュース__プライシング
☞ 破裂音 [t] の脱落

⑦ **that you** — ザット・ユー ▶ ザッチュー
☞ [t] と [j] が同化

⑧ **that will** — ザット・ウィル ▶ ザッ__ウィル；ザッドゥ[ル]ル
☞ 破裂音 [t] の脱落。また、短縮形 that'll [ザットゥル] の [t] が弾音化する場合もある

⑨ **it be** — イット・ビー ▶ イッ__ビー
☞ 破裂音 [t] の脱落

⑩ **finished product** — フィニッシュト・プラーダクト ▶ フィニッシュ__プラーダクト
☞ 破裂音 [t] の脱落

⑪ **It's not** — イッツ・ナット ▶ __スナッ__
☞ it's は [s] の音あるいは [ts] の音が残る。not の末尾の破裂音 [t] も脱落することがある

⑫ **will be** — ウィル・ビー ▶ ウィ__ビ
☞ [l] 音の脱落

⑬ **certain** — スートゥン ▶ スーんン
☞ 破裂音の [t] 声門閉鎖音化

⑭ **will not be** — ウィル・ナット・ビー ▶ ウィルナッ__ビ
☞ 破裂音 [t] の脱落

⑮ **control** — カントゥロウル ▶ カンチュロウル
☞ [ntr] の音が [ntʃr] に変化

⑯ **contact you** — カンタクト・ユー ▶ カンタクチュー
☞ [t] と [j] が同化

🔊 ビジネス・リスニング（5回目）

Unit 25

契約内容への同意
Contract Detail Agreement

Stage 01 — 穴埋めビジネス・リスニング

音声変化に注意してCDでビジネスのダイアローグを聴きながら、空欄部分を埋めてみよう。

ダイアローグ音声収録 （CD 2-22）

May: Hi Mike. I just ① _____ _____ email.

Mike: Yes, we were able to make most of the revisions you requested. Unfortunately, as I suspected we ② _____ _____ to purchase a ③ _____ ④ _____ _____ units per year, but we will make our best effort to ⑤ _____ _____ with at least six months' notice if the project is to be discontinued.

May: I did not see any attachment with your email.

Mike: Sorry ⑥ _____ _____. I ⑦ _____ _____ forgot to ⑧ _____ _____. I will ⑨ _____ _____ when I ⑩ _____ _____ to the office. I sent two copies of the revised agreement by Fed-Ex to your attention. They have already been ⑪ _____ _____ our company president, so have one of your executives sign them both and return one original copy to us, and keep one copy for your records.

May: Okay. Our management team is not here today, ⑫ _____ _____ ⑬ _____ _____ able to get the agreement signed and ⑭ _____ _____ to you tomorrow. In China ⑮ _____ _____ common to use a stamp ⑯ _____ _____ a signature, is ⑰ _____ _____?

Mike: Either is fine.

🔊 ビジネス・リスニング（1回目）

Stage 02 ビジネス・ボキャビル

ビジネスのボキャブラリーをCDで確認しよう。そのあとでもう一度、ビジネス・リスニングにチャレンジ。Stage 01 でできなかったところをもう一度聴き取って、穴埋めを完成させよう。

英日 音声収録

1	most of the revisions	変更のほとんど
2	unfortunately	残念ながら
3	suspect	疑問視する；疑う
4	promise	約束する
5	effort	努力
6	be discontinued	継続されない
7	attachment	添付ファイル
8	two copies	2部
9	agreement	契約書
10	to your attention	あなた宛に
11	executive	取締役
12	original copy	原本
13	for one's records	記録用に
14	send out	発送する
15	common	一般的な
16	stamp	印鑑
17	instead of ...	…の代わりに
18	signature	署名
19	either	どちらでも

🔊 ビジネス・リスニング（2回目）

Stage 03　日本語トランスレーション

ビジネス・ダイアローグの日本語を確認してみよう！ その上で、ダイアローグを聴きながら、まだできていない部分の穴埋めに再チャレンジしよう。

May: こんにちは、マイク。いまメールを受領したところです。
Mike: そうですね。御社の要求されているほとんどの改訂を採用することができました。残念ながら、私が疑っていたとおり、毎年の決まった数量の購入を約束することはできませんでした。しかし、もしプロジェクトが停止になる場合は、6 カ月前の通知を提供できるよう最大限の努力をします。
May: メールに添付ファイルがついていないようですが。
Mike: それはすみません。添付するのを忘れてしまったようです。オフィスに戻ったらお送りしますね。あなた宛に FedEx で改訂版の契約書を 2 通お送りしました。当社の社長がすでに署名していますので、御社の取締役のおひとりに両方にご署名いただき、1 通の原本をこちらにご返送ください。もう 1 通は御社の記録のために保存をお願いします。
May: 了解しました。弊社の経営陣は本日不在ですが、明日にはサインを入れて御社に発送できると思います。中国では署名の代わりに印鑑を使うのが一般的ですが、それで大丈夫でしょうか？
Mike: どちらでもかまいませんよ。

🔊 ビジネス・リスニング（3 回目）

Stage 04　英文トランスクリプション

ビジネス・ダイアローグの原稿を確認してみよう！ 穴埋め部分の正解をチェックして、英文を理解し直そう。そのあとで、もう一度ダイアローグを聴いてみよう。

May: Hi Mike. I just ① got your email.
Mike: Yes, we were able to make most of the revisions you requested. Unfortunately, as I suspected we ② couldn't promise to purchase a ③ certain ④ number of units per year, but we will make our best effort to ⑤ provide you with at least six months' notice if the project is to be discontinued.
May: I did not see any attachment with your email.
Mike: Sorry ⑥ about that. I ⑦ must have forgot to ⑧ attach it. I will ⑨ send it when I ⑩ get back to the office. I sent two copies of the revised agreement by Fed-Ex to your attention. They have already been ⑪ signed by our company president, so have one of your executives sign them both and return one original copy to us, and keep one copy for your records.
May: Okay. Our management team is not here today, ⑫ but I ⑬ should be able to get the agreement signed and ⑭ sent out to you tomorrow. In China ⑮ it is common to use a stamp ⑯ instead of a signature, is ⑰ that okay?
Mike: Either is fine.

🔊 ビジネス・リスニング（4 回目）

Stage 05 音声変化をチェック

まとめとして、穴埋め部分の音声変化の特徴をスロースピードとナチュラルスピードで確認しよう。下記に示したカタカナ表記で音声変化を確認して、もう一度ビジネス・ダイアローグを聴き直してみよう。発音変化のルールは適宜復習しよう。

2種類の音声を収録　　CD 2-24

① **got your** 　　　　　　　　ガット・ユア　　　　　　▶ ガッチュア
　☞ [t] と [j] が同化

② **couldn't promise** 　　　　クドゥント・プラミス　　▶ クドゥン＿プラミス
　☞ 破裂音 [t] の脱落

③ **certain** 　　　　　　　　　スートゥン　　　　　　　▶ スーンン
　☞ 破裂音 [t] の声門閉鎖音化

④ **number of** 　　　　　　　 ナンバー・アヴ　　　　　▶ ナンバラヴ
　☞ 2語が連結。末尾の [v] も脱落することがある

⑤ **provide you** 　　　　　　 プラヴァイド・ユー　　　▶ プラヴァイジュー
　☞ [d] と [j] が同化

⑥ **about that** 　　　　　　　 アバウト・ザット　　　　▶ アバウ＿ザッ＿
　☞ 1カ所あるいは2カ所で破裂音 [t] の脱落

⑦ **must have** 　　　　　　　 マスト・ハヴ　　　　　　▶ マスタヴ
　☞ must が弱化した have [アヴ] に連結

⑧ **attach it** 　　　　　　　　アタッチ・イット　　　　▶ アタッチット
　☞ 2語が連結

⑨ **send it** 　　　　　　　　　センド・イット　　　　　▶ センディット；セニット
　☞ 2語が連結。破裂音 [d] が脱落して連結することもある

⑩ **get back** 　　　　　　　　 ゲット・バック　　　　　▶ ゲッ＿バック
　☞ 破裂音 [t] の脱落

⑪ **signed by** 　　　　　　　 サインド・バイ　　　　　▶ サイン＿バイ
　☞ 破裂音 [d] の脱落

⑫ **but I** 　　　　　　　　　　バット・アイ　　　　　　▶ バッダ [ラ] イ
　☞ 2語が連結。連結部の破裂音 [t] が弾音化

⑬ **should be** 　　　　　　　 シュッド・ビー　　　　　▶ シュッ＿ビ
　☞ 破裂音 [d] の脱落

⑭ **sent out** 　　　　　　　　セント・アウト　　　　　▶ セナウト；センタウト
　☞ 2語が連結。連結部の破裂音の [t] が脱落することもある

⑮ **it is** 　　　　　　　　　　イット・イズ　　　　　　▶ イッディ [リ] イズ；イッツ
　☞ 2語が連結し、連結部の破裂音 [t] が弾音化。短縮形の it's [イッツ] の発音になることもある

⑯ **instead of** 　　　　　　　 インステッド・アヴ　　　▶ インステッダヴ
　☞ 2語が連結。連結部の破裂音 [d] は弾音化することもある

⑰ **that okay** 　　　　　　　 ザット・オウケイ　　　　▶ ザッド [ロ] ウケイ
　☞ 2語が連結。連結部の破裂音 [t] の弾音化

🔊 ビジネス・リスニング（5回目）

Unit 26

試作品発注の訂正依頼
Requesting Correction of Sample Purchase Order

Stage 01　穴埋めビジネス・リスニング

音声変化に注意してCDでビジネスのダイアローグを聴きながら、空欄部分を埋めてみよう。

ダイアローグ音声収録

Mike: This is Mike speaking, how can I help you?

May: Mike, this is May with China Semicon.

Mike: Good morning. ① _____ _____ get my purchase order?

May: We ② _____ _____ . But the ③ _____ _____ on the order form was wrong. It shows the mass production piece-price of $0.045, but ④ _____ _____ know we ⑤ _____ _____ a sample fee of $1000 for the initial lot of 100 pcs.

Mike: Oh ... You're right May. I see that now. I am sorry I ⑥ _____ catch that when the PO was ⑦ _____ . I'll change that in the system and ⑧ _____ _____ new one ⑨ _____ _____ you ⑩ _____ _____ . I'm really sorry for the inconvenience.

May: Another thing is the due date. The ⑪ _____ _____ on these parts is ⑫ _____-five days. Your purchase order is showing a due ⑬ _____ _____ only sixty days. We will do our best to expedite sample production, but we cannot guarantee anything under ⑭ _____-five days.

Mike: Our system automatically generates a due date of sixty days. ⑮ _____ _____ change that manually and list the ⑯ _____ _____ on the revised PO. ⑰ _____ _____ _____ .

May: No problem, I look ⑱ _____ _____ receiving the new order.

🔊 ビジネス・リスニング（1回目）

Stage 02　ビジネス・ボキャビル

ビジネスのボキャブラリーを CD で確認しよう。そのあとでもう一度、ビジネス・リスニングにチャレンジ。Stage 01 でできなかったところをもう一度聴き取って、穴埋めを完成させよう。

英日 音声収録

1. purchase order　　　　　注文書；発注書
2. unit price　　　　　　　（1 ユニットの）単価
3. wrong　　　　　　　　　間違った
4. piece-price　　　　　　　単価
5. sample fee　　　　　　　サンプル代
6. initial lot　　　　　　　　初期ロット
7. PO　　　　　　　　　　　注文書（Purchase Order の略）
8. generate　　　　　　　　（機器・PC などで）作成する
9. right away　　　　　　　すぐに；即座に
10. inconvenience　　　　　迷惑；不便
11. due date　　　　　　　　期日；締め切り日
12. expedite　　　　　　　　はかどらせる；スピードを上げさせる
13. guarantee　　　　　　　保証する
14. automatically　　　　　自動的に
15. manually　　　　　　　　手動で
16. correct date　　　　　　正しい日付
17. revised　　　　　　　　　修正された
18. look forward to ...　　　…を楽しみに待つ
19. receive　　　　　　　　　受領する
20. order　　　　　　　　　　注文

◀)) ビジネス・リスニング（2回目）

Stage 03　日本語トランスレーション

ビジネス・ダイアローグの日本語を確認してみよう！　その上で、ダイアローグを聴きながら、まだできていない部分の穴埋めに再チャレンジしよう。

Mike: マイクです。ご用件は？
May: マイク、チャイナ・セミコンのメイです。
Mike: おはようございます。発注書を受け取ってくれましたか？
May: 受領しました。しかし、注文書のユニット単価が間違っていました。大量生産の単品価格が0.045ドルとなっていますが、ご存じのとおり、最初の100ロットのサンプル代金は1000ドルで合意しています。
Mike: ああ…そのとおりですね、メイ、いま気づきました。すみません、発注書が作成されたとき、その点を見落としました。システムで変更して、すぐに新しいものをお送りします。不便をおかけしてほんとうにすみません。
May: もう一点、期日の件ですが、このパーツの準備期間は75日です。御社の発注書では、期日が60日しかありません。サンプル製造を急がせるようベストを尽くしますが、75日未満の日数は保証できかねます。
Mike: 弊社のシステムが自動的に60日の期日を作成しているんです。手動で変更して、変更した注文書に正しい日付を記載しておきます。申し訳ない。
May: 大丈夫です。新しい注文書をお待ちしていますね。

🔊 ビジネス・リスニング（3回目）

Stage 04　英文トランスクリプション

ビジネス・ダイアローグの原稿を確認してみよう！　穴埋め部分の正解をチェックして、英文を理解し直そう。そのあとで、もう一度ダイアローグを聴いてみよう。

Mike: This is Mike speaking, how can I help you?
May: Mike, this is May with China Semicon.
Mike: Good morning. ① Did you get my purchase order?
May: We ② got it. But the ③ unit price on the order form was wrong. It shows the mass production piece-price of $0.045, but ④ as you know we ⑤ agreed to a sample fee of $1000 for the initial lot of 100 pcs.
Mike: Oh … You're right May. I see that now. I am sorry I ⑥ didn't catch that when the PO was ⑦ generated. I'll change that in the system and ⑧ have a new one ⑨ sent to you ⑩ right away. I'm really sorry for the inconvenience.
May: Another thing is the due date. The ⑪ lead time on these parts is ⑫ seventy-five days. Your purchase order is showing a due ⑬ date of only sixty days. We will do our best to expedite sample production, but we cannot guarantee anything under ⑭ seventy-five days.
Mike: Our system automatically generates a due date of sixty days. ⑮ I will change that manually and list the ⑯ correct date on the revised PO. ⑰ Sorry about that.
May: No problem, I look ⑱ forward to receiving the new order.

🔊 ビジネス・リスニング（4回目）

Stage 05 音声変化をチェック

まとめとして、穴埋め部分の音声変化の特徴をスロースピードとナチュラルスピードで確認しよう。下記に示したカタカナ表記で音声変化を確認して、もう一度ビジネス・ダイアローグを聴き直してみよう。発音変化のルールは適宜復習しよう。

2種類の音声を収録
CD 2-27

① **Did you**   ディッド・ユー ▶ ディッジュー
 ☞ [d] 音と [j] 音が同化

② **got it**   ガット・イット ▶ ガディ [リ] ット ; ガッティット
 ☞ 2語が連結。連結部の破裂音 [t] の弾音化

③ **unit price**   ユニット・プライス ▶ ユニッ＿プライス
 ☞ 破裂音 [t] の脱落

④ **as you**   アズ・ユー ▶ アジュー
 ☞ [z] 音と [j] 音が同化

⑤ **agreed to**   アグリード・トゥー ▶ アグリー＿トゥー
 ☞ 破裂音 [d] の脱落

⑥ **didn't**   ディドゥント ▶ ディんン＿
 ☞ [d] 音の声門閉鎖音化。末尾の破裂音 [t] の脱落

⑦ **generated**   ジェネレイティッド ▶ ジェネレイディ [リ] ッド
 ☞ 破裂音 [t] の弾音化

⑧ **have a**   ハヴ・ア ▶ ハヴァ
 ☞ 2語が連結

⑨ **sent to**   セント・トゥー ▶ セン＿トゥー
 ☞ [t] 音が片方脱落

⑩ **right away**   ライト・アウェイ ▶ ライダ [ラ] ウェイ
 ☞ 2語の連結。連結部の破裂音 [t] の弾音化

⑪ **lead time**   リード・タイム ▶ リー＿タイム
 ☞ 破裂音 [d] の脱落

⑫ **seventy**   セヴンティー ▶ セヴニー
 ☞ 破裂音 [t] の脱落

⑬ **date of**   デイト・アヴ ▶ デイダ [ラ] ヴ
 ☞ 2語が連結。連結部の破裂音 [t] の弾音化

⑭ **seventy**   セヴンティー ▶ セヴニー
 ☞ 破裂音 [t] の脱落

⑮ **I will**   アイ・ウィル ▶ アイル ; アイウァ
 ☞ 短縮形 I'll の発音、あるいは will が弱化

⑯ **correct date**   コレクト・デイト ▶ コレク＿デイト
 ☞ 破裂音 [t] の脱落

⑰ **Sorry about that**   サーリー・アバウト・ザット ▶ サーリーアバウ＿ザッ＿
 ☞ 2カ所で破裂音 [t] の脱落

⑱ **forward to**   フォーワード・トゥー ▶ フォーワー＿トゥー
 ☞ 破裂音 [d] の脱落

🔊 ビジネス・リスニング（5回目）

Unit 27

進捗の報告
Progress Report

Stage 01 穴埋めビジネス・リスニング

音声変化に注意してCDでビジネスのダイアローグを聴きながら、空欄部分を埋めてみよう。

ダイアローグ音声収録

Mike: Good morning, May. I just ① _____ _____ ② _____ _____ the ③ _____ of our samples. I realize they are not ④ _____ _____ be finished for another month, ⑤ _____ _____ have ⑥ _____-five components in the mix and I am ⑦ _____ _____ with each supplier to confirm we are on schedule.

May: Well, we have the raw materials and are ⑧ _____ _____ finished ⑨ _____ _____ the production line. I just ⑩ _____ _____ meeting with Mr. Chang and he ⑪ _____ indicate that there were any issues ⑫ _____ _____ cause a delay.

Mike: When ⑬ _____ _____ expect actual production to begin?

May: ⑭ _____ it is scheduled to start next Monday. Of course the testing process is almost as lengthy as the production.

Mike: This is something I ⑮ _____ _____ ask, but when you submit the PPAP documents they ⑯ _____ _____ in English, right?

May: Yes, we will translate them and I will send them electronically when the samples are shipped.

Mike: Okay then. I will check back with you ⑰ _____ _____ week or so.

🔊 ビジネス・リスニング（1回目）

Stage 02 ビジネス・ボキャビル

ビジネスのボキャブラリーを CD で確認しよう。そのあとでもう一度、ビジネス・リスニングにチャレンジ。Stage 01 でできなかったところをもう一度聴き取って、穴埋めを完成させよう。

英日 音声収録

1. check on ...　　…を確認する
2. status　　現状
3. be scheduled to ...　　…する予定になっている
4. have ... in the mix　　…を同時に動かしている；手配中だ
5. touch base with ...　　…と連絡を取る
6. confirm　　確認する
7. on schedule　　スケジュールどおりの
8. set up　　設置する；組み上げる
9. production line　　生産ライン
10. cause　　生じさせる
11. delay　　遅延
12. expect　　予期する；予測する
13. actual production　　実際の生産
14. currently　　現在；いまのところ
15. testing process　　検査の工程
16. lengthy　　長時間の
17. submit　　提出する
18. electronically　　電子的に；E メールで
19. in a week or so　　1 週間くらいあとで

ビジネス・リスニング（2 回目）

Stage 03 　日本語トランスレーション

ビジネス・ダイアローグの日本語を確認してみよう！ その上で、ダイアローグを聴きながら、まだできていない部分の穴埋めに再チャレンジしよう。

Mike: おはよう、メイ。サンプルの状況を知りたいんですが。あと1カ月はできあがらないのはわかってますが、45もの部品のを同時に手配中なので、スケジュールどおりなのか下請け各社と連絡を取っているところなのです。

May: ええ、原料は入手していまして、ちょうど生産ラインの組み立てが終わるところです。先ほどチャンさんと打ち合わせを行いましたが、遅延につながるような問題点についてはなにも聞かされませんでした。

Mike: 実際の生産が開始されるのはいつ頃になりそうですか？

May: 現在、次の月曜の予定です。もちろん、検査の過程でも製造と同じくらい時間がかかりますが。

Mike: それについてお聞きするのを忘れていましたが、御社が生産部品承認プロセスの書類を提出する際は英語でいただけるんですよね？

May: はい、こちらで翻訳して、サンプル発送時に電子メールでお送りいたします。

Mike: そうですか。では、1週間ほどしたらまたご連絡しますね。

🔊 ビジネス・リスニング（3回目）

Stage 04 　英文トランスクリプション

ビジネス・ダイアローグの原稿を確認してみよう！ 穴埋め部分の正解をチェックして、英文を理解し直そう。そのあとで、もう一度ダイアローグを聴いてみよう。

Mike: Good morning, May. I just ① wanted to ② check on the ③ status of our samples. I realize they are not ④ scheduled to be finished for another month, ⑤ but we have ⑥ forty-five components in the mix and I am ⑦ touching base with each supplier to confirm we are on schedule.

May: Well, we have the raw materials and are ⑧ just about finished ⑨ setting up the production line. I just ⑩ had a meeting with Mr. Chang and he ⑪ didn't indicate that there were any issues ⑫ that would cause a delay.

Mike: When ⑬ do you expect actual production to begin?

May: ⑭ Currently it is scheduled to start next Monday. Of course the testing process is almost as lengthy as the production.

Mike: This is something I ⑮ forgot to ask, but when you submit the PPAP documents they ⑯ will be in English, right?

May: Yes, we will translate them and I will send them electronically when the samples are shipped.

Mike: Okay then. I will check back with you ⑰ in a week or so.

🔊 ビジネス・リスニング（4回目）

Stage 05 音声変化をチェック

まとめとして、穴埋め部分の音声変化の特徴をスロースピードとナチュラルスピードで確認しよう。下記に示したカタカナ表記で音声変化を確認して、もう一度ビジネス・ダイアローグを聴き直してみよう。発音変化のルールは適宜復習しよう。

2種類の音声を収録

① **wanted to**　　　ワンティッド・トゥー　　▶ ワニッ__トゥー
☞ 破裂音 [t] と [d] の脱落。to の破裂音 [t] が弾音化することもある

② **check on**　　　チェック・オン　　▶ チェッコン
☞ 2語が連結

③ **status**　　　ステイタス　　▶ ステイダ [ラ] ス
☞ 破裂音 [t] の弾音化

④ **scheduled to**　　　スケジュールド・トゥー　　▶ スケジュール__トゥー
☞ 破裂音 [d] の脱落

⑤ **but we**　　　バット・ウィ　　▶ バッ__ウィ
☞ 破裂音 [t] の脱落

⑥ **forty**　　　フォーティー　　▶ フォーディ [リ] ー
☞ 破裂音 [t] の弾音化

⑦ **touching base**　　　タッチング・ベイス　　▶ タッチン__ベイス
☞ 破裂音 [g] の脱落

⑧ **just about**　　　ジャスト・アバウト　　▶ ジャスタバウト
☞ 2語が連結。破裂音 [t] が脱落する場合もある

⑨ **setting up**　　　セッティング・アップ　　▶ セッディ [リ] ン__アップ
☞ setting の [t] 音が弾音化、[g] 音の脱落。さらに2語が連結する場合もある

⑩ **had a**　　　ハッド・ア　　▶ ハッダ [ラ]
☞ 2語が連結。破裂音 [d] は弾音化することもある

⑪ **didn't**　　　ディドゥント　　▶ ディンン__
☞ [d] 音の声門閉鎖音化。末尾の破裂音 [t] の脱落

⑫ **that would**　　　ザット・ウッド　　▶ ザッ__ウッド
☞ 破裂音 [t] の脱落

⑬ **do you**　　　ドゥー・ユー　　▶ ドゥユ；ジュ
☞ do の弱化。さらに [d] と [j] が同化することもある

⑭ **Currently**　　　カレントゥリー　　▶ カレン__リー
☞ 破裂音 [t] の脱落

⑮ **forgot to**　　　フォーガット・トゥー　　▶ フォーガッ__トゥー
☞ 破裂音の [t] が脱落。to の [t] 音は弾音化することもある

⑯ **will be**　　　ウィル・ビー　　▶ ウィ__ビ
☞ [l] 音の脱落

⑰ **in a**　　　イン・ア　　▶ イナ
☞ 2語が連結

🔊 ビジネス・リスニング（5回目）

Unit 28

計画の大幅な見直し依頼 ①
Major Plan Revision Request 1

Stage 01 穴埋めビジネス・リスニング

音声変化に注意してCDでビジネスのモノローグを聴きながら、空欄部分を埋めてみよう。

モノローグ音声収録

Mike: May, this is Mike with AAA Safety Systems. I have some bad news. We just ① _____ _____ that there was ② _____ _____ on the part diagram ③ _____ _____ customer sent. I have just ④ _____ _____ a revised diagram via email. I have marked the relevant changes in red. I realize this is a huge issue, and I ⑤ _____ _____ be leaving this message on your voicemail. Please review the information and the prints and ⑥ _____ _____ a call as soon as possible. We really ⑦ _____ _____ know if these changes will affect pricing or the production conditions and schedule. Also, please check and ⑧ _____ _____ know if the samples ⑨ _____ in production can be reworked to address this problem. If not, ⑩ _____ _____ know what the cost is to dispose of the in-production parts. We will be having a ⑪ _____ on this tomorrow afternoon. So please ⑫ _____ _____ to me before then with ⑬ _____ information ⑭ _____ _____ available. You can ⑮ _____ _____ anytime on my cell phone, ⑯ _____ _____ ⑰ _____ _____ time difference. Thanks.

🔊 ビジネス・リスニング（1回目）

Stage 02 ビジネス・ボキャビル

ビジネスのボキャブラリーをCDで確認しよう。そのあとでもう一度、ビジネス・リスニングにチャレンジ。Stage 01でできなかったところをもう一度聴き取って、穴埋めを完成させよう。

英日 音声収録

CD 2-32

1	bad news	悪い知らせ
2	find out	発見する
3	error	間違い；エラー
4	part diagram	部品の設計図；図表
5	mark	印をつける
6	relevant changes	関連する変更
7	in red	赤い文字で
8	huge issue	大きな問題
9	hate to …	…したくない
10	voicemail	音声メール（システム）
11	as soon as possible	できるだけ早く
12	affect	影響を与える
13	production conditions	生産条件
14	in production	生産中の
15	rework	手直しする；手を加える
16	address	（困難・問題など）に対処する
17	dispose of …	…を廃棄する
18	whatever information	どんな情報でも
19	available	手に入る；入手可能な
20	cell phone	携帯電話
21	time difference	時差

🔊 ビジネス・リスニング（2回目）

Stage 03　日本語トランスレーション

ビジネス・モノローグの日本語を確認してみよう！ その上で、モノローグを聴きながら、まだできていない部分の穴埋めに再チャレンジしよう。

Mike: メイ、AAA セーフティー・システムズのマイクです。ちょっと悪い知らせがあるのですが。弊社の顧客が送ってきた部品の設計図に1カ所間違いがあることがわかりました。更新した設計図をメールであなたに送信したところです。変更箇所には赤字で印をつけておきました。大きな問題であることはわかっていますし、この件を留守電に残すのは避けたかったのですが。情報と図面を確認してできるだけ早めに折り返しご連絡ください。この変更が値付けや生産条件、あるいはスケジュールに影響を与えるのかどうかを知りたいのです。また、現在製造中のサンプルを手直ししてこの問題に対処することが可能かどうかも調べて教えてください。もし無理なら、生産に入っている部品を廃棄する費用がどのくらいなのかを教えてください。弊社では、明日の午後この件についてミーティングをする予定です。ですから、その時間までに、使える情報であればなんでも私にお知らせください。私の携帯にはいつでもご連絡ください。時差は考えに入れないでかまいません。それでは、失礼します。

🔊 ビジネス・リスニング（3回目）

Stage 04　英文トランスクリプション

ビジネス・モノローグの原稿を確認してみよう！ 穴埋め部分の正解をチェックして、英文を理解し直そう。そのあとで、もう一度モノローグを聴いてみよう。

Mike: May, this is Mike with AAA Safety Systems. I have some bad news. We just ① found out that there was ② an error on the part diagram ③ that our customer sent. I have just ④ sent you a revised diagram via email. I have marked the relevant changes in red. I realize this is a huge issue, and I ⑤ hate to be leaving this message on your voicemail. Please review the information and the prints and ⑥ give me a call as soon as possible. We really ⑦ need to know if these changes will affect pricing or the production conditions and schedule. Also, please check and ⑧ let me know if the samples ⑨ currently in production can be reworked to address this problem. If not, ⑩ let me know what the cost is to dispose of the in-production parts. We will be having a ⑪ meeting on this tomorrow afternoon. So please ⑫ get back to me before then with ⑬ whatever information ⑭ that is available. You can ⑮ call me anytime on my cell phone, ⑯ don't worry ⑰ about the time difference. Thanks.

🔊 ビジネス・リスニング（4回目）

Stage 05 音声変化をチェック

まとめとして、穴埋め部分の音声変化の特徴をスロースピードとナチュラルスピードで確認しよう。下記に示したカタカナ表記で音声変化を確認して、もう一度ビジネス・モノローグを聴き直してみよう。発音変化のルールは適宜復習しよう。

2種類の音声を収録　　CD 2-33

① **found out**　　ファウンド・アウト　▶ ファウンダ [ラ] ウト
　☞ 2語が連結。連結部の破裂音 [d] の弾音化

② **an error**　　アン・エラー　▶ アネラー
　☞ 2語が連結

③ **that our**　　ザット・アウァ　▶ ザッダ [ラ] ウァ
　☞ 2語が連結。連結部の破裂音 [t] の弾音化

④ **sent you**　　セント・ユー　▶ センチュー
　☞ [t] 音と [j] 音が同化

⑤ **hate to**　　ヘイト・トゥー　▶ ヘイ＿トゥー
　☞ 破裂音 [t] の脱落

⑥ **give me**　　ギヴ・ミー　▶ ギ＿ミ
　☞ [v] 音の脱落

⑦ **need to**　　ニード・トゥー　▶ ニードゥ[ル] ー；ニー＿トゥー
　☞ need to の破裂音 [d] が脱落。to の破裂音 [t] が弾音化することもある

⑧ **let me**　　レット・ミー　▶ レッ＿ミ
　☞ 破裂音 [t] の脱落

⑨ **currently**　　カレントゥリー　▶ カレン＿リー
　☞ 破裂音 [t] の脱落

⑩ **let me**　　レット・ミー　▶ レッ＿ミ
　☞ 破裂音 [t] の脱落

⑪ **meeting**　　ミーティング　▶ ミーディ [リ] ング
　☞ 破裂音 [t] の弾音化

⑫ **get back**　　ゲット・バック　▶ ゲッ＿バック
　☞ 破裂音 [t] の脱落

⑬ **whatever**　　ワットエヴァー　▶ ワッデ [レ] ヴァー
　☞ 破裂音 [t] の弾音化

⑭ **that is**　　ザット・イズ　▶ ザッディ [リ] ズ
　☞ 2語が連結。連結部の破裂音 [t] の弾音化

⑮ **call me**　　コール・ミー　▶ コー＿ミ
　☞ [l] 音の脱落

⑯ **don't worry**　　ドウント・ワーリー　▶ ドウン＿ワーリー
　☞ 破裂音 [t] の脱落。don't は弱化して [ドン＿] と発音されることもある

⑰ **about the**　　アバウト・ザ　▶ アバウ＿ザ
　☞ 破裂音 [t] の脱落

🔊 ビジネス・リスニング（5回目）

Unit 29

計画の大幅な見直し依頼 ②
Major Plan Revision Request 2

Stage 01　穴埋めビジネス・リスニング

音声変化に注意してCDでビジネスのダイアローグを聴きながら、空欄部分を埋めてみよう。

ダイアローグ音声収録

Mike: Hello?

May: Mike, this is May. Sorry to ① _____ _____ at ② _____ _____ late hour. I ③ _____ _____ message, ④ _____ _____ just ⑤ _____ _____ a ⑥ _____ with our design and production team. I have some good news and some bad news. The good news is ⑦ _____ _____ changes you indicate can be done and won't impact the price of the product.

Mike: Okay, ⑧ _____ _____ relief. What's the bad news?

May: ⑨ _____ _____ _____ _____ have to adjust the tooling and start from scratch with sample production. The tooling ⑩ _____ _____ ⑪ _____ _____ $1000. We are still crunching the numbers as to when samples ⑫ _____ _____ available.

Mike: There is no way to salvage the current samples?

May: Unfortunately not. Since the revisions ⑬ _____ _____ the materials, I would think that we are looking at an additional week or so. Like I said, though, our production team is still ⑭ _____ _____ ⑮ _____ _____ with a timetable. I ⑯ _____ _____ able to give you a drop-dead date by tomorrow.

Mike: Okay. Thanks. I will pass that information along and ⑰ _____ _____ to you if any other questions ⑱ _____ _____.

◀)) ビジネス・リスニング (1回目)

Stage 02 ビジネス・ボキャビル

ビジネスのボキャブラリーを CD で確認しよう。そのあとでもう一度、ビジネス・リスニングにチャレンジ。Stage 01 でできなかったところをもう一度聴き取って、穴埋めを完成させよう。

英日 音声収録

1	late hour	遅い時間
2	design and production team	デザイン（設計）・製造チーム
3	impact	影響を与える
4	relief	安堵
5	adjust	調整する
6	tooling	機械設備
7	start from scratch	一から始める
8	crunch	（大量に）計算する
9	as to ...	…に関して
10	there is no way to ...	…する方法がない
11	salvage	救い出す
12	unfortunately	残念ながら
13	additional	追加の
14	though	しかしながら
15	come up with ...	…を考え出す
16	timetable	予定表；スケジュール
17	drop-dead date	締め切り日
18	information	情報
19	question	質問；疑問
20	come up	出てくる

◆)) ビジネス・リスニング（2回目）

Stage 03　日本語トランスレーション

ビジネス・ダイアローグの日本語を確認してみよう！　その上で、ダイアローグを聴きながら、まだできていない部分の穴埋めに再チャレンジしよう。

Mike: もしもし。
May: マイク、メイです。こんな遅い時間にお電話してすみません。メッセージをいただいています。いま設計・製造チームとの打ち合わせが終わったところです。いいお知らせと悪いお知らせがあります。いいお知らせのほうは、御社からご指摘いただいた変更が可能で、価格には跳ね返らないということです。
Mike: そうですか、それはほっとしました。悪い知らせとは？
May: 機械設備を調整しなければならないことになるため、サンプルの生産を一からやり直さなければならないんです。機械設備の調整は1000ドルかかります。サンプルがいつアップするかについてはまだ計算中です。
Mike: 現在のサンプルを使ってなんとかする方法はないのですね？
May: 残念ながらありません。変更は原材料に影響を与えないため、追加で1週間ほどと見ています。申し上げましたように、弊社の製作チームはいまもスケジュールについて検討中です。明日には仕上がり可能な期限をお知らせできるはずですので。
Mike: わかりました。ありがとう。情報をみんなに伝えて、なにかほかの質問が出てきたらご連絡しますので。

🔊 ビジネス・リスニング（3回目）

Stage 04　英文トランスクリプション

ビジネス・ダイアローグの原稿を確認してみよう！　穴埋め部分の正解をチェックして、英文を理解し直そう。そのあとで、もう一度ダイアローグを聴いてみよう。

Mike: Hello?
May: Mike, this is May. Sorry to ① call you at ② such a late hour. I ③ got your message, ④ and I just ⑤ got out of a ⑥ meeting with our design and production team. I have some good news and some bad news. The good news is ⑦ that the changes you indicate can be done and won't impact the price of the product.
Mike: Okay, ⑧ that's a relief. What's the bad news?
May: ⑨ We are going to have to adjust the tooling and start from scratch with sample production. The tooling ⑩ adjustment cost ⑪ will be $1000. We are still crunching the numbers as to when samples ⑫ will be available.
Mike: There is no way to salvage the current samples?
May: Unfortunately not. Since the revisions ⑬ don't affect the materials, I would think that we are looking at an additional week or so. Like I said, though, our production team is still ⑭ trying to ⑮ come up with a timetable. I ⑯ should be able to give you a drop-dead date by tomorrow.
Mike: Okay. Thanks. I will pass that information along and ⑰ get back to you if any other questions ⑱ come up.

🔊 ビジネス・リスニング（4回目）

Stage 05 音声変化をチェック

まとめとして、穴埋め部分の音声変化の特徴をスロースピードとナチュラルスピードで確認しよう。下記に示したカタカナ表記で音声変化を確認して、もう一度ビジネス・ダイアローグを聴き直してみよう。発音変化のルールは適宜復習しよう。

2種類の音声を収録　　CD 2-36

① **call you**　　　　　　　コール・ユー　　　　　　▶ コー＿ユ
　☞ [l] 音の脱落

② **such a**　　　　　　　　サッチ・ア　　　　　　　▶ サッチャ
　☞ 2 語が連結

③ **got your**　　　　　　　ガット・ユア　　　　　　▶ ガッチュア
　☞ [t] 音と [j] 音が同化

④ **and I**　　　　　　　　 アンド・アイ　　　　　　▶ アンナイ
　☞ and の破裂音 [d] が脱落し、2 語が連結

⑤ **got out of**　　　　　　ガット・アウト・アヴ　　 ▶ ガッダ [ラ] ウダ [ラ] ヴ
　☞ 3 語が連結。それぞれの連結部で破裂音 [t] が弾音化

⑥ **meeting**　　　　　　　ミーティング　　　　　　▶ ミーディ [リ] ング
　☞ 破裂音 [t] の弾音化

⑦ **that the**　　　　　　　ザット・ザ　　　　　　　▶ ザッ＿ザ
　☞ 破裂音 [t] の脱落

⑧ **that's a**　　　　　　　ザッツ・ア　　　　　　　▶ ザッツァ
　☞ 2 語が連結

⑨ **We are going to**　　　ウィ・アー・ゴウイング・トゥー ▶ ウィァゴナ
　☞ are は弱化。going to は [ゴナ] と発音

⑩ **adjustment cost**　　　アジャストゥメント・コウスト ▶ アジャストゥメン＿コウスト
　☞ 破裂音 [t] の脱落

⑪ **will be**　　　　　　　　ウィル・ビー　　　　　　▶ ウィ＿ビ
　☞ [l] 音の脱落

⑫ **will be**　　　　　　　　ウィル・ビー　　　　　　▶ ウィ＿ビ
　☞ [l] 音の脱落

⑬ **don't affect**　　　　　ドゥント・アフェクト　　　▶ ドウナフェクト
　☞ 破裂音 [t] が脱落した don't に affect が連結

⑭ **trying to**　　　　　　　トゥライング・トゥー　　　▶ トゥライイン＿トゥー
　☞ 破裂音 [g] の脱落。さらに [t] 音が脱落し [トゥライヌー] と発音されることもある

⑮ **come up**　　　　　　　カム・アップ　　　　　　▶ カマップ
　☞ 2 語が連結

⑯ **should be**　　　　　　シュッド・ビー　　　　　　▶ シュッ＿ビ
　☞ 破裂音 [d] の脱落

⑰ **get back**　　　　　　　ゲット・バック　　　　　　▶ ゲッ＿バック
　☞ 破裂音 [t] の脱落

⑱ **come up**　　　　　　　カム・アップ　　　　　　▶ カマップ
　☞ 2 語が連結

🔊 ビジネス・リスニング (5 回目)

Unit 30

注文数の緊急増加
Sudden Order Increase

Stage 01 　穴埋めビジネス・リスニング

音声変化に注意してCDでビジネスのダイアローグを聴きながら、空欄部分を埋めてみよう。

ダイアローグ音声収録　　　　　　　　　　　　　　　　　　　CD 2-37

Mike: May, I just ① _____ _____ email ② _____ _____ sample production schedule. Our customer has ③ _____ _____ their trial process one week due to the design change. So your new due date is ④ _____ _____ problem.

May: Good. We did our best to expedite the tooling adjustment, so as I indicated the delay ⑤ _____ _____ _____ more than five days. I took the liberty of sending you ⑥ _____ _____ for the tooling fee, so please issue a PO for the $1000.

Mike: Unfortunately we have another issue. Because of the design change there is a need for additional testing by our customer so we are going to need an additional fifty samples. ⑦ _____ _____ make the ⑧ _____ sample quantity one ⑨ _____ _____ fifty pieces. ⑩ _____ _____ think ⑪ _____ _____ present any problems with respect to cost or timing?

May: ⑫ _____ _____ service to you we can provide the fifty extra parts for the same $1000 sample fee you already paid. It ⑬ _____ _____ a difference with respect to the completion deadline.

Mike: Well, we ⑭ _____ appreciate that. I'm truly sorry for ⑮ _____ _____ changes.

🔊 ビジネス・リスニング（1回目）

Stage 02　ビジネス・ボキャビル

ビジネスのボキャブラリーを CD で確認しよう。そのあとでもう一度、ビジネス・リスニングにチャレンジ。Stage 01 でできなかったところをもう一度聴き取って、穴埋めを完成させよう。

英日 音声収録　　CD 2-38

1	move back	遅らせる
2	trial process	試験工程
3	due to ...	…による
4	design change	デザイン変更
5	due date	締め切り日
6	expedite	はかどらせる
7	tooling adjustment	設備の調整
8	more than ...	…を超えて
9	take the liberty of ...	勝手ながら…する
10	invoice	インボイス；送り状；請求書
11	issue	発行する
12	PO	発注書
13	additional testing	追加検査
14	quantity	量
15	present	（困難などを）引き起こす
16	with respect to ...	…に関して
17	as a service to ...	…へのサービスとして
18	extra	追加の；余分の
19	completion	完了
20	certainly	ほんとうに
21	truly	実に；ほんとうに

◀)) ビジネス・リスニング（2回目）

注文数の緊急増加

Stage 03　日本語トランスレーション

ビジネス・ダイアローグの日本語を確認してみよう！　その上で、ダイアローグを聴きながら、まだできていない部分の穴埋めに再チャレンジしよう。

Mike: メイ、サンプル製造のスケジュールに関するメールをいま受け取りました。デザイン変更のため、顧客がトライアルのプロセスを1週間延期したんです。ですから御社の新しい期限は問題になりません。

May: よかったです。機械設備の調整を急がせるためにベストを尽くしました。ですから、ちらっと申し上げましたように、遅延は5日を超えることはありません。勝手ながら機械設備費のインボイスをお送りいたしましたので、1000ドルの発注書をご作成ください。

Mike: 恐縮ですが、もうひとつ問題があります。デザイン変更によって顧客による追加のテストが必要になりますから、追加でさらに50のサンプルが必要になるんです。そうすると、トータルでは150ユニットのサンプル数になります。コストやタイミングの面で、なにか問題が生じると思いますか？

May: 御社へのサービスとして50の追加のパーツはすでにお支払いいただいている1000ドルのサンプル代でご提供できます。仕上げの締め切りに関しては、変わりは生じません。

Mike: ほんとうに助かります。今回の変更についてはほんとうにすみませんでした。

🔊 ビジネス・リスニング（3回目）

Stage 04　英文トランスクリプション

ビジネス・ダイアローグの原稿を確認してみよう！　穴埋め部分の正解をチェックして、英文を理解し直そう。そのあとで、もう一度ダイアローグを聴いてみよう。

Mike: May, I just ① got your email ② about the sample production schedule. Our customer has ③ moved back their trial process one week due to the design change. So your new due date is ④ not a problem.

May: Good. We did our best to expedite the tooling adjustment, so as I indicated the delay ⑤ will not be more than five days. I took the liberty of sending you ⑥ an invoice for the tooling fee, so please issue a PO for the $1000.

Mike: Unfortunately we have another issue. Because of the design change there is a need for additional testing by our customer so we are going to need an additional fifty samples. ⑦ That would make the ⑧ total sample quantity one ⑨ hundred and fifty pieces. ⑩ Do you think ⑪ that will present any problems with respect to cost or timing?

May: ⑫ As a service to you we can provide the fifty extra parts for the same $1000 sample fee you already paid. It ⑬ shouldn't make a difference with respect to the completion deadline.

Mike: Well, we ⑭ certainly appreciate that. I'm truly sorry for ⑮ all the changes.

🔊 ビジネス・リスニング（4回目）

Stage 05 音声変化をチェック

まとめとして、穴埋め部分の音声変化の特徴をスロースピードとナチュラルスピードで確認しよう。下記に示したカタカナ表記で音声変化を確認して、もう一度ビジネス・ダイアローグを聴き直してみよう。発音変化のルールは適宜復習しよう。

2種類の音声を収録　　CD 2-39

① **got your**　　ガット・ユア　▶ ガッチュア
　☞ [t] 音と [j] 音が同化

② **about the**　　アバウト・ザ　▶ アバウ＿ザ
　☞ 破裂音 [t] の脱落

③ **moved back**　　ムーヴド・バック　▶ ムーヴ＿バック
　☞ 破裂音 [d] の脱落

④ **not a**　　ナット・ア　▶ ナッダ [ラ]
　☞ 2 語の連結。連結部の破裂音 [t] の弾音化

⑤ **will not be**　　ウィル・ナット・ビー　▶ ウィルナッ＿ビ
　☞ 破裂音 [t] の脱落。be は弱化することもある

⑥ **an invoice**　　アン・インヴォイス　▶ アニンヴォイス
　☞ 2 語の連結

⑦ **That would**　　ザット・ウッド　▶ ザッ＿ウッド
　☞ 破裂音 [t] の脱落

⑧ **total**　　トウトゥル　▶ トウドゥ [ル] ル
　☞ 破裂音 [t] の弾音化

⑨ **hundred and**　　ハンドレッド・アンド　▶ ハンドレッダ [ラ] ン＿
　☞ 2 語の連結。連結部の破裂音 [d] の弾音化。末尾の破裂音 [d] の脱落

⑩ **Do you**　　ドゥー・ユー　▶ ドゥユ；ヂュ
　☞ do の弱化。さらに [d] と [j] が同化することもある

⑪ **that will**　　ザット・ウィル　▶ ザッ＿ウィル；ザドゥ [ル] ル
　☞ 破裂音 [t] の脱落。また、短縮形 that'll [ザットゥル] の [t] が弾音化する場合もある

⑫ **As a**　　アズ・ア　▶ アザ
　☞ 2 語の連結

⑬ **shouldn't make**　　シュドウント・メイク　▶ シュドウン＿メイク
　☞ 破裂音の [t] の脱落

⑭ **certainly**　　スートゥンリー　▶ スーんンリー
　☞ 破裂音 [t] の声門閉鎖音化

⑮ **all the**　　オール・ザ　▶ オー＿ザ
　☞ [l] 音の脱落

🔊 ビジネス・リスニング（5 回目）

注文数の緊急増加

Unit 31

新スケジュールでの進捗報告
New Schedule Progress Report

Stage 01 穴埋めビジネス・リスニング

音声変化に注意して CD でビジネスのダイアローグを聴きながら、空欄部分を埋めてみよう。

ダイアローグ音声収録 CD 2-40

May: Mike, I am calling because I ① _____ get a response to my email. The one hundred-fifty samples you ordered are ready to ship.

Mike: ② _____ _____ _____ . ③ _____ ④ _____ _____ _____ out sick for the ⑤ _____ _____ days. I ⑥ _____ _____ cold from ⑦ _____ _____ _____ sons.

May: Oh, I hope you're feeling better.

Mike: Much, thanks. You can ship the parts Fedex international ⑧ _____ to my attention. As I ⑨ _____ _____ , we are pulling in many new components for this project so please clearly mark the product with my name and "T2A program." ⑩ _____ _____ make sure the parts ⑪ _____ _____ the ⑫ _____ _____ ⑬ _____ _____ I am not here to receive them myself.

May: Okay then, I will have them sent out today. You should get them tomorrow or the next day ⑭ _____ _____ _____ . How long ⑮ _____ _____ say it ⑯ _____ _____ before you have the final prototype finished?

Mike: We are a ⑰ _____ behind schedule but it ⑱ _____ _____ more than two weeks or so.

🔊 ビジネス・リスニング (1回目)

Stage 02 ビジネス・ボキャビル

ビジネスのボキャブラリーを CD で確認しよう。そのあとでもう一度、ビジネス・リスニングにチャレンジ。Stage 01 でできなかったところをもう一度聴き取って、穴埋めを完成させよう。

英日 音声収録　CD 2-41

1	response	返信；返事
2	be ready to ...	…する準備ができている
3	actually	実は
4	catch a cold	風邪をひく
5	feel better	具合・気分がよくなる
6	ship ... (by) Fedex international priority	…をフェデックス・インターナショナル・プライオリティーで発送する
7	to someone's attention	…宛に
8	pull in	取り寄せる
9	clearly	鮮明に；はっきりと
10	mark	印をつける
11	program	計画
12	make sure	確実にする
13	right person	ふさわしい人物
14	receive	受領する
15	send out	発送する
16	at the latest	遅くとも
17	final prototype	最終試作品
18	finish	終える；完成する
19	behind schedule	スケジュールが遅れて

🔊 ビジネス・リスニング（2回目）

新スケジュールでの進捗報告

Stage 03 日本語トランスレーション

ビジネス・ダイアローグの日本語を確認してみよう！ その上で、ダイアローグを聴きながら、まだできていない部分の穴埋めに再チャレンジしよう。

May: マイク、メールの返事をいただいていないのでお電話しました。ご注文の 150 のサンプルはすでに発送準備ができています。

Mike: 申し訳ない。実は、この 2 日間病気で休んでいたんです。息子のひとりに風邪をうつされまして。

May: あら、だいぶよくなっているといいんですけど。

Mike: ずいぶんいいですよ。ありがとう。部品はフェデックス・インターナショナル・プライオリティーで私宛に発送してください。以前にも申し上げましたが、弊社ではこのプロジェクトのために多くの部品を取り寄せていますので、製品に私の名前と「T2A プログラム」（という文字）をはっきりと目立つように記載しておいてください。そうすれば、私が不在で自分で受け取れないときにも、確実に適切な人のところに渡りますので。

May: わかりました。では、本日発送いたします。明日か、遅くとも明後日にはお受け取りになれると思います。最終的なプロトタイプができるまでに、どのくらいかかるとおっしゃっていましたっけ？

Mike: 少々スケジュールが遅れてはいますが、2 週間前後を超えることはないと思います。

🔊 ビジネス・リスニング (3回目)

Stage 04 英文トランスクリプション

ビジネス・ダイアローグの原稿を確認してみよう！ 穴埋め部分の正解をチェックして、英文を理解し直そう。そのあとで、もう一度ダイアローグを聴いてみよう。

May: Mike, I am calling because I ① didn't get a response to my email. The one hundred-fifty samples you ordered are ready to ship.

Mike: ② Sorry about that. ③ Actually ④ I've been out sick for the ⑤ past two days. I ⑥ caught a cold from ⑦ one of my sons.

May: Oh, I hope you're feeling better.

Mike: Much, thanks. You can ship the parts Fedex international ⑧ priority to my attention. As I ⑨ said before, we are pulling in many new components for this project so please clearly mark the product with my name and "T2A program." ⑩ That will make sure the parts ⑪ get to the ⑫ right person ⑬ even if I am not here to receive them myself.

May: Okay then, I will have them sent out today. You should get them tomorrow or the next day ⑭ at the latest. How long ⑮ did you say it ⑯ would be before you have the final prototype finished?

Mike: We are a ⑰ little behind schedule but it ⑱ shouldn't be more than two weeks or so.

🔊 ビジネス・リスニング (4回目)

Stage 05 音声変化をチェック

まとめとして、穴埋め部分の音声変化の特徴をスロースピードとナチュラルスピードで確認しよう。下記に示したカタカナ表記で音声変化を確認して、もう一度ビジネス・ダイアローグを聴き直してみよう。発音変化のルールは適宜復習しよう。

2種類の音声を収録　　CD 2-42

① **didn't**　　ディドゥント　　▶ ディンント
☞ 破裂音 [d] の声門閉鎖音化。末尾の破裂音 [t] が脱落することもある

② **Sorry about that**　　サーリー・アバウト・ザット　　▶ サーリー＿バウ＿ザット
☞ about の曖昧母音 [ə] の脱落、破裂音 [t] の脱落。that 末尾の [t] も脱落することがある

③ **Actually**　　アクチュアリー　　▶ アクシュァリー
☞ [ktʃu] から [t] 音の脱落

④ **I've been**　　アイヴ・ビン　　▶ アイ＿ビン
☞ 摩擦音 [v] の脱落

⑤ **past two**　　パスト・トゥー　　▶ パス＿トゥー
☞ 破裂音 [t] の脱落

⑥ **caught a**　　コート・ア　　▶ コーダ [ラ]
☞ 2語の連結。連結部で破裂音 [t] の弾音化

⑦ **one of my**　　ワン・アヴ・マイ　　▶ ワナ＿マイ
☞ one と of が連結。摩擦音 [v] の脱落

⑧ **priority**　　プライオーラティー　　▶ プライオーラディ [リ] ー
☞ 破裂音 [t] の弾音化

⑨ **said before**　　セッド・ビフォー　　▶ セッ＿ビフォー
☞ 破裂音 [d] の脱落

⑩ **That will**　　ザット・ウィル　　▶ ザッ＿ウィル；ザドゥ [ル] ル
☞ 破裂音 [t] の脱落。また、短縮形 that'll [ザットゥル] の [t] が弾音化する場合もある

⑪ **get to**　　ゲット・トゥー　　▶ ゲッ＿トゥー
☞ 破裂音 [t] の脱落

⑫ **right person**　　ライト・プースン　　▶ ライ＿プースン
☞ 破裂音 [t] の脱落

⑬ **even if**　　イーヴン・イフ　　▶ イーヴニフ
☞ 2語の連結

⑭ **at the latest**　　アット・ザ・レイティスト　　▶ アッ＿ザレイディ [リ] スト
☞ 破裂の [t] の脱落。latest の [t] 音の弾音化

⑮ **did you**　　ディド・ユー　　▶ ディッジュー
☞ [d] 音と [j] 音が同化

⑯ **would be**　　ウッド・ビー　　▶ ウッ＿ビ
☞ 破裂音 [d] の脱落

⑰ **little**　　リトゥル　　▶ リドゥ [ル] ル
☞ 破裂音 [t] の弾音化

⑱ **shouldn't be**　　シュドゥント・ビー　　▶ シュドゥン＿ビ
☞ 破裂音 [t] の脱落

🔊 ビジネス・リスニング（5回目）

新スケジュールでの進捗報告

Unit 32

製品の完成
Product Completion

Stage 01 穴埋めビジネス・リスニング

音声変化に注意してCDでビジネスのダイアローグを聴きながら、空欄部分を埋めてみよう。

ダイアローグ音声収録

Mike: Well, production ① _____ _____ prototypes is complete. The ② _____ control team will start testing the initial batch tomorrow.

Tom: When do they ③ _____ _____ to be complete?

Mike: ④ _____ _____ _____ less than 8 hours from start to finish.

Tom: We have to submit the results of the inspection to Jack at AA Auto by close of business Wednesday ⑤ _____ _____ _____. How are things coming along ⑥ _____ _____ expo preparations?

Mike: Our booth space is reserved, and ⑦ _____ _____ outsourcing the posters and printed materials. They ⑧ _____ _____ finished within the next two weeks.

Tom: Is there a list of exhibitors on the expo website?

Mike: ⑨ _____ _____ get my email? I checked and the site says they will ⑩ _____ _____ downloadable file of all exhibiting vendors ⑪ _____ _____ floor plan by Thursday.

Tom: I am still having network issues with my computer. The IT guys have supposedly been working ⑫ _____ _____ all morning, ⑬ _____ _____ can't seem to figure out ⑭ _____ _____ problem is. I have to leave early today, but ⑮ _____ _____ know the testing results as soon as possible.

Mike: Will do.

◀)) ビジネス・リスニング（1回目）

Stage 02 ビジネス・ボキャビル

ビジネスのボキャブラリーを CD で確認しよう。そのあとでもう一度、ビジネス・リスニングにチャレンジ。Stage 01 でできなかったところをもう一度聴き取って、穴埋めを完成させよう。

英日 音声収録

CD 2-44

#	英語	日本語
1	complete	完了した
2	quality control	品質管理
3	initial batch	最初の分
4	less than ...	…よりも少ない
5	from start to finish	開始から終了まで
6	submit	提出する
7	inspection	検査
8	by close of business	終業時間までに
9	come along	進行する
10	preparation	準備
11	booth space	ブースのスペース
12	reserved	予約の取れた
13	outsource	外注する
14	printed material	印刷物
15	list of exhibitors	展示(出店)社のリスト
16	website	ウェブサイト
17	downloadable	ダウンロード可能な
18	vendor	メーカー；業者
19	floor plan	間取り案
20	network issues	ネットワーク回線の問題
21	IT guy	IT 担当者
22	supposedly	おそらく；推定するところでは
23	figure out	理解する

◀)) ビジネス・リスニング(2回目)

Stage 03　日本語トランスレーション

ビジネス・ダイアローグの日本語を確認してみよう！　その上で、ダイアローグを聴きながら、まだできていない部分の穴埋めに再チャレンジしよう。

Mike: さて、プロトタイプの製造は完了です。品質管理チームが最初の分のテストを明日始めることになっています。
Tom: テストはいつ頃終わると言っているの？
Mike: 開始してから終了まで8時間はかからないはずですよ。
Tom: 検査結果は、遅くとも水曜日の営業終了までにAAオートのジャックに提出しないといけないからね。エキスポの準備のほうはどうなっているんだい？
Mike: ブースは確保してあります。それに、ポスターや印刷物は外部に発注しているところです。2週間以内にはできあがるはずです。
Tom: エキスポのウェブサイトに出展者のリストはあるのかな？
Mike: メールを見ませんでした？　サイトをチェックしましたが、すべての出店メーカーのリストとフロアマップのダウンロード可能なファイルを、木曜日までに準備すると書いてありましたよ。
Tom: 僕のコンピューターは、まだネットワークの問題があってね。IT部の連中が午前中ずっと作業していたはずなんだけど、なにが問題なのかわからないみたいなんだ。今日は早く出なければならないけど、テスト結果はできるだけ早く知らせてね。
Mike: そうします。

🔊 ビジネス・リスニング（3回目）

Stage 04　英文トランスクリプション

ビジネス・ダイアローグの原稿を確認してみよう！　穴埋め部分の正解をチェックして、英文を理解し直そう。そのあとで、もう一度ダイアローグを聴いてみよう。

Mike: Well, production ① of the prototypes is complete. The ② quality control team will start testing the initial batch tomorrow.
Tom: When do they ③ expect testing to be complete?
Mike: ④ It should be less than 8 hours from start to finish.
Tom: We have to submit the results of the inspection to Jack at AA Auto by close of business Wednesday ⑤ at the latest. How are things coming along ⑥ with the expo preparations?
Mike: Our booth space is reserved, and ⑦ we are outsourcing the posters and printed materials. They ⑧ should be finished within the next two weeks.
Tom: Is there a list of exhibitors on the expo website?
Mike: ⑨ Didn't you get my email? I checked and the site says they will ⑩ have a downloadable file of all exhibiting vendors ⑪ and a floor plan by Thursday.
Tom: I am still having network issues with my computer. The IT guys have supposedly been working ⑫ on it all morning, ⑬ but they can't seem to figure out ⑭ what the problem is. I have to leave early today, but ⑮ let me know the testing results as soon as possible.
Mike: Will do.

🔊 ビジネス・リスニング（4回目）

Unit 32

Stage 05 音声変化をチェック

まとめとして、穴埋め部分の音声変化の特徴をスロースピードとナチュラルスピードで確認しよう。下記に示したカタカナ表記で音声変化を確認して、もう一度ビジネス・ダイアローグを聴き直してみよう。発音変化のルールは適宜復習しよう。

2種類の音声を収録
CD 2-45

① **of the**
☞ 摩擦音 [v] の脱落
アヴ・ザ ▶ ア_ザ

② **quality**
☞ 破裂音 [t] の弾音化
クァラティー ▶ クァラディ [リ] ー

③ **expect testing**
☞ 破裂音 [t] の脱落
イクスペクト・テスティング ▶ イクスペク_テスティング

④ **It should be**
☞ 破裂音 [t] と [d] がそれぞれ脱落。ダイアローグでは、さらに it の音がすべて脱落している
イット・シュッド・ビー ▶ イッ_シュッ_ビ

⑤ **at the latest**
☞ at の破裂音 [t] の脱落。latest の破裂音 [t] の弾音化
アット・ザ・レイティスト ▶ アッ_ザレイディ [リ] スト

⑥ **with the**
☞ 重なった [ð] の片方の音が脱落
ウィズ・ズィ ▶ ウィ_ズィ

⑦ **we are**
☞ 短縮形 we're の発音
ウィ・アー ▶ ウィアー

⑧ **should be**
☞ 破裂音 [d] の脱落
シュッド・ビー ▶ シュッ_ビ

⑨ **Didn't you**
☞ [t] 音と [j] 音が同化
ディドゥント・ユー ▶ ディドゥンチュー

⑩ **have a**
☞ 2語の連結
ハヴ・ア ▶ ハヴァ

⑪ **and a**
☞ and の破裂音 [d] が脱落し、2語が連結
アンド・ア ▶ アナ

⑫ **on it**
☞ 2語の連結
オン・イット ▶ オニット

⑬ **but they**
☞ 破裂音の [t] の脱落
バット・ゼイ ▶ バッ_ゼイ

⑭ **what the**
☞ 破裂音 [t] の脱落
ワット・ザ ▶ ワッ_ザ

⑮ **let me**
☞ 破裂音 [t] の脱落
レット・ミー ▶ レッ_ミ

🔊 ビジネス・リスニング (5回目)

製品の完成

Unit 33

プロトタイプでトラブル発生
Trouble with the Prototype

Stage 01　穴埋めビジネス・リスニング

音声変化に注意してCDでビジネスのダイアローグを聴きながら、空欄部分を埋めてみよう。

ダイアローグ音声収録

Tom: Okay, Steve, what's the issue?

Steve: We ran the initial prototypes through the inspection process, and ① _____ of the first ② _____ units ③ _____ _____ function.

Tom: Do we know which component is causing the failure?

Steve: We ④ _____ _____ complete disassembly of the rejected parts, and individual testing shows ⑤ _____ _____ semiconductors are the source of the problem, ⑥ _____ _____ don't have the testing ⑦ _____ _____ determine ⑧ _____ _____ issue is.

Tom: Mike, get China Semicon on the phone. I want a ⑨ _____ engineer here no ⑩ _____ than Thursday. I'll file a report with AA Auto and ⑪ _____ _____ ⑫ _____ _____ a ⑬ _____ for next Monday.

Mike: I'll email May immediately and follow up with a phone call tomorrow.

Tom: Steve, have your team test the rest of the prototypes so we can ⑭ _____ _____ complete ⑮ _____ of the failure to function ratio. Don't waste any more time on disassembly though. As soon as you ⑯ _____ _____ numbers give them to Mike and I so we can convey ⑰ _____ _____ China Semicon.

◀)) ビジネス・リスニング（1回目）

Stage 02 ビジネス・ボキャビル

ビジネスのボキャブラリーを CD で確認しよう。そのあとでもう一度、ビジネス・リスニングにチャレンジ。Stage 01 でできなかったところをもう一度聴き取って、穴埋めを完成させよう。

英日 音声収録 CD 2-47

1	run ... through ...	…を…にかける
2	inspection process	検査工程
3	fail to ...	…することに失敗する
4	function	（正常に）機能する
5	component	部品
6	cause	引き起こす
7	failure	失敗
8	complete	完全な
9	disassembly	分解
10	rejected parts	不良部品
11	individual	個々の；個別の
12	source of the problem	問題の原因
13	testing equipment	検査器具
14	determine	決定する；結論する
15	no later than ...	（遅くとも）…までには
16	file a report	報告書を提出する
17	immediately	すぐに
18	the rest of ...	残りの…
19	complete	完全な
20	waste	無駄にする
21	convey	（情報を）伝える

🔊 ビジネス・リスニング（2回目）

Stage 03　日本語トランスレーション

ビジネス・ダイアローグの日本語を確認してみよう！　その上で、ダイアローグを聴きながら、まだできていない部分の穴埋めに再チャレンジしよう。

Tom: えーと、スティーヴ、なにが問題になってるの？
Steve: 初期のプロトタイプを検査にかけたんですが、最初の30台のうち20台が機能しなかったんです。
Tom: どの部品が失敗の原因かわかっているの？
Steve: 不良品を完全に分解し、それぞれのテスト結果から半導体が問題の原因だとわかっています。しかし、問題がなんなのかを判断する検査器具がないんです。
Tom: マイク、チャイナ・セミコンに電話をしてよ。品質管理技術者を1名、木曜までにはここに呼び出したいんだ。僕はAAオートに報告書を書いて、次の月曜に打ち合わせを設定するから。
Mike: すぐにメイにメールを書いて、明日フォローの電話をしておきますね。
Tom: スティーヴ、君のチームに残りのプロトタイプをテストさせてほしい。不良品と優良品の割合を完全に把握したいんだ。しかし、分解でこれ以上時間を無駄にしないでほしい。数がわかり次第、マイクと僕に伝えてほしい。チャイナ・セミコンに数値を伝えたいからね。

🔊 ビジネス・リスニング（3回目）

Stage 04　英文トランスクリプション

ビジネス・ダイアローグの原稿を確認してみよう！　穴埋め部分の正解をチェックして、英文を理解し直そう。そのあとで、もう一度ダイアローグを聴いてみよう。

Tom: Okay, Steve, what's the issue?
Steve: We ran the initial prototypes through the inspection process, and ① twenty of the first ② thirty units ③ failed to function.
Tom: Do we know which component is causing the failure?
Steve: We ④ did a complete disassembly of the rejected parts, and individual testing shows ⑤ that the semiconductors are the source of the problem, ⑥ but we don't have the testing ⑦ equipment to determine ⑧ what the issue is.
Tom: Mike, get China Semicon on the phone. I want a ⑨ quality engineer here no ⑩ later than Thursday. I'll file a report with AA Auto and ⑪ we will ⑫ set up a ⑬ meeting for next Monday.
Mike: I'll email May immediately and follow up with a phone call tomorrow.
Tom: Steve, have your team test the rest of the prototypes so we can ⑭ get a complete ⑮ picture of the failure to function ratio. Don't waste any more time on disassembly though. As soon as you ⑯ get those numbers give them to Mike and I so we can convey ⑰ that to China Semicon.

🔊 ビジネス・リスニング（4回目）

Stage 05　音声変化をチェック

まとめとして、穴埋め部分の音声変化の特徴をスロースピードとナチュラルスピードで確認しよう。下記に示したカタカナ表記で音声変化を確認して、もう一度ビジネス・ダイアローグを聴き直してみよう。発音変化のルールは適宜復習しよう。

2種類の音声を収録　　　　　　　　　　　　　　　　　　　　　CD 2-48

① **twenty**　　　　　トゥエンティー　　　▶　トゥエニー
　☞ 破裂音 [t] の脱落

② **thirty**　　　　　サーティー　　　　　▶　サーディ [リ] ー
　☞ 破裂音 [t] の弾音化

③ **failed to**　　　　フェイルド・トゥー　　▶　フェイル＿トゥー
　☞ 破裂音 [d] の脱落

④ **did a**　　　　　ディッド・ア　　　　　▶　ディダ [ラ]
　☞ 2 語の連結。連結部の破裂音 [d] は弾音化することもある

⑤ **that the**　　　　ザット・ザ　　　　　▶　ザッ＿ザ
　☞ 破裂音 [t] の脱落

⑥ **but we**　　　　バット・ウィ　　　　　▶　バッ＿ウィ
　☞ 破裂音 [t] の脱落

⑦ **equipment to**　　イクィプメント・トゥー　▶　イクィプメン＿トゥー
　☞ 破裂音 [t] の脱落

⑧ **what the**　　　ワット・ズィ　　　　　▶　ワッ＿ズィ
　☞ 破裂音 [t] の脱落

⑨ **quality**　　　　クァラティー　　　　　▶　クァラディ [リ] ー
　☞ 破裂音 [t] の弾音化

⑩ **later**　　　　　レイター　　　　　　▶　レイダ [ラ] ー
　☞ 破裂音 [t] の弾音化

⑪ **we will**　　　　ウィ・ウィル　　　　　▶　ウィル；ウィゥ
　☞ 短縮形 we'll [ウィル] の発音。さらに弱化して [ウィゥ] のように発音されることもある

⑫ **set up**　　　　セット・アップ　　　　▶　セダ [ラ] ップ
　☞ 2 語が連結。連結部の破裂音 [t] の弾音化

⑬ **meeting**　　　ミーティング　　　　　▶　ミーディ [リ] ング
　☞ 破裂音 [t] の弾音化

⑭ **get a**　　　　　ゲット・ア　　　　　　▶　ゲッタ；ゲッダ [ラ]
　☞ 2 語の連結。連結部の破裂音 [t] が弾音化することもある

⑮ **picture**　　　　ピクチャー　　　　　▶　ピクシャー
　☞ [ktʃu] から [t] 音の脱落

⑯ **get those**　　　ゲット・ゾウズ　　　　▶　ゲッ＿ゾウズ
　☞ 破裂音 [t] の脱落

⑰ **that to**　　　　ザット・トゥー　　　　▶　ザッ＿トゥー
　☞ 破裂音 [t] の脱落

◀)) ビジネス・リスニング（5 回目）

Unit 34

アメリカへの出張依頼
Request for Overseas Business Trip

Stage 01 穴埋めビジネス・リスニング

音声変化に注意してCDでビジネスのダイアローグを聴きながら、空欄部分を埋めてみよう。

ダイアローグ音声収録 ··· CD 2-49

Mike: May, we have a big problem.

May: What happened?

Mike: We ① _____ the prototype production, ② _____ _____ are having ③ _____ issues ④ _____ _____ large percentage of the products. Our quality engineering team has traced it to your product. ⑤ _____ _____ _____ _____ ⑥ _____ _____ quality engineer and member of management here as soon as possible. ⑦ _____, we need them here by the day after tomorrow. This has ⑧ _____ _____ ⑨ _____ _____ _____ place with our customer.

May: I will make arrangements for Mr. Chen, Mr. Chang and myself to be there as soon as possible. I will ⑩ _____ _____ back within three hours to inform you of our ⑪ _____ _____. In the meantime, if you could ⑫ _____ _____ ⑬ _____ _____ information you have on the inspection failures that would help. ⑭ _____, failure percentages and any other ⑮ _____ you have.

Mike: I will send you ⑯ _____ _____ have, but we do not have the equipment to ⑰ _____ _____ product properly, nor do we have the expertise in your product field to properly evaluate the situation.

May: Okay. I am really sorry ⑱ _____ _____, ⑲ _____ _____ send me that info and I will get back to you as soon as possible.

🔊 ビジネス・リスニング（1回目）

Stage 02 ビジネス・ボキャビル

ビジネスのボキャブラリーを CD で確認しよう。そのあとでもう一度、ビジネス・リスニングにチャレンジ。Stage 01 でできなかったところをもう一度聴き取って、穴埋めを完成させよう。

英日 音声収録

1	quality issues	品質の問題
2	percentage	割合；パーセント
3	trace ... to ...	…（の原因）が…だと突き止める
4	the day after tomorrow	明後日
5	awkward place	まずい状況
6	as soon as possible	できるだけ早く
7	inform	（情報などを）伝える
8	flight details	フライトの詳細
9	in the meantime	その間に
10	inspection failure	検査の失敗
11	equipment	機器
12	properly	適切に
13	product field	製品分野
14	evaluate	評価する
15	situation	状況
16	info	情報（information の略）

🔊 ビジネス・リスニング（2回目）

アメリカへの出張依頼

Stage 03　日本語トランスレーション

ビジネス・ダイアローグの日本語を確認してみよう！　その上で、ダイアローグを聴きながら、まだできていない部分の穴埋めに再チャレンジしよう。

Mike: メイ、大問題です。
May: どうしたんです？
Mike: プロトタイプの製造を完了したのですが、かなりの率で品質に問題が出ているんです。弊社の品質管理技術チームが調査して、御社の製品に問題があるとわかりました。品質管理技術者と経営陣にできるだけ早くこちらに来ていただく必要が出てきます。実は明後日までにこちらに来てもらいたいんですよ。この件で、顧客に対してまずい状況になっているんです。
May: チェンさんとチャンさん、それに私ができるだけ早くそちらへ行けるように手配いたします。3時間以内に電話を折り返して、フライトの詳細をお伝えします。その間に、検査での不合格に関するお手元にあるすべての情報を私宛に送っていただけると助かります。写真、不合格率、ほかにもお持ちのデータならなんでもお願いします。
Mike: 手持ちのデータは送りますが、弊社には御社の製品を適切に調べる器具がありませんし、状況を適切に評価するための御社の製品分野の専門知識もないのです。
May: わかりました。今回の件はほんとうに申し訳ありません。どうか情報をお送りください。できるだけ早く折り返しますので。

🔊 ビジネス・リスニング（3回目）

Stage 04　英文トランスクリプション

ビジネス・ダイアローグの原稿を確認してみよう！　穴埋め部分の正解をチェックして、英文を理解し直そう。そのあとで、もう一度ダイアローグを聴いてみよう。

Mike: May, we have a big problem.
May: What happened?
Mike: We ① completed the prototype production, ② but we are having ③ quality issues ④ with a large percentage of the products. Our quality engineering team has traced it to your product. ⑤ We are going to ⑥ need a quality engineer and member of management here as soon as possible. ⑦ Actually, we need them here by the day after tomorrow. This has ⑧ put us ⑨ in an awkward place with our customer.
May: I will make arrangements for Mr. Chen, Mr. Chang and myself to be there as soon as possible. I will ⑩ call you back within three hours to inform you of our ⑪ flight details. In the meantime, if you could ⑫ send me ⑬ all the information you have on the inspection failures that would help. ⑭ Pictures, failure percentages and any other ⑮ data you have.
Mike: I will send you ⑯ what I have, but we do not have the equipment to ⑰ test your product properly, nor do we have the expertise in your product field to properly evaluate the situation.
May: Okay. I am really sorry ⑱ about this, ⑲ but please send me that info and I will get back to you as soon as possible.

🔊 ビジネス・リスニング（4回目）

Stage 05 音声変化をチェック

まとめとして、穴埋め部分の音声変化の特徴をスロースピードとナチュラルスピードで確認しよう。下記に示したカタカナ表記で音声変化を確認して、もう一度ビジネス・ダイアローグを聴き直してみよう。発音変化のルールは適宜復習しよう。

2種類の音声を収録

CD 2-51

① **completed** — カンプリーティッド ▶ カンプリーディ [リ] ッド
  ☞ 破裂音 [t] の弾音化

② **but we** — バット・ウィ ▶ バッ＿ウィ
  ☞ 破裂音 [t] の脱落

③ **quality** — クァラティー ▶ クァラディ [リ] ー
  ☞ 破裂音 [t] の弾音化

④ **with a** — ウィズ・ア ▶ ウィザ
  ☞ 2語の連結

⑤ **We are going to** — ウィ・アー・ゴウイング・トゥー ▶ ウィアゴナ
  ☞ are は弱化。going to は [ゴナ] と発音

⑥ **need a** — ニード・ア ▶ ニーダ [ラ]
  ☞ 2語の連結。連結部の破裂音 [t] の弾音化

⑦ **Actually** — アクチュアリー ▶ アクシュアリー
  ☞ [ktʃu] から [t] 音の脱落

⑧ **put us** — プット・アス ▶ プッダ [ラ] ス
  ☞ 2語の連結。連結部の破裂音 [t] が弾音化

⑨ **in an awkward** — イン・アン・オークワード ▶ イナノークワード
  ☞ 3語の連結

⑩ **call you** — コール・ユー ▶ コー＿ユ
  ☞ [l] 音の脱落

⑪ **flight details** — フライト・デーテイルズ ▶ フライ＿ディーテイルズ
  ☞ 破裂音 [t] の脱落

⑫ **send me** — センド・ミー ▶ セン＿ミ
  ☞ 破裂音 [d] の脱落

⑬ **all the** — オール・ズィ ▶ オー＿ズィ
  ☞ [l] 音の脱落

⑭ **Pictures** — ピクチャーズ ▶ ピクシャーズ
  ☞ [ktʃu] から [t] 音の脱落

⑮ **data** — デイタ；ダータ ▶ デイダ [ラ]；ダーダ [ラ]
  ☞ 破裂音 [t] の弾音化

⑯ **what I** — ワット・アイ ▶ ワッダ [ラ] イ
  ☞ 2語が連結。連結部で破裂音 [t] が弾音化

⑰ **test your** — テスト・ユア ▶ テスチュア
  ☞ [t] 音と [j] 音が同化

⑱ **about this** — アバウト・ズィス ▶ アバウ＿ズィス
  ☞ 破裂音 [t] の脱落

⑲ **but please** — バット・プリーズ ▶ バッ＿プリーズ
  ☞ 破裂音 [t] の脱落

🔊 ビジネス・リスニング（5回目）

Unit 35

緊急の海外出張
Urgent Overseas Business Trip

Stage 01 穴埋めビジネス・リスニング

音声変化に注意してCDでビジネスのダイアローグを聴きながら、空欄部分を埋めてみよう。

ダイアローグ音声収録

May: We just ① _____ _____ from AAA Safety Systems ② _____ _____ that their prototypes are failing final inspection. They have ③ _____ traced the root of the problem to our product. They are requesting ④ _____ _____ member of management and someone from ⑤ _____ control fly over there to help them assess the problem.

Mr. Chen: Clear my schedule, and ⑥ _____ _____ flight for you, Mr. Chang and I to leave tomorrow. ⑦ _____ _____ have the inspection reports ⑧ _____ _____ generated prior to shipment?

May: Yes. We conducted detailed inspection on ⑨ _____ two of the one hundred and fifty pieces. Every part passed and was ⑩ _____ _____ be completely within specifications.

Mr. Chen: Have they sent any detailed information with ⑪ _____ _____ the problem?

May: They sent ⑫ _____ of the product and failure ratio ⑬ _____. Mr. Chang is reviewing ⑭ _____ _____ but he was under the impression that perhaps something ⑮ _____ _____ transport.

Mr. Chen: In any event, this is too large a ⑯ _____ _____ jeopardize. Make the trip arrangements and communicate to AAA Safety that we will do everything we can to ⑰ _____ _____ for this.

🔊 ビジネス・リスニング（1回目）

Stage 02 ビジネス・ボキャビル

ビジネスのボキャブラリーを CD で確認しよう。そのあとでもう一度、ビジネス・リスニングにチャレンジ。Stage 01 でできなかったところをもう一度聴き取って、穴埋めを完成させよう。

英日 音声収録

CD 3-02

1	word	連絡；言葉
2	fail	失敗する；不合格になる
3	final inspection	最終検査
4	apparently	おそらく…のようだ
5	root of the problem	問題の根底
6	assess	評価する；見極める；鑑定する
7	clear	片づける
8	book	予約する
9	inspection report	検査報告書
10	prior to ...	…に先だって
11	shipment	発送
12	conducted	実行された
13	detailed inspection	詳細な検査
14	pass	通過する；合格する
15	completely	完全に
16	within specifications	仕様どおりで
17	with respect to ...	…に関して
18	failure ratio data	不合格率のデータ
19	under the impression that ...	…という印象をもつ
20	perhaps	おそらく
21	during transport	輸送中に
22	in any event	いずれにせよ
23	jeopardize	危険にさらす
24	make up for ...	…を埋め合わせる

🔊 ビジネス・リスニング（2回目）

Stage 03　日本語トランスレーション

ビジネス・ダイアログの日本語を確認してみよう！ その上で、ダイアローグを聴きながら、まだできていない部分の穴埋めに再チャレンジしよう。

May: アメリカの AAA セーフティー・システムズからいま連絡がありまして、プロトタイプが最終検査に合格しないそうなのです。問題の原因を弊社の製品だと割り出した様子です。問題の評価を補助するために、経営陣 1 名と品質管理技術者をあちらへこしてほしいと要求してきています。

Mr. Chen: 私のスケジュールを空けて、君とチャンさんと私の明日出発のフライトを予約してください。発送前に作成した検査報告書はあるかな？

May: ええ、150 台のうち 32 台で詳細な検査を実施しました。すべてのパーツが合格で、完全に仕様どおりであると判断されました。

Mr. Chen: 問題に関して AAA セーフティーさんは詳細な情報を送ってくれましたか？

May: 製品の写真と不合格率のデータを送ってきました。チャンさんがいまチェックしていますが、輸送中になにか生じたのではないかという印象のようでした。

Mr. Chen: いずれにせよ、これは危険にさらすには大きすぎる契約だ。旅行の手配を行い、AAA セーフティーに連絡し、失敗を埋め合わせるためにできることはなんでもすると伝えてください。

🔊 ビジネス・リスニング（3回目）

Stage 04　英文トランスクリプション

ビジネス・ダイアログの原稿を確認してみよう！ 穴埋め部分の正解をチェックして、英文を理解し直そう。そのあとで、もう一度ダイアローグを聴いてみよう。

May: We just ① got word from AAA Safety Systems ② in America that their prototypes are failing final inspection. They have ③ apparently traced the root of the problem to our product. They are requesting ④ that a member of management and someone from ⑤ quality control fly over there to help them assess the problem.

Mr. Chen: Clear my schedule, and ⑥ book a flight for you, Mr. Chang and I to leave tomorrow. ⑦ Do you have the inspection reports ⑧ that we generated prior to shipment?

May: Yes. We conducted detailed inspection on ⑨ thirty two of the one hundred and fifty pieces. Every part passed and was ⑩ determined to be completely within specifications.

Mr. Chen: Have they sent any detailed information with ⑪ respect to the problem?

May: They sent ⑫ pictures of the product and failure ratio ⑬ data. Mr. Chang is reviewing ⑭ that now but he was under the impression that perhaps something ⑮ happened during transport.

Mr. Chen: In any event, this is too large a ⑯ contract to jeopardize. Make the trip arrangements and communicate to AAA Safety that we will do everything we can to ⑰ make up for this.

🔊 ビジネス・リスニング（4回目）

Stage 05 音声変化をチェック

まとめとして、穴埋め部分の音声変化の特徴をスロースピードとナチュラルスピードで確認しよう。下記に示したカタカナ表記で音声変化を確認して、もう一度ビジネス・ダイアローグを聴き直してみよう。発音変化のルールは適宜復習しよう。

2種類の音声を収録

CD 3-03

① **got word**
☞ 破裂音 [t] の脱落
ガット・ワード ▶ ガッ＿ワード

② **in America**
☞ 2語の連結
イン・アメリカ ▶ イナメリカ

③ **apparently**
☞ 破裂音 [t] の脱落
アパラントリー ▶ アパラン＿リー

④ **that a**
☞ 2語の連結。連結部で破裂音 [t] の弾音化
ザット・ア ▶ ザッダ [ラ]

⑤ **quality**
☞ 破裂音 [t] の弾音化
クァラティー ▶ クァラディ [リ] ー

⑥ **book a**
☞ 2語が連結
ブック・ア ▶ ブッカ

⑦ **Do you**
☞ do の弱化。さらに [d] と [j] が同化することもある
ドゥー・ユー ▶ ドゥユ；ジュ

⑧ **that we**
☞ 破裂音 [t] の脱落
ザット・ウィ ▶ ザッ＿ウィ

⑨ **thirty**
☞ 破裂音 [t] の弾音化
サーティー ▶ サーディ [リ] ー

⑩ **determined to**
☞ 破裂音 [d] の脱落
ディターミンド・トゥー ▶ ディターミン＿トゥー

⑪ **respect to**
☞ 破裂音 [t] の脱落
リスペクト・トゥー ▶ リスペク＿トゥー

⑫ **pictures**
☞ [ktʃu] から [t] 音の脱落
ピクチャーズ ▶ ピクシャーズ

⑬ **data**
☞ 破裂音 [t] の弾音化
デイタ；ダータ ▶ デイダ [ラ]；ダーダ [ラ]

⑭ **that now**
☞ 破裂音の [t] の脱落
ザット・ナウ ▶ ザッ＿ナウ

⑮ **happened during**
☞ 破裂音の [d] の脱落
ハップンド・デューリング ▶ ハップン＿デューリング

⑯ **contract to**
☞ [ntr] の音が [ntʃr] に変化。破裂音の [t] の脱落
カーントゥラクト・トゥー ▶ カーンチュラク＿トゥー

⑰ **make up**
☞ 2語の連結
メイク・アップ ▶ メイカップ

🔊 ビジネス・リスニング (5回目)

Unit 36

アメリカ行きのフライト
Flight to America

Stage 01 穴埋めビジネス・リスニング

音声変化に注意してCDでビジネスのモノローグを聴きながら、空欄部分を埋めてみよう。

モノローグ音声収録 (CD 3-04)

Attendant: Ladies and gentlemen, the Captain has turned on the fasten ① _____ _____ sign. If you haven't already done so, please stow your carry-on luggage underneath the seat in front of you or ② _____ _____ _____ bin. Please take your seat and fasten your ③ _____ _____. Please make sure your ④ _____ _____ and folding ⑤ _____ are in their full ⑥ _____ _____.

If you are ⑦ _____ ⑧ _____ _____ ⑨ _____ _____ exit, please read the special instructions card ⑩ _____ by your seat. If you do not wish to perform the actions described in the event of ⑪ _____ _____, please ask a flight attendant to ⑫ _____ _____.

⑬ _____ _____ time, we request that all mobile phones be turned off for the duration ⑭ _____ _____ flight, as these items might interfere with the navigational and communication equipment on this aircraft. We request that all other electronic devices be ⑮ _____ _____ until we fly above 10,000 feet. We will ⑯ _____ you when ⑰ _____ _____ safe to use such devices.

This is a non-smoking flight. Smoking is prohibited on the entire aircraft, including the lavatories. Tampering with or disabling the lavatory smoke detectors is prohibited by law.

🔊 ビジネス・リスニング（1回目）

Stage 02　ビジネス・ボキャビル

ビジネスのボキャブラリーを CD で確認しよう。そのあとでもう一度、ビジネス・リスニングにチャレンジ。Stage 01 でできなかったところをもう一度聴き取って、穴埋めを完成させよう。

英日 音声収録

CD 3-05

1	turn on	点灯する
2	fasten	締める
3	stow	しまう；片づける
4	carry-on luggage	手荷物
5	underneath ...	…の下に
6	overhead bin	頭上の荷物棚
7	folding tray	折りたたみトレー
8	upright	直立した
9	emergency exit	非常出口
10	instructions	指示
11	perform	行う
12	actions	動作；行動
13	describe	説明する；記述する
14	in the event of an emergency	非常時に
15	reseat	席を変えさせる
16	for the duration of ...	…の間
17	interfere with ...	…を妨げる
18	navigational	航行の
19	electronic devices	電子機器
20	prohibit	禁止する
21	disable	機能を停止させる
22	smoke detector	煙探知機

🔊 ビジネス・リスニング（2回目）

アメリカ行きのフライト

Stage 03　日本語トランスレーション

ビジネス・モノローグの日本語を確認してみよう！　その上で、モノローグを聴きながら、まだできていない部分の穴埋めに再チャレンジしよう。

Attendant: みなさま、機長がシートベルトサインを点灯いたしました。シートベルトを締めていないお客さまは、手荷物を前の座席の下か頭上の荷物棚にお入れください。座席に着きシートベルトを締めてください。シートを戻し、折りたたみのトレーが完全に上を向いていることをご確認ください。

非常口の隣におかけのお客さまは、そばにある特別指示のカードをお読みください。非常時に説明されている行動を取りたくない方は、アテンダントに座席の変更をお申し出ください。

現在、フライト中はすべての携帯電話の電源をお切りいただいております。航空機の航行および通信機器に影響を与える恐れがあるためです。その他すべての電子機器は高度1万フィートに達するまではお切りください。機器の使用が安全になりましたらお知らせいたします。

本機は禁煙のフライトとなっております。トイレを含みましてすべての機内での喫煙が禁止されております。トイレの煙探知機をいじったり停止したりすることは法律によって禁止されております。

🔊 ビジネス・リスニング（3回目）

Stage 04　英文トランスクリプション

ビジネス・モノローグの原稿を確認してみよう！　穴埋め部分の正解をチェックして、英文を理解し直そう。そのあとで、もう一度モノローグを聴いてみよう。

Attendant: Ladies and gentlemen, the Captain has turned on the fasten ① seat belt sign. If you haven't already done so, please stow your carry-on luggage underneath the seat in front of you or ② in an overhead bin. Please take your seat and fasten your ③ seat belt. Please make sure your ④ seat back and folding ⑤ trays are in their full ⑥ upright position. If you are ⑦ seated ⑧ next to ⑨ an emergency exit, please read the special instructions card ⑩ located by your seat. If you do not wish to perform the actions described in the event of ⑪ an emergency, please ask a flight attendant to ⑫ reseat you.

⑬ At this time, we request that all mobile phones be turned off for the duration ⑭ of the flight, as these items might interfere with the navigational and communication equipment on this aircraft. We request that all other electronic devices be ⑮ turned off until we fly above 10,000 feet. We will ⑯ notify you when ⑰ it is safe to use such devices. This is a non-smoking flight. Smoking is prohibited on the entire aircraft, including the lavatories. Tampering with or disabling the lavatory smoke detectors is prohibited by law.

🔊 ビジネス・リスニング（4回目）

Stage 05 音声変化をチェック

まとめとして、穴埋め部分の音声変化の特徴をスロースピードとナチュラルスピードで確認しよう。下記に示したカタカナ表記で音声変化を確認して、もう一度ビジネス・モノローグを聴き直してみよう。発音変化のルールは適宜復習しよう。

2種類の音声を収録

① **seat belt** — シート・ベルト ▶ シー__ベルト
  ☞ 破裂音 [t] の脱落

② **in an overhead** — イン・アン・オウヴァーヘッド ▶ イナノウヴァーヘッド
  ☞ 3語の連結

③ **seat belt** — シート・ベルト ▶ シー__ベルト
  ☞ 破裂音 [t] の脱落

④ **seat back** — シート・バック ▶ シー__バック
  ☞ 破裂音 [t] の脱落

⑤ **trays** — トゥレイズ ▶ チュレイズ
  ☞ [tr] の音が [tʃr] に変化

⑥ **upright position** — アップライト・パズィシャン ▶ アップライ__パズィシャン
  ☞ 破裂音 [t] の脱落

⑦ **seated** — シーティッド ▶ シーディ[リ]ッド
  ☞ 破裂音 [t] の弾音化

⑧ **next to** — ネクスト・トゥー ▶ ネクス__トゥー
  ☞ 破裂音 [t] の脱落

⑨ **an emergency** — アン・イマージェンシー ▶ アニマージェンシー
  ☞ 2語の連結

⑩ **located** — ロウケイティッド ▶ ロウケイディ[リ]ッド
  ☞ 破裂音 [t] の弾音化

⑪ **an emergency** — アン・イマージェンシー ▶ アニマージェンシー
  ☞ 2語の連結

⑫ **reseat you** — リシート・ユー ▶ リシーチュー
  ☞ [t] 音と [j] 音が同化

⑬ **At this** — アット・ズィス ▶ アッ__ズィス
  ☞ 破裂音 [t] の脱落

⑭ **of the** — アヴ・ザ ▶ ア__ザ
  ☞ 摩擦音 [v] の脱落

⑮ **turned off** — ターンド・オフ ▶ ターンドフ
  ☞ 2語の連結。連結部は弾音化することもある

⑯ **notify** — ノウタファイ ▶ ノウダ[ラ]ファイ
  ☞ 破裂音 [t] の弾音化

⑰ **it is** — イット・イズ ▶ イッディ[リ]ズ；イッツ
  ☞ 2語が連結し、連結部の破裂音 [t] が弾音化。短縮形の it's [イッツ] の発音になることもある

🔊 ビジネス・リスニング（5回目）

Unit 37

入国審査
Clearing Immigration

Stage 01　穴埋めビジネス・リスニング

音声変化に注意してCDでビジネスのダイアローグを聴きながら、空欄部分を埋めてみよう。

ダイアローグ音声収録　　CD 3-07

Officer: Welcome to Atlanta. May I see your ① _____ _____?
May: Sure, here you go.
Officer: Where are you ② _____ _____?
May: Shanghai, China.
Officer: ③ _____ _____ the purpose of your trip?
May: We are here on business.
Officer: How long ④ _____ _____ be here?
May: We ⑤ _____ _____ here for two days.
Officer: Where will you be staying?
May: We have reservations ⑥ _____ _____ Hilton downtown.
Officer: ⑦ _____ _____ have any items to declare?
May: No sir.
Officer: I don't see your disembarkation card ... ⑧ _____ _____ fill one out on the airplane?
May: Yes, I did. I'm sorry I ⑨ _____ _____ left it on the plane.
Officer: That's okay. I have one here you can fill out.
May: Thank you.
Officer: Have you been to the U.S. before?
May: Yes. I ⑩ _____ went to college here as ⑪ _____ _____ student.
Officer: Are those gentlemen in line behind you traveling with you?
May: Yes, we work together. Here is the card. Sorry ⑫ _____ _____.
Officer: No problem. ⑬ _____ _____ nice day ⑭ _____ _____ your stay here in Atlanta.
May: Thank you. I am sure I will.

◀)) ビジネス・リスニング（1回目）

Stage 02　ビジネス・ボキャビル

ビジネスのボキャブラリーを CD で確認しよう。そのあとでもう一度、ビジネス・リスニングにチャレンジ。Stage 01 でできなかったところをもう一度聴き取って、穴埋めを完成させよう。

英日 音声収録　　CD 3-08

1	passport	パスポート
2	purpose	目的
3	on business	仕事で
4	reservation	予約
5	downtown	市街の
6	item	項目；品目
7	declare	（課税品などを）申告する
8	sir	目上の男性や知らない男性への呼びかけの言葉
9	disembarkation card	入国カード
10	fill out	記入する
11	leave	残す
12	exchange student	交換留学生
13	in line	列にいる
14	travel with ...	…とともに出張する
15	Here is ...	こちらが…です
16	Sorry about ...	…について申し訳ありません
17	no problem	問題ない
18	enjoy one's stay	滞在を楽しむ

🔊 ビジネス・リスニング（2回目）

入国審査

Stage 03　日本語トランスレーション

ビジネス・ダイアローグの日本語を確認してみよう！　その上で、ダイアローグを聴きながら、まだできていない部分の穴埋めに再チャレンジしよう。

Officer:	アトランタへようこそ。パスポートを拝見できますか？
May:	もちろん、どうぞ。
Officer:	どちらからお越しですか？
May:	中国の上海です。
Officer:	ご旅行の目的は？
May:	こちらにはビジネスできています。
Officer:	どのくらいのご滞在ですか？
May:	2日です。
Officer:	どちらにご宿泊でしょうか？
May:	市街のヒルトンに予約を入れてあります。
Officer:	申告する品物はありますか？
May:	いいえ、ありません。
Officer:	入国カードが見当たりませんが…機内で記入しましたか？
May:	ええ、しました。すみません、飛行機に忘れてきたようです。
Officer:	大丈夫ですよ。こちらにありますのでご記入いただけます。
May:	どうも。
Officer:	アメリカにいらしたことはありますか？
May:	ええ、実は交換留学生としてこちらの大学に来ていたんです。
Officer:	列の後ろの男性たちはごいっしょにご出張ですか？
May:	ええ、いっしょに仕事をしております。はい、カードです。すみませんでした。
Officer:	大丈夫です。よい一日を、アトランタ滞在を楽しんでください。
May:	ありがとう、楽しんできます。

🔊 ビジネス・リスニング（3回目）

Stage 04　英文トランスクリプション

ビジネス・ダイアローグの原稿を確認してみよう！　穴埋め部分の正解をチェックして、英文を理解し直そう。そのあとで、もう一度ダイアローグを聴いてみよう。

Officer:	Welcome to Atlanta. May I see your ① passport please?
May:	Sure, here you go.
Officer:	Where are you ② coming from?
May:	Shanghai, China.
Officer:	③ What is the purpose of your trip?
May:	We are here on business.
Officer:	How long ④ will you be here?
May:	We ⑤ will be here for two days.
Officer:	Where will you be staying?
May:	We have reservations ⑥ at the Hilton downtown.
Officer:	⑦ Do you have any items to declare?
May:	No sir.
Officer:	I don't see your disembarkation card … ⑧ did you fill one out on the airplane?
May:	Yes, I did. I'm sorry I ⑨ must have left it on the plane.
Officer:	That's okay. I have one here you can fill out.
May:	Thank you.
Officer:	Have you been to the U.S. before?
May:	Yes. I ⑩ actually went to college here as ⑪ an exchange student.
Officer:	Are those gentlemen in line behind you traveling with you?
May:	Yes, we work together. Here is the card. Sorry ⑫ about that.
Officer:	No problem. ⑬ Have a nice day ⑭ and enjoy your stay here in Atlanta.
May:	Thank you. I am sure I will.

🔊 ビジネス・リスニング（4回目）

Stage 05　音声変化をチェック

まとめとして、穴埋め部分の音声変化の特徴をスロースピードとナチュラルスピードで確認しよう。下記に示したカタカナ表記で音声変化を確認して、もう一度ビジネス・ダイアローグを聴き直してみよう。発音変化のルールは適宜復習しよう。

2種類の音声を収録

① **passport please**
☞ 破裂音 [t] の脱落
パスポート・プリーズ　▶　パスポー＿プリーズ

② **coming from**
☞ 破裂音 [g] の脱落
カミング・フラム　▶　カミン＿フラム

③ **What is**
☞ 2 語が連結。連結部の破裂音 [t] の弾音化
ワット・イズ　▶　ワッディ [リ] ズ

④ **will you**
☞ [l] 音の脱落
ウィル・ユー　▶　ウィ＿ユー

⑤ **will be**
☞ [l] 音の脱落
ウィル・ビー　▶　ウィ＿ビ

⑥ **at the**
☞ 破裂音 [t] の脱落
アット・ザ　▶　アッ＿ザ

⑦ **Do you**
☞ do の弱化。さらに [d] と [j] が同化することもある
ドゥー・ユー　▶　ドゥユ；ジュ

⑧ **did you**
☞ [d] 音と [j] 音が同化
ディッド・ユー　▶　ディッジュー

⑨ **must have**
☞ must が弱化した have [アヴ] に連結
マスト・ハヴ　▶　マスタヴ

⑩ **actually**
☞ [ktʃu] から [t] 音の脱落
アクチュアリー　▶　アクシュアリー

⑪ **an exchange**
☞ 2 語が連結
アン・イクスチェインジ　▶　アニクスチェインジ

⑫ **about that**
☞ 破裂音 [t] の脱落
アバウト・ザット　▶　アバウ＿ザット

⑬ **Have a**
☞ 2 語の連結
ハヴ・ア　▶　ハヴァ

⑭ **and enjoy**
☞ and の破裂音 [d] が脱落し、2 語が連結
アンド・エンジョイ　▶　アネンジョイ

🔊 ビジネス・リスニング（5 回目）

Unit 38

ホテルへのチェックイン
Checking Into the Hotel

Stage 01 　穴埋めビジネス・リスニング

音声変化に注意してCDでビジネスのダイアローグを聴きながら、空欄部分を埋めてみよう。

ダイアローグ音声収録　CD 3-10

Clerk: Good afternoon.

May: Hello. We have reservations for one night.

Clerk: What name is the reservation under?

May: Ms. Chang, Mr. Chen and Mr. Chang.

Clerk: ① _____ _____ check our system ... Yes, here ② _____ _____ three rooms for one night. We have rooms with king beds available or two queen beds. ③ _____ _____ have a preference?

May: King beds please. ④ _____ _____ have smoking rooms available?

Clerk: I'm sorry ⑤ _____ _____ of our rooms are non-smoking. We do ⑥ _____ _____ smoking area ⑦ _____ _____ lobby to the left.

May: I see.

Clerk: Will these rooms be ⑧ _____ _____ or separately?

May: Separately. Please use this card for my room.

Clerk: There will be a $200 hold placed on the card as a ⑨ _____ deposit. This will fall off within ⑩ _____-four hours after checkout.

May: ⑪ _____ _____ fine. By the way, you do have wireless access ⑫ _____ _____ room, right?

Clerk: We sure do. The access code is listed right here on your room key. Okay, you're all set. We ⑬ _____ _____ complimentary breakfast served from 6:00 a.m. to 9:00 a.m.

🔊 ビジネス・リスニング（1回目）

Stage 02 ビジネス・ボキャビル

ビジネスのボキャブラリーを CD で確認しよう。そのあとでもう一度、ビジネス・リスニングにチャレンジ。Stage 01 でできなかったところをもう一度聴き取って、穴埋めを完成させよう。

英日 音声収録

1	for one night	1泊の
2	under ...	…という名前で
3	king bed	キングサイズのベッド
4	queen bed	クィーンサイズのベッド
5	preference	好み
6	available	利用可能な
7	non-smoking	禁煙の
8	smoking area	喫煙所
9	outside ...	…の外に
10	separately	別々に
11	hold	留保；差し押さえ
12	security deposit	保証金
13	fall off	解消する
14	checkout	（ホテルの）チェックアウト
15	wireless access	無線ネット接続
16	access code	アクセスコード
17	all set	（準備などが）すべて整った
18	complimentary	無料の；招待の
19	serve	（食事を）出す；提供する

◀)) ビジネス・リスニング（2回目）

Stage 03　日本語トランスレーション

ビジネス・ダイアローグの日本語を確認してみよう！　その上で、ダイアローグを聴きながら、まだできていない部分の穴埋めに再チャレンジしよう。

Clerk: こんにちは。
May: こんにちは、1泊の予約をしているのですが。
Clerk: どちらさまのお名前でご予約でしょうか？
May: ミズ・チャン、ミスター・チェン、ミスター・チャンです。
Clerk: システムで確認いたします…はい、こちらですね、1泊で3部屋のご予約。キングサイズのベッドのお部屋とクイーンサイズのベッドが2つあるお部屋がございます。どちらがお好みでしょうか？
May: キングサイズでお願いします。喫煙のお部屋はありますか？
Clerk: すみませんが、すべてのお部屋が禁煙となっております。ロビーの外の左側に喫煙所がありますので。

May: わかりました。
Clerk: お部屋の代金はまとめてお支払いですか？　それとも別々でしょうか？
May: 別々にお願いします。私の部屋はこちらのカードでお願いします。
Clerk: 保証金としてカードから200ドルを押さえさせていただきます。これは、チェックアウト後24時間で解消されます。
May: かまいません。ところで、それぞれの部屋にはインターネットのWi-Fi アクセスがありますよね？
Clerk: 確かにございます。アクセスコードはルームキーのこちらに掲載されています。では、これですべて大丈夫です。午前6時から9時の間に無料の朝食をご用意しております。

🔊 ビジネス・リスニング（3回目）

Stage 04　英文トランスクリプション

ビジネス・ダイアローグの原稿を確認してみよう！　穴埋め部分の正解をチェックして、英文を理解し直そう。そのあとで、もう一度ダイアローグを聴いてみよう。

Clerk: Good afternoon.
May: Hello. We have reservations for one night.
Clerk: What name is the reservation under?
May: Ms. Chang, Mr. Chen and Mr. Chang.
Clerk: ① Let me check our system … Yes, here ② it is three rooms for one night. We have rooms with king beds available or two queen beds. ③ Do you have a preference?
May: King beds please. ④ Do you have smoking rooms available?
Clerk: I'm sorry ⑤ but all of our rooms are non-smoking. We do ⑥ have a smoking area ⑦ outside the lobby to the left.

May: I see.
Clerk: Will these rooms be ⑧ paid together or separately?
May: Separately. Please use this card for my room.
Clerk: There will be a $200 hold placed on the card as a ⑨ security deposit. This will fall off within ⑩ twenty-four hours after checkout.
May: ⑪ That is fine. By the way, you do have wireless access ⑫ in each room, right?
Clerk: We sure do. The access code is listed right here on your room key. Okay, you're all set. We ⑬ have a complimentary breakfast served from 6:00 a.m. to 9:00 a.m.

🔊 ビジネス・リスニング（4回目）

Stage 05 音声変化をチェック

まとめとして、穴埋め部分の音声変化の特徴をスロースピードとナチュラルスピードで確認しよう。下記に示したカタカナ表記で音声変化を確認して、もう一度ビジネス・ダイアローグを聴き直してみよう。発音変化のルールは適宜復習しよう。

2種類の音声を収録   CD 3-12

① **Let me**　　　　　　　　　　レット・ミー　　　　　▶　レッ＿ミー
　☞ 破裂音 [t] の脱落

② **it is**　　　　　　　　　　　イット・イズ　　　　　▶　イッディ [リ] ズ；イッツ
　☞ 2語が連結し、連結部の破裂音 [t] が弾音化。短縮形の it's [イッツ] の発音になることもある

③ **Do you**　　　　　　　　　ドゥー・ユー　　　　　▶　ドゥユ；ジュ
　☞ do の弱化。さらに [d] と [j] が同化することもある

④ **Do you**　　　　　　　　　ドゥー・ユー　　　　　▶　ドゥユ；ジュ
　☞ do の弱化。さらに [d] と [j] が同化することもある

⑤ **but all**　　　　　　　　　バット・オール　　　　▶　バッド [ロ] ール
　☞ 2語が連結。連結部の破裂音 [t] が弾音化

⑥ **have a**　　　　　　　　　ハヴ・ア　　　　　　　▶　ハヴァ
　☞ 2語が連結

⑦ **outside the**　　　　　　アウトサイド・ザ　　　▶　アウトサイ＿ザ
　☞ 破裂音 [d] の脱落。破裂音 [t] と [d] の両方が脱落することもある

⑧ **paid together**　　　　　ペイド・トゥゲザー　　▶　ペイ＿トゥゲザー
　☞ 破裂音 [d] の脱落

⑨ **security**　　　　　　　　セキュラティー　　　　▶　セキュァラディ [リ] ー
　☞ 破裂音 [t] の弾音化

⑩ **twenty**　　　　　　　　　トゥエンティー　　　　▶　トゥエニー
　☞ 破裂音 [t] の脱落

⑪ **That is**　　　　　　　　　ザット・イズ　　　　　▶　ザッディ [リ] ズ；ザッツ
　☞ 2語が連結。連結部の破裂音 [t] の弾音化。短縮形の that's の発音になることもある

⑫ **in each**　　　　　　　　　イン・イーチ　　　　　▶　イニーチ
　☞ 2語が連結

⑬ **have a**　　　　　　　　　ハヴ・ア　　　　　　　▶　ハヴァ
　☞ 2語が連結

◀)) ビジネス・リスニング (5回目)

Unit 39

顧客のオフィスを訪問する
Visit to the Customer Office

Stage 01　穴埋めビジネス・リスニング

音声変化に注意してCDでビジネスのダイアローグを聴きながら、空欄部分を埋めてみよう。

ダイアローグ音声収録　CD 3-13

Mike:　　　① _____ _____. Welcome to Atlanta.

Mr. Chen:　Thank you. We are happy to be here ② _____ _____ _____ the circumstances.

Mike:　　　③ _____ _____ show you around. This is our main office area, of course. The production floor is ④ _____ _____ way. Before we enter the plant area I will ⑤ _____ _____ ⑥ _____ _____ to ⑦ _____ _____ your shoes and replace them with these slippers. You can use the lockers ⑧ _____ _____ there. Also, ⑨ _____ _____ jackets you can wear right over your clothes.

May:　　　Do we need safety glasses?

Mike:　　　If you ⑩ _____ _____ ⑪ _____ _____ fine, ⑫ _____ ⑬ _____ _____ _____ required. Follow me please. Okay, here is the primary line where the ⑭ _____ _____ and other components are assembled to make the sensors. They are then ⑮ _____ _____ this line where they are ⑯ _____ _____ a bracket that goes under the car seats. Back there is our receiving and warehousing area where raw materials and other components are stored.

May:　　　⑰ _____ _____ like you are doing some construction outside.

Mike:　　　Yes, we are ⑱ _____ _____ expand our production area to twice its current size.

🔊 ビジネス・リスニング（1回目）

Stage 02 ビジネス・ボキャビル

ビジネスのボキャブラリーを CD で確認しよう。そのあとでもう一度、ビジネス・リスニングにチャレンジ。Stage 01 でできなかったところをもう一度聴き取って、穴埋めを完成させよう。

英日 音声収録

#	英語	日本語
1	be happy to ...	…できてうれしい
2	circumstance	環境
3	show ... around	…を案内する
4	enter	入る；入場する
5	plant	工場；施設
6	take off	脱ぐ
7	replace	取り替える
8	safety glasses	安全のための眼鏡
9	be required	要求される；必要とされる
10	follow	従う；ついていく
11	primary	最初の；第一の
12	line	生産ライン
13	circuit board	回路基板
14	assemble	組み立てる
15	transfer	移動させる；移す
16	fasten to ...	…に留める
17	warehouse	保管する
18	raw materials	原材料
19	store	保存する
20	construction	建設工事
21	plan to ...	…することを計画する
22	expand	拡大する
23	twice its current size	現在のサイズの 2 倍

🔊 ビジネス・リスニング（2回目）

Stage 03　日本語トランスレーション

ビジネス・ダイアログの日本語を確認してみよう！　その上で、ダイアログを聴きながら、まだできていない部分の穴埋めに再チャレンジしよう。

Mike:　　おはようございます。アトランタへようこそ。
Mr. Chen:　ありがとうございます。こちらへ来られてうれしいです。状況は別ですけれども。
Mike:　　ご案内いたしましょう。ここは、当然ですが弊社の本社エリアです。製造はこちらへまっすぐのところですね。工場エリアに入る前に、靴を脱いでスリッパに履き替えていただく必要があります。あちらのロッカーをお使いください。それから、服の上に着ていただくジャケットもありますので。
May:　　セーフティー・グラスはかける必要がありますか？
Mike:　　お持ちでしたらかけてもいいですが、必要はありません。こちらです。えー、こちらが回路基板と他の部品を組み立ててセンサーを作る最初の製造ラインです。そのあと、こちらのラインに移され、車の座席の下に入るブラケットに留められます。あちらの奥のほうが受け取りと保管のエリアになります。原材料やその他の部品が保管されているんです。
May:　　外ではなにか工事をなさっているようですね。
Mike:　　そうなんです。製造エリアを現在のサイズの2倍にする予定なんですよ。

🔊 ビジネス・リスニング（3回目）

Stage 04　英文トランスクリプション

ビジネス・ダイアログの原稿を確認してみよう！　穴埋め部分の正解をチェックして、英文を理解し直そう。そのあとで、もう一度ダイアログを聴いてみよう。

Mike:　　① Good morning. Welcome to Atlanta.
Mr. Chen:　Thank you. We are happy to be here ② but not about the circumstances.
Mike:　　③ Let me show you around. This is our main office area, of course. The production floor is ④ right this way. Before we enter the plant area I will ⑤ need to ⑥ ask you to ⑦ take off your shoes and replace them with these slippers. You can use the lockers ⑧ right over there. Also, ⑨ there are jackets you can wear right over your clothes.
May:　　Do we need safety glasses?
Mike:　　If you ⑩ have them ⑪ that is fine, ⑫ but ⑬ they are not required. Follow me please. Okay, here is the primary line where the ⑭ circuit boards and other components are assembled to make the sensors. They are then ⑮ transferred to this line where they are ⑯ fastened to a bracket that goes under the car seats. Back there is our receiving and warehousing area where raw materials and other components are stored.
May:　　⑰ It looks like you are doing some construction outside.
Mike:　　Yes, we are ⑱ planning to expand our production area to twice its current size.

🔊 ビジネス・リスニング（4回目）

Stage 05　音声変化をチェック

まとめとして、穴埋め部分の音声変化の特徴をスロースピードとナチュラルスピードで確認しよう。下記に示したカタカナ表記で音声変化を確認して、もう一度ビジネス・ダイアローグを聴き直してみよう。発音変化のルールは適宜復習しよう。

2種類の音声を収録　　CD 3-15

① **Good morning** 　　グッド・モーニング　　▶ グッ__モーニング
　☞ 破裂音 [d] の脱落

② **but not about** 　　バット・ナット・アバウト　　▶ バッ__ナダ [ラ] バウ__
　☞ but と about の末尾の破裂音 [t] の脱落。not と about が連結し、連結部の破裂音 [t] は弾音化

③ **Let me** 　　レット・ミー　　▶ レッ__ミー
　☞ 破裂音 [t] の脱落

④ **right this** 　　ライト・ズィス　　▶ ライ__ズィス
　☞ 破裂音 [t] の脱落

⑤ **need to** 　　ニード・トゥー　　▶ ニードゥ [ル] ー；ニー__トゥー
　☞ need to の破裂音 [d] が脱落。to の破裂音 [t] が弾音化することもある

⑥ **ask you** 　　アスク・ユー　　▶ アスキュー
　☞ 2語が連結

⑦ **take off** 　　テイク・オフ　　▶ テイコフ
　☞ 2語が連結

⑧ **right over** 　　ライト・オウヴァー　　▶ ライド [ロ] ウヴァー
　☞ 2語が連結。連結部の破裂音 [t] の弾音化

⑨ **there are** 　　ゼァ・アー　　▶ ゼァラー
　☞ 短縮形 there're の発音

⑩ **have them** 　　ハヴ・ゼム　　▶ ハヴェム
　☞ have が弱化した them [ェム] に連結

⑪ **that is** 　　ザット・イズ　　▶ ザッディ [リ] ズ
　☞ 2語が連結。連結部の破裂音 [t] の弾音化。短縮形の that's の発音になることもある

⑫ **but** 　　バット　　▶ バッ__
　☞ 破裂音 [t] の脱落

⑬ **they are not** 　　ゼイ・アー・ナット　　▶ ゼァナッ__
　☞ they are は弱く [ゼァ] と発音。not は末尾の破裂音 [t] が脱落

⑭ **circuit boards** 　　スーカット・ボーズ　　▶ スーカッ__ボーズ
　☞ 破裂音の [t] の脱落

⑮ **transferred to** 　　トゥランスファード・トゥー　　▶ トゥランスファー__トゥー
　☞ 破裂音の [d] の脱落

⑯ **fastened to** 　　ファスンド・トゥー　　▶ ファスン__トゥー
　☞ 破裂音の [d] の脱落

⑰ **It looks** 　　イット・ルックス　　▶ イッ__ルックス
　☞ 破裂音の [t] の脱落

⑱ **planning to** 　　プラニング・トゥー　　▶ プラニン__トゥー
　☞ 破裂音の [g] の脱落

🔊 ビジネス・リスニング（5回目）

Unit 40

製品の問題箇所を検証する
Determining the Product Issue

Stage 01 穴埋めビジネス・リスニング

音声変化に注意してCDでビジネスのダイアローグを聴きながら、空欄部分を埋めてみよう。

ダイアローグ音声収録

Mike: Mr. Chang this is Steve Jones, our ① _____ control manager.

Mr. Chang: Nice to ② _____ _____.

Steve: As you know, we are ③ _____ _____ with the prototype sensor units, ④ _____ _____ large percentage of them are failing at final inspection. I have ⑤ _____ _____ some space for you to work ⑥ _____ _____ ⑦ _____ lab, where we have samples of the ⑧ _____ parts.

Mr. Chang: Good. I brought some testing equipment I can use to evaluate the semi-conductors. I will just ⑨ _____ _____ table and electric power.

Steve: That's no problem ⑩ _____ _____.

Mike: May, while they are doing the testing and inspection, I would like to go over some numbers with you and Mr. Chen if we ⑪ _____ _____ replace these parts.

Mr. Chen: ⑫ _____ if ⑬ _____ _____ okay, ⑭ _____ _____ like to see the parts as well. May can work with you on some preliminary scheduling for replacement parts.

Mike: That's fine. Steve, ⑮ _____ _____ show them to the lab. ⑯ _____ _____ _____ ⑰ _____ _____ in conference room B.

🔊 ビジネス・リスニング(1回目)

Stage 02　ビジネス・ボキャビル

ビジネスのボキャブラリーを CD で確認しよう。そのあとでもう一度、ビジネス・リスニングにチャレンジ。Stage 01 でできなかったところをもう一度聴き取って、穴埋めを完成させよう。

英日 音声収録

CD 3-17

1	quality control	品質管理
2	have problems with ...	…に問題がある
3	prototype	試作品
4	sensor unit	センサー部
5	large percentage	高い割合
6	fail	失格する
7	final inspection	最終検査
8	quality lab	品質試験場
9	problematic	問題のある
10	testing equipment	テスト用機材
11	evaluate	評価する
12	semi-conductor	半導体
13	electric power	電力
14	numbers	数値；数字
15	replace	交換する
16	Actually, ...	というか…；実は…
17	preliminary	仮の
18	conference room	会議室

🔊 ビジネス・リスニング（2回目）

製品の問題箇所を検証する

Stage 03　日本語トランスレーション

ビジネス・ダイアローグの日本語を確認してみよう！　その上で、ダイアローグを聴きながら、まだできていない部分の穴埋めに再チャレンジしよう。

Mike:	チャンさん、こちらが弊社の品質管理部長のスティーヴ・ジョーンズです。
Mr. Chang:	はじめまして。
Steve:	ご存じのように、プロトタイプのセンサー部に問題が発生しています。最終検査でかなりの率のパーツが失格になっています。弊社の品質試験場に作業できるスペースを確保しました。そちらに問題のある部品のサンプルを置いてあります。
Mr. Chang:	わかりました。半導体を検査するのに使える機器をいくつか持参しました。テーブルと電源さえあればかまいません。
Steve:	それはまったく問題ありませんよ。
Mike:	メイ、彼らがテストと検査をしている間に、この部品の交換が必要になった場合の数字についてあなたとチェンさんといっしょに話しておきたいのですが。
Mr. Chen:	というか、問題なければ、私にも部品を見せていただきたいのですが。交換部品の仮のスケジュールに関しては、まずはメイのほうであなたとお話しできると思います。
Mike:	いいですよ。スティーヴ、みなさんをラボに案内してください。メイと私はB会議室にいますから。

🔊 ビジネス・リスニング（3回目）

Stage 04　英文トランスクリプション

ビジネス・ダイアローグの原稿を確認してみよう！　穴埋め部分の正解をチェックして、英文を理解し直そう。そのあとで、もう一度ダイアローグを聴いてみよう。

Mike:	Mr. Chang this is Steve Jones, our ① quality control manager.
Mr. Chang:	Nice to ② meet you.
Steve:	As you know, we are ③ having problems with the prototype sensor units, ④ as a large percentage of them are failing at final inspection. I have ⑤ set up some space for you to work ⑥ in our ⑦ quality lab, where we have samples of the ⑧ problematic parts.
Mr. Chang:	Good. I brought some testing equipment I can use to evaluate the semiconductors. I will just ⑨ need a table and electric power.
Steve:	That's no problem ⑩ at all.
Mike:	May, while they are doing the testing and inspection, I would like to go over some numbers with you and Mr. Chen if we ⑪ need to replace these parts.
Mr. Chen:	⑫ Actually if ⑬ it is okay, ⑭ I would like to see the parts as well. May can work with you on some preliminary scheduling for replacement parts.
Mike:	That's fine. Steve, ⑮ would you show them to the lab. ⑯ May and I ⑰ will be in conference room B.

🔊 ビジネス・リスニング（4回目）

Stage 05 音声変化をチェック

まとめとして、穴埋め部分の音声変化の特徴をスロースピードとナチュラルスピードで確認しよう。下記に示したカタカナ表記で音声変化を確認して、もう一度ビジネス・ダイアローグを聴き直してみよう。発音変化のルールは適宜復習しよう。

2種類の音声を収録

CD 3-18

① **quality** クァラティー ▶ クァラディ [リ] ー
☞ 破裂音 [t] の弾音化

② **meet you** ミート・ユー ▶ ミーチュー
☞ [t] 音と [j] 音が同化

③ **having problems** ハヴィング・プラーブラムズ ▶ ハヴィン__プラーブラムズ
☞ 破裂音 [g] の脱落

④ **as a** アズ・ア ▶ アザ
☞ 2語の連結

⑤ **set up** セットアップ ▶ セッダ [ラ] ップ
☞ 2語の連結。連結部の破裂音 [t] の弾音化

⑥ **in our** イン・アウァ ▶ イナウァ
☞ 2語の連結

⑦ **quality** クァラティー ▶ クァラディ [リ] ー
☞ 破裂音 [t] の弾音化

⑧ **problematic** プラーブラマティック ▶ プラーブラマディ [リ] ック
☞ 破裂音 [t] の弾音化

⑨ **need a** ニード・ア ▶ ニーダ [ラ]
☞ 2語の連結。連結部で破裂音 [t] の弾音化

⑩ **at all** アット・オール ▶ アッド [ロ] ー__
☞ 2語の連結。連結部の破裂音 [t] の弾音化。末尾の [l] 音は脱落することもある

⑪ **need to** ニード・トゥー ▶ ニードゥ [ル] ー ; ニー__トゥー
☞ need to の破裂音 [d] が脱落。to の破裂音 [t] が弾音化することもある

⑫ **Actually** アクチュアリー ▶ アクシュアリー
☞ [ktʃu] から [t] 音の脱落

⑬ **it is** イット・イズ ▶ イッディ [リ] ズ ; イッツ
☞ 2語が連結し、連結部の破裂音 [t] が弾音化。短縮形の it's [イッツ] の発音になることもある

⑭ **I would** アイ・ウッド ▶ アイド
☞ 短縮形 I'd の発音

⑮ **would you** ウッド・ユー ▶ ウッジュー
☞ [d] 音と [j] 音が同化

⑯ **May and I** メイ・アンド・アイ ▶ メイアナイ
☞ and の破裂音 [d] が脱落し I が連結

⑰ **will be** ウィル・ビー ▶ ウィ__ビ
☞ [l] 音の脱落

🔊 ビジネス・リスニング（5回目）

製品の問題箇所を検証する

Unit 41

製品のトラブルシューティング
Troubleshooting the Product

Stage 01 　穴埋めビジネス・リスニング

音声変化に注意して CD でビジネスのダイアローグを聴きながら、空欄部分を埋めてみよう。

ダイアローグ音声収録　CD 3-19

Mr. Chang: So you are having a large ① _____ _____ failures at final inspection, ② _____ _____ all of the parts are being rejected?

Steve: Yes. At first I thought maybe some parts had been damaged in transit, ③ _____ _____ could not see any appearance flaws. Our receiving department ④ _____ report any damage to the packaging either.

Mr. Chang: This computer and machine uses several different ⑤ _____ _____ to illuminate the surface of the wafer and allow us to check ⑥ _____ _____ defects.

Mr. Chen: If they were ⑦ _____ _____ or ⑧ _____ _____ ⑨ _____ charge, my guess is the problem is contamination of some kind. ⑩ _____ _____ explain why some chips work and some do not.

Steve: Here are the component samples.

Mr. Chang: Look here. ⑪ _____ _____ the problem ⑫ _____ _____. Somehow dust ⑬ _____ _____ the surface of the wafer and is causing a malfunction.

Mr. Chen: Send that ⑭ _____ to our plant in Shanghai ⑮ _____ _____. Have them do an immediate inspection of the production line to find the cause and implement countermeasures.

🔊 ビジネス・リスニング（1回目）

Stage 02 ビジネス・ボキャビル

ビジネスのボキャブラリーを CD で確認しよう。そのあとでもう一度、ビジネス・リスニングにチャレンジ。Stage 01 でできなかったところをもう一度聴き取って、穴埋めを完成させよう。

英日 音声収録

CD 3-20

#	英語	日本語
1	failure	（機能の）不適格；失格
2	reject	拒否する；却下する
3	damage	損傷を与える
4	transit	輸送；運送
5	appearance flaw	外的損傷
6	receiving department	受領部門；受け入れ部門
7	report	報告する
8	packaging	パッケージ
9	light pattern	光線パターン
10	illuminate	照らす
11	surface	表面
12	wafer	（集積回路の）基板
13	defect	欠陥
14	be subjected to ...	…に晒される
15	electrostatic	静電気の
16	guess	推測；推量
17	contamination	汚染
18	explain	説明する
19	somehow	どういうわけか；なんらかの方法で
20	dust	埃
21	malfunction	機能不全
22	implement	実行する
23	countermeasure	対策

🔊 ビジネス・リスニング（2回目）

製品のトラブルシューティング

Stage 03　日本語トランスレーション

ビジネス・ダイアローグの日本語を確認してみよう！　その上で、ダイアローグを聴きながら、まだできていない部分の穴埋めに再チャレンジしよう。

Mr. Chang: それで、最終検査では多くの不適格が出ているということですが、すべてのパーツが不合格となったわけではないのですね？

Steve: ええ、最初はおそらく部品のいくつかが輸送中に壊れたのだと思ったのですが、外的な損傷が見つからなかったのです。受領部門でもパッケージへの損傷を報告してきませんでした。

Mr. Chang: このコンピューターと機材は異なる光線パターンを使って基板の表面を照らすことができます。欠陥をチェックするのに利用できるんです。

Mr. Chen: もしダメージもなく、静電気に晒されていなければ、私の推測では、なんらかの汚染が原因ではないかと思います。そう考えると、チップの一部が動作して、一部がしなかったことの説明になりますね。

Steve: こちらが部品サンプルです。

Mr. Chang: ここを見てください。ちょうどこの部分に問題がありますね。なんらかの原因で埃が基板の表面に付着して誤動作を引き起こしているんです。

Mr. Chen: そのデータをすぐに上海のうちのプラントに送りなさい。原因を見つけて対策を講じるために、生産ラインをすぐに検査させるように。

🔊 ビジネス・リスニング（3回目）

Stage 04　英文トランスクリプション

ビジネス・ダイアローグの原稿を確認してみよう！　穴埋め部分の正解をチェックして、英文を理解し直そう。そのあとで、もう一度ダイアローグを聴いてみよう。

Mr. Chang: So you are having a large ① number of failures at final inspection, ② but not all of the parts are being rejected?

Steve: Yes. At first I thought maybe some parts had been damaged in transit, ③ but I could not see any appearance flaws. Our receiving department ④ didn't report any damage to the packaging either.

Mr. Chang: This computer and machine uses several different ⑤ light patterns to illuminate the surface of the wafer and allow us to check ⑥ for any defects.

Mr. Chen: If they were ⑦ not damaged or ⑧ subjected to ⑨ electrostatic charge, my guess is the problem is contamination of some kind. ⑩ That would explain why some chips work and some do not.

Steve: Here are the component samples.

Mr. Chang: Look here. ⑪ There is the problem ⑫ right there. Somehow dust ⑬ got onto the surface of the wafer and is causing a malfunction.

Mr. Chen: Send that ⑭ data to our plant in Shanghai ⑮ right away. Have them do an immediate inspection of the production line to find the cause and implement countermeasures.

🔊 ビジネス・リスニング（4回目）

Unit 41

Stage 05　音声変化をチェック

まとめとして、穴埋め部分の音声変化の特徴をスロースピードとナチュラルスピードで確認しよう。下記に示したカタカナ表記で音声変化を確認して、もう一度ビジネス・ダイアローグを聴き直してみよう。発音変化のルールは適宜復習しよう。

2種類の音声を収録　　CD 3-21

① **number of** 　　　　ナンバー・アヴ　　　　▶ ナンバーラヴ
　☞ 2語が連結

② **but not** 　　　　バット・ナット　　　　▶ バッ＿ナット
　☞ but の破裂音 [t] が脱落。CD では not の末尾の破裂音 [t] も all につながることで弾音化

③ **but I** 　　　　バット・アイ　　　　▶ バッダ [ラ] イ
　☞ 2語が連結。連結部の破裂音 [t] 音の弾音化

④ **didn't** 　　　　ディドント　　　　▶ ディんン＿
　☞ 破裂音 [d] の声門閉鎖音化。末尾の破裂音 [t] の脱落

⑤ **light patterns** 　　　　ライト・パターンズ　　　　▶ ライ＿パダ [ラ] ーンズ
　☞ light の破裂音 [t] の脱落。patterns の破裂音 [t] の弾音化

⑥ **for any** 　　　　フォー・エニイ　　　　▶ フォレニイ
　☞ 2語の連結

⑦ **not damaged** 　　　　ナット・ダメジド　　　　▶ ナッ＿ダメジド
　☞ 破裂音 [t] の脱落

⑧ **subjected to** 　　　　サブジェクティッド・トゥー　　　　▶ サブジェクティッ＿トゥー
　☞ 破裂音 [d] の脱落

⑨ **electrostatic** 　　　　イレクトゥロウスタティック　　　　▶ イレクトゥロウスタディ [リ] ック
　☞ 破裂の [t] の弾音化

⑩ **That would** 　　　　ザット・ウッド　　　　▶ ザッ＿ウッド
　☞ 破裂音 [t] の脱落

⑪ **There is** 　　　　ゼア・イズ　　　　▶ ゼアリズ
　☞ 短縮形 there's の発音

⑫ **right there** 　　　　ライト・ゼア　　　　▶ ライ＿ゼア
　☞ 破裂音 [t] の脱落

⑬ **got onto** 　　　　ゴット・オントゥー　　　　▶ ゴッド [ロ] ントゥー
　☞ 2語の連結。連結部の破裂音の [t] が弾音化

⑭ **data** 　　　　デイタ；ダータ　　　　▶ デイダ [ラ]；ダーダ [ラ]
　☞ 破裂音 [t] の弾音化

⑮ **right away** 　　　　ライト・アウェイ　　　　▶ ライダ [ラ] ウェイ
　☞ 2語の連結。連結部の破裂音の [t] が弾音化

🔊 ビジネス・リスニング (5回目)

製品のトラブルシューティング　173

Unit 42

不具合についての打ち合わせ
Meeting About the Defective Parts

Stage 01 穴埋めビジネス・リスニング

音声変化に注意してCDでビジネスのダイアローグを聴きながら、空欄部分を埋めてみよう。

ダイアローグ音声収録

Mr. Chang: We were able to verify that somehow foreign ① _____ such as dust ② _____ _____ way into the production line and contaminated ③ _____ _____ _____ wafers. This is the root cause ④ _____ _____ problem.

Mr. Chen: Mike, I realize this is a terrible way to ⑤ _____ relationship, ⑥ _____ _____ assure you we are already ⑦ _____ things in motion to rectify this situation. Immediately upon our return we will submit a corrective action report and ⑧ _____ _____ with a schedule for delivering ⑨ _____ _____.

Mike: What ⑩ _____ _____ _____ time-frame are we ⑪ _____ _____?

Mr. Chen: I can't say until we find the cause of the contamination, ⑫ _____ _____ would say ten days.

Mike: That's ⑬ _____ _____ _____ _____ good enough. We will need product here ⑭ _____ _____ week to stay on schedule to build our exhibits for the expo.

May: ⑮ _____ _____ use ⑯ _____ _____ _____ parts ⑰ _____ _____ inspection and are functioning properly for the display?

Mike: There is no way to be sure that it will continue to function, if it fails ⑱ _____ _____ expo, we are sunk. We just can't take that chance.

🔊 ビジネス・リスニング（1回目）

Stage 02 ビジネス・ボキャビル

ビジネスのボキャブラリーを CD で確認しよう。そのあとでもう一度、ビジネス・リスニングにチャレンジ。Stage 01 でできなかったところをもう一度聴き取って、穴埋めを完成させよう。

英日 音声収録　CD 3-23

#	英	日
1	verify	（調査などで）確認・立証する
2	foreign matter	異物
3	production line	生産ライン
4	contaminate	汚染する
5	root cause	根本原因
6	terrible	ひどい
7	relationship	関係
8	rectify	改正する；正す
9	Immediately upon ...	…したらすぐに
10	corrective action report	修正のための行動報告
11	provide	提供する
12	replacement product	交換品
13	time-frame	時間枠；タイムスパン
14	stay on schedule	スケジュールを保つ
15	exhibit	展示品
16	pass	合格する
17	function	機能する
18	properly	適切に
19	display	展示
20	continue to ...	…し続ける
21	fail	失敗する
22	be sunk	沈む；おしまいだ
23	can't take that chance	そんな賭には出られない

🔊 ビジネス・リスニング（2回目）

不具合についての打ち合わせ

Stage 03　日本語トランスレーション

ビジネス・ダイアローグの日本語を確認してみよう！　その上で、ダイアローグを聴きながら、まだできていない部分の穴埋めに再チャレンジしよう。

Mr. Chang: 埃のような異物が生産ラインに混入して基板の一部を汚染したことは確認できました。これが問題の根源です。
Mr. Chen: マイク、最初の取引としてはひどいものになりましたが、弊社ではすでに今回の状況を修正するために動きを取り始めています。戻り次第すぐに、修正のための行動報告を提出し、交換品の配送スケジュールをお送りします。
Mike: どのくらいのタイムスパンの話をしているのでしょうか？
Mr. Chen: 汚染の原因を見つけるまでははっきり言えませんが、10日ほどかと。
Mike: それでは問題が残ります。エキスポの展示の作成スケジュールを守るためには、1週間で製品が必要になるのです。
May: 展示には、検査を通過してきちんと動いている部品を使っていただくことはできないでしょうか？
Mike: それが引き続き動き続ける保証はありません。エキスポで失敗すれば、おしまいなんですよ。そんな危険な賭に出ることはできません。

🔊 ビジネス・リスニング（3回目）

Stage 04　英文トランスクリプション

ビジネス・ダイアローグの原稿を確認してみよう！　穴埋め部分の正解をチェックして、英文を理解し直そう。そのあとで、もう一度ダイアローグを聴いてみよう。

Mr. Chang: We were able to verify that somehow foreign ① matter such as dust ② found its way into the production line and contaminated ③ some of the wafers. This is the root cause ④ of the problem.
Mr. Chen: Mike, I realize this is a terrible way to ⑤ start our relationship, ⑥ but I assure you we are already ⑦ setting things in motion to rectify this situation. Immediately upon our return we will submit a corrective action report and ⑧ provide you with a schedule for delivering ⑨ replacement product.
Mike: What ⑩ kind of a time-frame are we ⑪ talking about?
Mr. Chen: I can't say until we find the cause of the contamination, ⑫ but I would say ten days.
Mike: That's ⑬ not going to be good enough. We will need product here ⑭ within a week to stay on schedule to build our exhibits for the expo.
May: ⑮ Couldn't you use ⑯ some of the parts ⑰ that passed inspection and are functioning properly for the display?
Mike: There is no way to be sure that it will continue to function, if it fails ⑱ at the expo, we are sunk. We just can't take that chance.

🔊 ビジネス・リスニング（4回目）

Stage 05 音声変化をチェック

まとめとして、穴埋め部分の音声変化の特徴をスロースピードとナチュラルスピードで確認しよう。下記に示したカタカナ表記で音声変化を確認して、もう一度ビジネス・ダイアローグを聴き直してみよう。発音変化のルールは適宜復習しよう。

2種類の音声を収録　　CD 3-24

① **matter**　　マター　　▶ マダ [ラ] ー
　☞ 破裂音 [t] の弾音化

② **found its**　　ファウンド・イッツ　　▶ ファウンディ [リ] ッツ
　☞ 2語の連結。連結部の破裂音 [d] が弾音化することもある

③ **some of the**　　サム・アヴ・ザ　　▶ サマ＿ザ
　☞ some と of は連結。of の摩擦音 [v] が脱落

④ **of the**　　アヴ・ザ　　▶ ア＿ザ
　☞ 摩擦音 [v] の脱落

⑤ **start our**　　スタート・アウァ　　▶ スターダ [ラ] ウァ
　☞ 2語の連結。連結部の破裂音 [t] が弾音化

⑥ **but I**　　バット・アイ　　▶ バッダ [ラ] イ
　☞ 2語の連結。連結部の破裂音 [t] が弾音化

⑦ **setting**　　セッティング　　▶ セッディ [リ] ング
　☞ 破裂音 [t] の弾音化

⑧ **provide you**　　プラヴァイド・ユー　　▶ プラヴァイジュー
　☞ [d] 音と [j] 音が同化

⑨ **replacement product**　　リプレイスメント・プラダクト　　▶ リプレイスメン＿プラダ [ラ] クト
　☞ replacement の破裂音 [t] の脱落。product の破裂音 [d] の弾音化

⑩ **kind of a**　　カインド・アヴ・ア　　▶ カイナヴァ
　☞ kind の破裂音 [d] が脱落して 3 語が連結

⑪ **talking about**　　トーキング・アバウト　　▶ トーキングアバウ＿
　☞ 末尾の破裂音 [t] の脱落

⑫ **but I**　　バット・アイ　　▶ バッダ [ラ] イ
　☞ 2語の連結。連結部の破裂音 [t] が弾音化

⑬ **not going to be**　　ナット・ゴウイング・トゥー・ビー　　▶ ナッ＿ゴナビ
　☞ not の破裂音 [t] の脱落。going to be は [ゴナビ] と短く発音

⑭ **within a**　　ウィズィン・ア　　▶ ウィズィナ
　☞ 2語が連結

⑮ **Couldn't you**　　クドゥント・ユー　　▶ クドゥンチュー：クんチュー
　☞ [t] 音と [j] 音が同化。破裂音 [d] は声門閉鎖音化あるいは脱落することもある

⑯ **some of the**　　サム・アヴ・ザ　　▶ サマ＿ザ
　☞ some と of が連結。of の摩擦音 [v] の脱落

⑰ **that passed**　　ザット・パスト　　▶ ザッ＿パスト
　☞ 破裂音 [t] の脱落

⑱ **at the**　　アット・ズィ　　▶ アッ＿ズィ
　☞ 破裂音 [t] の脱落

◀)) ビジネス・リスニング（5回目）

Unit 43

ホテルのチェックアウト
Checking Out of the Hotel

Stage 01　穴埋めビジネス・リスニング

音声変化に注意してCDでビジネスのダイアローグを聴きながら、空欄部分を埋めてみよう。

ダイアローグ音声収録

May:　I'm checking ① _____ _____ Room number 432.
Clerk:　⑫ _____ _____ enjoy your stay with us?
May:　Yes. Everything was fine, thank you. Although, you should know that the ③ _____ _____ in the bathroom burned out this morning.
Clerk:　Oh? I'm very sorry for the inconvenience. We'll have that replaced ④ _____ _____. I see that you have a room service charge of $15.
May:　There ⑤ _____ _____ some mistake. I ⑥ _____ order anything from room service, ⑦ _____ _____ did not return until very late. Those charges ⑧ _____ _____ for someone else.
Clerk:　Hmmm. That's strange. ⑨ _____ _____ ⑩ _____ _____ real quick. I'll be ⑪ _____ _____.
Clerk:　I'm very sorry ⑫ _____ _____. Apparently that was for another room. After taking the room service off your bill, the total comes to $135.55. ⑬ _____ _____ like me to leave this ⑭ _____ _____ ⑮ _____ _____?
May:　Yes please.
Clerk:　Here is your receipt. If you'll just sign here you'll be all set. Do you need a shuttle to take you to the airport?
May:　No thanks. We have a ⑯ _____ car.

🔊 ビジネス・リスニング（1回目）

Stage 02 ビジネス・ボキャビル

ビジネスのボキャブラリーをCDで確認しよう。そのあとでもう一度、ビジネス・リスニングにチャレンジ。Stage 01でできなかったところをもう一度聴き取って、穴埋めを完成させよう。

英日 音声収録

1	although	しかしながら
2	light bulb	電球
3	burn out	（電球が）切れる
4	inconvenience	不便
5	replace	交換する
6	right away	即座に；すぐに
7	room service charge	ルームサービス料
8	strange	不思議な
9	real quick	大急ぎで
10	apparently	おそらく
11	bill	請求書；伝票；明細
12	come to ...	合計で…になる
13	leave ... on credit card	…をクレジットカード払いにする
14	receipt	レシート；領収書
15	sign	署名する
16	all set	すべて完了した
17	shuttle	シャトルバス
18	rental car	レンタカー

🔊 ビジネス・リスニング（2回目）

Stage 03　日本語トランスレーション

ビジネス・ダイアローグの日本語を確認してみよう！ その上で、ダイアローグを聴きながら、まだできていない部分の穴埋めに再チャレンジしよう。

May: 432号室をチェックアウトします。
Clerk: ご宿泊はいかがでしたでしょうか？
May: よかったですよ、ありがとう。ただ、バスルームの電球が今朝切れてしまったのでお伝えしておきますね。
Clerk: そうですか。ご不便をおかけして申し訳ありませんでした。すぐに取り替えさせておきます。15ドルのルームサービスの料金がございますね。
May: なにかの間違いだと思います。私は、部屋ではなにも頼んでいませんし、すごく遅くに戻りましたので。ほかの方のものだと思います。
Clerk: うーん、変ですね。急いで調べてみます。すぐに戻りますので。
Clerk: すみませんでした。ほかの部屋のものだったようです。ルームサービスの料金を除きますと、合計で135ドル55セントになります。クレジットカードからのお支払いにしますか？
May: はい、お願いします。
Clerk: こちらが領収書でございます。こちらにサインいただければ大丈夫です。空港までのシャトルバスをご利用ですか？
May: いいえ、けっこうです。レンタカーがありますので。

🔊 ビジネス・リスニング（3回目）

Stage 04　英文トランスクリプション

ビジネス・ダイアローグの原稿を確認してみよう！ 穴埋め部分の正解をチェックして、英文を理解し直そう。そのあとで、もう一度ダイアローグを聴いてみよう。

May: I'm checking ① out of Room number 432.
Clerk: ⑫ Did you enjoy your stay with us?
May: Yes. Everything was fine, thank you. Although, you should know that the ③ light bulb in the bathroom burned out this morning.
Clerk: Oh? I'm very sorry for the inconvenience. We'll have that replaced ④ right away. I see that you have a room service charge of $15.
May: There ⑤ must be some mistake. I ⑥ didn't order anything from room service, ⑦ and I did not return until very late. Those charges ⑧ must be for someone else.
Clerk: Hmmm. That's strange. ⑨ Let me ⑩ check on that real quick. I'll be ⑪ right back.
Clerk: I'm very sorry ⑫ about that. Apparently that was for another room. After taking the room service off your bill, the total comes to $135.55. ⑬ Would you like me to leave this ⑭ on your ⑮ credit card?
May: Yes please.
Clerk: Here is your receipt. If you'll just sign here you'll be all set. Do you need a shuttle to take you to the airport?
May: No thanks. We have a ⑯ rental car.

🔊 ビジネス・リスニング（4回目）

Stage 05 音声変化をチェック

まとめとして、穴埋め部分の音声変化の特徴をスロースピードとナチュラルスピードで確認しよう。下記に示したカタカナ表記で音声変化を確認して、もう一度ビジネス・ダイアローグを聴き直してみよう。発音変化のルールは適宜復習しよう。

2種類の音声を収録
CD 3-27

① **out of** アウト・アヴ ▶ アウダ [ラ] ヴ
☞ 2語が連結。連結部の破裂音 [t] が弾音化。末尾の摩擦音 [v] も脱落することがある

② **Did you** ディッド・ユー ▶ ディジュー; __ジュ
☞ [d] 音と [j] 音が同化。[ジュ] の音だけが残ることもある

③ **light bulb** ライト・バルブ ▶ ライ__バルブ
☞ 破裂音 [t] の脱落

④ **right away** ライト・アウェイ ▶ ライダ [ラ] ウェイ
☞ 2語が連結。連結部の破裂音 [t] が弾音化

⑤ **must be** マスト・ビー ▶ マス__ビ
☞ 破裂音 [t] の脱落

⑥ **didn't** ディドゥント ▶ ディンン__
☞ 破裂音 [d] の声門閉鎖音化。末尾の破裂音 [t] も脱落することがある

⑦ **and I** アンド・アイ ▶ アナイ
☞ and の破裂音 [d] が脱落し、2語が連結

⑧ **must be** マスト・ビー ▶ マス__ビ
☞ 破裂音 [t] の脱落

⑨ **Let me** レット・ミー ▶ レッ__ミ
☞ 破裂音 [t] の脱落

⑩ **check on that** チェック・オン・ザット ▶ チェッコンザット
☞ check に on が連結

⑪ **right back** ライト・バック ▶ ライ__バック
☞ 破裂音 [t] の脱落

⑫ **about that** アバウト・ザット ▶ アバウ__ザッ__
☞ 2カ所で破裂音 [t] の脱落

⑬ **Would you** ウッド・ユー ▶ ウッジュー
☞ [d] 音と [j] 音が同化

⑭ **on your** オン・ユア ▶ オニュア
☞ 2語が連結

⑮ **credit card** クレディット・カード ▶ クレディ [リ] ッ__カード
☞ credit の破裂音 [d] が弾音化、[t] は脱落

⑯ **rental** レンタル ▶ レナル
☞ 破裂音 [t] の脱落

🔊 ビジネス・リスニング (5回目)

Unit 44

問題解決に関する連絡
Confirmation of the Problem Resolution

Stage 01　穴埋めビジネス・リスニング

音声変化に注意して CD でビジネスのダイアローグを聴きながら、空欄部分を埋めてみよう。

ダイアローグ音声収録

May: ① _____ _____ Mike. This is May Chang.

Mike: Hi May, ② _____ _____ have a ③ _____ _____ home?

May: Yes, thank you. Did you ④ _____ _____ email?

Mike: Yes. ⑤ _____ _____ like you found the cause of the problem?

May: Yes, one of our air filters was ⑥ _____, and ⑦ _____ _____ to the dust ⑧ _____ into the system. We have replaced the filter unit. As I noted in my report, we have changed our production manual to include a daily inspection of each filter, as ⑨ _____ _____ ⑩ _____ _____ as we previously did.

Mike: When do you expect to begin production?

May: We already have. ⑪ _____ _____ _____ _____ close, but we should have parts to you by the end of the week. We will overnight them to you ⑫ _____ _____ expense, of course.

Mike: ⑬ _____ _____ need a new purchase ⑭ _____?

May: Yes. Since we will issue a ⑮ _____ for the initial batch of samples ⑯ _____ _____ defective.

🔊 ビジネス・リスニング（1回目）

Stage 02 ビジネス・ボキャビル

ビジネスのボキャブラリーを CD で確認しよう。そのあとでもう一度、ビジネス・リスニングにチャレンジ。Stage 01 でできなかったところをもう一度聴き取って、穴埋めを完成させよう。

英日 音声収録

CD 3-29

1	find the cause of the problem	問題の原因を見つける
2	defective	欠陥のある
3	lead to ...	…につながる
4	replace	交換する
5	filter unit	フィルター部
6	production manual	製造マニュアル
7	include	含む
8	daily	毎日の
9	as opposed to ...	…ではなく
10	previously	以前；前に
11	close	ぎりぎりの
12	by the end of ...	…の終わりまでに
13	overnight	翌日到着便で送る
14	expense	出費
15	purchase order	発注書；注文書
16	issue a credit for ...	…の控除書類を発行する
17	initial batch of ...	初回分の…

🔊 ビジネス・リスニング（2回目）

問題解決に関する連絡

Stage 03　日本語トランスレーション

ビジネス・ダイアローグの日本語を確認してみよう！ その上で、ダイアローグを聴きながら、まだできていない部分の穴埋めに再チャレンジしよう。

May: マイク、おはようございます。メイ・チャンです。
Mike: やあ、メイ、帰りの旅は順調でしたか？
May: ええ、ありがとう。私のメールは着いてますか？
Mike: ええ、問題の原因を特定したようですね。
May: はい。エアフィルターのひとつに欠陥があって、埃がシステムに入り込んでいたのです。フィルターを交換しました。報告書にも書いたとおり、製造マニュアルに変更を加えて、以前のように週1回ではなく毎日個々のフィルターを検査するようにしました。
Mike: いつ製造を始める予定ですか？
May: すでに開始しています。ぎりぎりですけれども、週の終わりまでには御社宛の部品ができあがるはずです。部品は、もちろん弊社の負担で、翌日到着便で発送します。
Mike: 新しい発注書は必要ですか？
May: はい。欠陥のあった最初のサンプル分には支払い控除の書類を発行しますので。

◆))ビジネス・リスニング（3回目）

Stage 04　英文トランスクリプション

ビジネス・ダイアローグの原稿を確認してみよう！ 穴埋め部分の正解をチェックして、英文を理解し直そう。そのあとで、もう一度ダイアローグを聴いてみよう。

May: ① Good morning Mike. This is May Chang.
Mike: Hi May, ② did you have a ③ good trip home?
May: Yes, thank you. Did you ④ get my email?
Mike: Yes. ⑤ It looks like you found the cause of the problem?
May: Yes, one of our air filters was ⑥ defective, and ⑦ that led to the dust ⑧ getting into the system. We have replaced the filter unit. As I noted in my report, we have changed our production manual to include a daily inspection of each filter, as ⑨ opposed to ⑩ checking weekly as we previously did.
Mike: When do you expect to begin production?
May: We already have. ⑪ It's going to be close, but we should have parts to you by the end of the week. We will overnight them to you ⑫ at our expense, of course.
Mike: ⑬ Do you need a new purchase ⑭ order?
May: Yes. Since we will issue a ⑮ credit for the initial batch of samples ⑯ that were defective.

◆))ビジネス・リスニング（4回目）

Stage 05 音声変化をチェック

まとめとして、穴埋め部分の音声変化の特徴をスロースピードとナチュラルスピードで確認しよう。下記に示したカタカナ表記で音声変化を確認して、もう一度ビジネス・ダイアローグを聴き直してみよう。発音変化のルールは適宜復習しよう。

2種類の音声を収録

① **Good morning** — グッド・モーニング ▶ グッ＿モーニン＿
☞ 破裂音 [d] と [g] が脱落

② **did you** — ディッド・ユー ▶ ディッジュー
☞ [d] 音と [j] 音が同化

③ **good trip** — グッド・トゥリップ ▶ グッ＿チュリップ
☞ 破裂音 [d] の脱落。[tr] 音が [tʃr] に変化

④ **get my** — ゲット・マイ ▶ ゲッ＿マイ
☞ 破裂音 [t] の脱落

⑤ **It looks** — イット・ルックス ▶ イッ＿ルックス
☞ 破裂音 [t] の脱落。ダイアローグでは、it の音がすべて脱落している

⑥ **defective** — ディフェクティヴ ▶ ディフェ＿ティヴ
☞ 破裂音 [k] の脱落

⑦ **that led** — ザット・レッド ▶ ザッ＿レッド
☞ 破裂音 [t] の脱落

⑧ **getting** — ゲッティング ▶ ゲッディ[リ]ング
☞ 破裂音 [t] の弾音化

⑨ **opposed to** — オポウズド・トゥー ▶ オポウズ＿トゥー
☞ 破裂音 [d] の脱落

⑩ **checking weekly** — チェッキング・ウィークリー ▶ チェッキン＿ウィークリー
☞ 破裂音 [g] の脱落

⑪ **It's going to be** — イッツ・ゴウイング・トゥー・ビー ▶ イスゴナビ；イッツゴナビ
☞ going to be は [ゴナビ] と発音。it's からは破裂音 [t] が脱落することもある

⑫ **at our** — アット・アウァ ▶ アッダ[ラ]ウァ
☞ 2語が連結。連結部の破裂音 [t] が弾音化

⑬ **Do you** — ドゥー・ユー ▶ ドゥユ；ジュ
☞ do の弱化。さらに [d] と [j] が同化することもある

⑭ **order** — オーダー ▶ オーダ[ラ]ー
☞ 破裂音 [d] の弾音化

⑮ **credit** — クレディット ▶ クレディ[リ]ット
☞ 破裂音 [d] の弾音化

⑯ **that were** — ザット・ワー ▶ ザッ＿ワー
☞ 破裂音 [t] の脱落

🔊 ビジネス・リスニング（5 回目）

Unit 45

代替品の検査合格の連絡
Replacement Parts Pass Inspection

Stage 01　穴埋めビジネス・リスニング

音声変化に注意してCDでビジネスのダイアローグを聴きながら、空欄部分を埋めてみよう。

ダイアローグ音声収録　CD 3-31

Mike: May, I am ① _____ _____ ② _____ _____ know that the ③ _____ _____ you sent passed inspection. We have ④ _____ the rebuild of the prototypes and there were zero rejects.

May: That's ⑤ _____ _____ hear. Once again, we are really sorry for the inconvenience we caused. The expo is only two weeks away. Have you ⑥ _____ ⑦ _____ _____ _____ preparations?

Mike: We are still tweaking the car mock-up and the booth itself, but ⑧ _____ _____ _____ printed materials and display items are ⑨ _____ _____ go. Are you and Mr. Chen going to attend?

May: I am looking ⑩ _____ _____ it, but unfortunately Mr. Chen has a schedule conflict and won't be able to be there. The expo will ⑪ _____ _____ a chance to meet with some of our other customers ⑫ _____ _____ have not seen ⑬ _____ _____ very long time or never ⑭ _____ _____. It's always ⑮ _____ _____ have a chance to see where and how our tiny ⑯ _____ products are being used.

Mike: Okay then, I'll see you in Detroit!

May: Thanks Mike. Have a great day.

🔊 ビジネス・リスニング（1回目）

Stage 02　ビジネス・ボキャビル

ビジネスのボキャブラリーをCDで確認しよう。そのあとでもう一度、ビジネス・リスニングにチャレンジ。Stage 01 でできなかったところをもう一度聴き取って、穴埋めを完成させよう。

英日 音声収録　　CD 3-32

1	pass inspection	検査に合格する
2	complete	完了する
3	rebuild	再構築
4	reject	不合格；失格
5	cause	生じさせる
6	preparation	準備
7	tweak	微調整する；手直しする
8	car mock-up	自動車の模型
9	printed material	印刷物
10	display item	ディスプレー品
11	attend	出席する
12	unfortunately	残念ながら
13	schedule conflict	スケジュールの重なり
14	chance to ...	…する機会
15	customer	顧客
16	in a very long time	長い間
17	where and how	どこでどのように
18	tiny	小さな
19	product	製品
20	be used	使用される

🔊 ビジネス・リスニング（2回目）

代替品の検査合格の連絡

Stage 03　日本語トランスレーション

ビジネス・ダイアローグの日本語を確認してみよう！ その上で、ダイアローグを聴きながら、まだできていない部分の穴埋めに再チャレンジしよう。

Mike: メイ、送ってくれた代替部品が検査に合格したので連絡しました。プロトタイプの再組み立てを終了して、不合格はゼロでした。
May: それはよかったです。ご迷惑をおかけしたことをもう一度お詫びいたします。エキスポはほんの2週間先ですね。準備はすべてできましたか？
Mike: まだ自動車の模型とブース自体を微調整していますが、印刷物と展示はすべて準備万端です。あなたとチェンさんは出席のご予定ですか？
May: 私は出席を楽しみにしていますが、あいにくチェンさんはスケジュールが重なっていて行けません。エキスポでは、長年お会いしていないほかの顧客やはじめての顧客と会うチャンスもあります。それに、どこでどのように弊社の小さな製品が使われているのかを見るのは、いつだっていいものですからね。
Mike: では、デトロイトで会いましょう！
May: ありがとう、マイク。今日もがんばって。

🔊 ビジネス・リスニング（3回目）

Stage 04　英文トランスクリプション

ビジネス・ダイアローグの原稿を確認してみよう！ 穴埋め部分の正解をチェックして、英文を理解し直そう。そのあとで、もう一度ダイアローグを聴いてみよう。

Mike: May, I am ① calling to ② let you know that the ③ replacement parts you sent passed inspection. We have ④ completed the rebuild of the prototypes and there were zero rejects.
May: That's ⑤ great to hear. Once again, we are really sorry for the inconvenience we caused. The expo is only two weeks away. Have you ⑥ completed ⑦ all of your preparations?
Mike: We are still tweaking the car mock-up and the booth itself, but ⑧ all of the printed materials and display items are ⑨ good to go. Are you and Mr. Chen going to attend?
May: I am looking ⑩ forward to it, but unfortunately Mr. Chen has a schedule conflict and won't be able to be there. The expo will ⑪ give me a chance to meet with some of our other customers ⑫ that I have not seen ⑬ in a very long time or never ⑭ met before. It's always ⑮ good to have a chance to see where and how our tiny ⑯ little products are being used.
Mike: Okay then, I'll see you in Detroit!
May: Thanks Mike. Have a great day.

🔊 ビジネス・リスニング（4回目）

Stage 05 　音声変化をチェック

まとめとして、穴埋め部分の音声変化の特徴をスロースピードとナチュラルスピードで確認しよう。下記に示したカタカナ表記で音声変化を確認して、もう一度ビジネス・ダイアローグを聴き直してみよう。発音変化のルールは適宜復習しよう。

2種類の音声を収録　CD 3-33

① **calling to**　コーリング・トゥー　▶ コーリン＿トゥー
　☞ 破裂音 [g] の脱落

② **let you**　レット・ユー　▶ レッチュー
　☞ [t] 音と [j] 音が同化

③ **replacement parts**　リプレイスメント・パーツ　▶ リプレイスメン＿パーツ
　☞ 破裂音 [t] の脱落

④ **completed**　カンプリーティッド　▶ カンプリーディ[リ]ッド
　☞ 破裂音 [t] の弾音化

⑤ **great to**　グレイト・トゥー　▶ グレイ＿トゥー
　☞ 破裂音 [t] の脱落

⑥ **completed**　カンプリーティッド　▶ カンプリーディ[リ]ッド
　☞ 破裂音 [t] の弾音化

⑦ **all of your**　オール・アヴ・ユア　▶ オーラヴァ；オーラ＿ャ
　☞ 3語が連結。of の摩擦音 [v] が脱落することもある

⑧ **all of the**　オール・アヴ・ザ　▶ オーラ＿ザ
　☞ 3語が連結。of の摩擦音 [v] が脱落

⑨ **good to**　グッド・トゥー　▶ グッ＿トゥー
　☞ 破裂音 [d] の脱落

⑩ **forward to**　フォーワード・トゥー　▶ フォーワー＿トゥ
　☞ 破裂音 [d] の脱落

⑪ **give me**　ギヴ・ミー　▶ ギ＿ミ
　☞ 摩擦音 [v] の脱落

⑫ **that I**　ザット・アイ　▶ ザッダ[ラ]イ
　☞ 2語の連結。連結部で破裂音 [t] が弾音化

⑬ **in a**　イン・ア　▶ イナ
　☞ 2語が連結

⑭ **met before**　メット・ビフォー　▶ メッ＿ビフォー
　☞ 破裂音 [t] の脱落

⑮ **good to**　グッド・トゥー　▶ グッ＿トゥー
　☞ 破裂音 [d] の脱落

⑯ **little**　リトゥル　▶ リドゥ[ル]ル
　☞ 破裂音 [t] の弾音化

🔊 ビジネス・リスニング（5回目）

代替品の検査合格の連絡

Unit 46

エキスポにて
At the Expo Booth

Stage 01 穴埋めビジネス・リスニング

音声変化に注意してCDでビジネスのダイアローグを聴きながら、空欄部分を埋めてみよう。

ダイアローグ音声収録

Visitor: ① _____ _____. This is a very ② _____ display. So your company manufactures air-bags?

Mike: We produce several products ③ _____ _____ passenger safety, primarily focused on air-bag ④ _____ systems. Here step over to our mockup ⑤ _____ _____ _____ show you. ⑥ _____ _____ _____ ⑦ _____ things about air-bag restraint systems is of course, deployment. Our new system on display here uses ⑧ _____ edge technology to ⑨ _____ communicate to the on-board ⑩ _____ what seats are occupied by passengers, and also employs eighteen different sensors ⑪ _____ _____ what air bags ⑫ _____ _____ deployed based on the force or direction of ⑬ _____ _____ impact.

Visitor: Wow. Air-bags are so common I never thought ⑭ _____ _____ how they ⑮ _____ work.

Mike: Well, here at AAA Safety Systems we do that for you!

Visitor: Which car manufacturer currently uses this new system?

Mike: ⑯ _____ _____ _____ available on several 2015 models of American Auto brand vehicles. We are hoping our system becomes a standard on many ⑰ _____ _____ and models in the years to come. That's why we are here.

Visitor: ⑱ _____ _____ have any brochures?

Mike: Here you go.

🔊 ビジネス・リスニング（1回目）

Stage 02 ビジネス・ボキャビル

ビジネスのボキャブラリーを CD で確認しよう。そのあとでもう一度、ビジネス・リスニングにチャレンジ。Stage 01 でできなかったところをもう一度聴き取って、穴埋めを完成させよう。

英日 音声収録

1. manufacture — 製造する
2. produce — 製造する；生み出す
3. relating to ... — …に関連する
4. passenger safety — 乗客の安全
5. focus on ... — …に焦点を絞る
6. air-bag restraint system — エアバッグシートのシステム
7. deployment — （エアバッグの）展開
8. cutting edge — 最新の
9. better communicate — より効率的に伝達する
10. on-board — 搭載された；内蔵された
11. occupy — 座席を占める；使用する
12. passenger — 乗客
13. employ — 利用する
14. determine — 決定する
15. based on ... — …に基づいて
16. force — 力
17. direction — 方向
18. accident impact — 事故の衝撃
19. actually — 実際に
20. vehicle — 乗り物；自動車
21. standard — 標準
22. brochures — パンフレット

◁)) ビジネス・リスニング（2回目）

Stage 03　日本語トランスレーション

ビジネス・ダイアローグの日本語を確認してみよう！　その上で、ダイアローグを聴きながら、まだできていない部分の穴埋めに再チャレンジしよう。

Visitor: こんにちは、非常に興味深い展示ですね。御社はエアバッグを製造していらっしゃるのですか？
Mike: 乗客の安全に関するいくつかの製品を製造していますが、エアバッグシートのシステムがおもな製品です。どうぞ模型にお乗りください。ご説明しますので。エアバッグシートのシステムで重要な点のひとつは、もちろんその開き方です。ここに展示されている新しいシステムは、どの座席に乗員がいるのかを搭載されているコンピューターに効率よく伝達するために、最新のテクノロジーを利用しています。また、18のセンサーを利用して、事故の衝撃の力や方向をもとに、どのエアバッグが展開されるべきかを決定します。
Visitor: へえ！ エアバッグはすごく一般的なのに、実際どうやって動いているのかをあまり考えたことがありませんでしたよ。
Mike: ええ、私ども AAA セーフティー・システムズでは、あなたのためにそれを行っているんですよ！
Visitor: どの自動車メーカーが、いま現在このシステムを使っているのですか？
Mike: アメリカン・オート・ブランドの自動車の 2015 年モデルのいくつかで使われます。今後、多くのメーカーやモデルで弊社のシステムがスタンダードになることを願っています。そのために出展している次第です。
Visitor: パンフレットはありますか？
Mike: どうぞ、こちらです。

🔊 ビジネス・リスニング（3回目）

Stage 04　英文トランスクリプション

ビジネス・ダイアローグの原稿を確認してみよう！　穴埋め部分の正解をチェックして、英文を理解し直そう。そのあとで、もう一度ダイアローグを聴いてみよう。

Visitor: ① Good afternoon. This is a very ② interesting display. So your company manufactures air-bags?
Mike: We produce several products ③ relating to passenger safety, primarily focused on air-bag ④ restraint systems. Here step over to our mockup ⑤ and let me show you. ⑥ One of the ⑦ important things about air-bag restraint systems is of course, deployment. Our new system on display here uses ⑧ cutting edge technology to ⑨ better communicate to the on-board ⑩ computer what seats are occupied by passengers, and also employs eighteen different sensors ⑪ that determine what air bags ⑫ should be deployed based on the force or direction of ⑬ an accident impact.
Visitor: Wow. Air-bags are so common I never thought ⑭ much about how they ⑮ actually work.
Mike: Well, here at AAA Safety Systems we do that for you!
Visitor: Which car manufacturer currently uses this new system?
Mike: ⑯ It will be available on several 2015 models of American Auto brand vehicles. We are hoping our system becomes a standard on many ⑰ different makers and models in the years to come. That's why we are here.
Visitor: ⑱ Do you have any brochures?
Mike: Here you go.

🔊 ビジネス・リスニング（4回目）

Stage 05　音声変化をチェック

まとめとして、穴埋め部分の音声変化の特徴をスロースピードとナチュラルスピードで確認しよう。下記に示したカタカナ表記で音声変化を確認して、もう一度ビジネス・ダイアローグを聴き直してみよう。発音変化のルールは適宜復習しよう。

2種類の音声を収録

CD 3-36

① **Good afternoon**　　グッド・アフタヌーン　　▶ グッダ [ラ] フタヌーン
☞ 2語の連結。連結部で破裂音 [d] が弾音化

② **interesting**　　インタラスティング　　▶ インチャラスティング
☞ [tər] の音が [tʃər] に変化

③ **relating to**　　リレイティング・トゥー　　▶ リレイディ [リ] ン_トゥー
☞ relating で、破裂音 [t] の弾音化と破裂音 [g] の脱落

④ **restraint**　　リストゥレイント　　▶ リスチュレイント
☞ [str] の音が [stʃr] に変化

⑤ **and let me**　　アンド・レット・ミー　　▶ アン_レッ_ミ
☞ and と let の末尾の破裂音 [d] と [t] がそれぞれ脱落

⑥ **One of the**　　ワン・アヴ・ズィ　　▶ ワナ_ズィ
☞ one と of が連結。of の摩擦音 [v] が脱落

⑦ **important**　　イムポータント　　▶ イムポーダ [ラ] ント
☞ 破裂音 [t] の弾音化

⑧ **cutting**　　カッティング　　▶ カッディ [リ] ング
☞ 破裂音 [t] の弾音化

⑨ **better**　　ベター　　▶ ベダ [ラ] ー
☞ 破裂音 [t] の弾音化

⑩ **computer**　　カンピューター　　▶ カンピューダ [ラ] ー
☞ 破裂音 [t] の弾音化

⑪ **that determine**　　ザット・ディターミン　　▶ ザッ_ディターミン
☞ 破裂音 [t] の脱落

⑫ **should be**　　シュッド・ビー　　▶ シュッ_ビ
☞ 破裂音 [d] の脱落

⑬ **an accident**　　アン・アクシデント　　▶ アナクシデント
☞ 2語の連結

⑭ **much about**　　マッチ・アバウト　　▶ マッチャバウ_
☞ 2語が連結。末尾の破裂音 [t] が脱落

⑮ **actually**　　アクチュアリー　　▶ アクシュアリー
☞ [ktʃu] から [t] 音の脱落

⑯ **It will be**　　イット・ウィル・ビー　　▶ イッ_ウィルビ；イドゥルビ
☞ 短縮形 it'll [イットル] の破裂音 [t] が弾音化し [イドゥル] と発音。it will から [t] 音だけが脱落することもある

⑰ **different makers**　　ディファラント・メイカーズ　　▶ ディファラン_メイカーズ
☞ 破裂音 [t] の脱落

⑱ **Do you**　　ドー・ユー　　▶ ドゥユ；ジュ
☞ do の弱化。さらに [d] と [j] が同化することもある

🔊 ビジネス・リスニング（5回目）

Unit 47

エキスポでの成果
Success Report on the Expo

Stage 01 穴埋めビジネス・リスニング

音声変化に注意してCDでビジネスのモノローグを聴きながら、空欄部分を埋めてみよう。

モノローグ音声収録 CD 3-37

Tom: Well, everyone, I want first and foremost to thank you and congratulate you all for your hard work these last three days ① _____ _____ expo and all the many months of preparation. Preliminary numbers show ② _____ _____ event had record attendance, by both regular visitors and ③ _____ related people. The ④ _____ ⑤ _____ _____ booth surpassed all of our expectations, and I am ⑥ _____ _____ inform you that ⑦ _____ _____ did we ⑧ _____ _____ _____ for ⑨ _____ _____ design; I have already been contacted by several auto manufacturers who are very ⑩ _____ ⑪ _____ _____ product. ⑫ _____ _____, based on the attention we gained here our current customer American Auto has ⑬ _____ to use our restraint system on all of their new vehicle models. ⑭ _____ _____ _____ ⑮ _____ _____ a fantastic weekend, and ⑯ _____ _____ all ⑰ _____ _____ your tireless ⑱ _____ and cooperation.

🔊 ビジネス・リスニング（1回目）

Stage 02 ビジネス・ボキャビル

ビジネスのボキャブラリーを CD で確認しよう。そのあとでもう一度、ビジネス・リスニングにチャレンジ。Stage 01 でできなかったところをもう一度聴き取って、穴埋めを完成させよう。

英日 音声収録

1	first and foremost	なによりもまず
2	congratulate	祝福する
3	preparation	準備
4	preliminary number	中間報告の数値
5	event	催し物
6	record attendance	記録的な出席数
7	regular visitor	一般客
8	industry related people	業界関連の人々
9	traffic	（人の）通行量
10	surpass	超過する
11	expectation	期待
12	inform	知らせる
13	award	賞
14	booth design	ブースデザイン
15	be contacted	接触を受ける
16	in addition	加えて
17	attention	注目
18	gain	獲得する
19	commit to ...	…すると約束する
20	all in all	総括的に；概して；全体に
21	due to ...	…による
22	tireless	たゆみない；不断の
23	commitment and cooperation	献身と協力

◀)) ビジネス・リスニング（2回目）

Stage 03　日本語トランスレーション

ビジネス・モノローグの日本語を確認してみよう！ その上で、モノローグを聴きながら、まだできていない部分の穴埋めに再チャレンジしよう。

Tom: さて、みなさん。なによりもまず、このエキスポ3日間と何カ月もの準備で懸命に働いてくださったみなさんに感謝と祝福の言葉を申し上げたいと思います。現時点での中間報告の数値で、今回のエキスポは、通常の来客と業界関連の人々で記録的な出席者の数となりました。弊社ブースへの来客もわれわれの期待を完全に上回りました。また、弊社がベストブースデザイン賞を受賞しただけではなく、弊社の製品に興味をもついくつかの自動車メーカーからすでにコンタクトを受けていることをご報告できるのはとてもよろこばしいことです。加えて、この会場で弊社が注目を集めたことで、弊社の現在のクライアントであるアメリカン・オートもすべての自動車の新型モデルで弊社のシートベルトシステムを使うことを約束してくれました。要するに、この週末は最高でした。そして、これはひとえにみなさんの献身と協力によるものです。

🔊 ビジネス・リスニング（3回目）

Stage 04　英文トランスクリプション

ビジネス・モノローグの原稿を確認してみよう！ 穴埋め部分の正解をチェックして、英文を理解し直そう。そのあとで、もう一度モノローグを聴いてみよう。

Tom: Well, everyone, I want first and foremost to thank you and congratulate you all for your hard work these last three days ① at the expo and all the many months of preparation. Preliminary numbers show ② that this event had record attendance, by both regular visitors and ③ industry related people. The ④ traffic ⑤ at our booth surpassed all of our expectations, and I am ⑥ pleased to inform you that ⑦ not only did we ⑧ win an award for ⑨ best booth design; I have already been contacted by several auto manufacturers who are very ⑩ interested ⑪ in our product. ⑫ In addition, based on the attention we gained here our current customer American Auto has ⑬ committed to use our restraint system on all of their new vehicle models. ⑭ All in all ⑮ it was a fantastic weekend, and ⑯ it was all ⑰ due to your tireless ⑱ commitment and cooperation.

🔊 ビジネス・リスニング（4回目）

Stage 05 音声変化をチェック

まとめとして、穴埋め部分の音声変化の特徴をスロースピードとナチュラルスピードで確認しよう。下記に示したカタカナ表記で音声変化を確認して、もう一度ビジネス・モノローグを聴き直してみよう。発音変化のルールは適宜復習しよう。

2種類の音声を収録　　CD 3-39

① **at the**　　アット・ズィ　　▶ アッ＿ズィ
　☞ 破裂音 [t] の脱落

② **that this**　　ザット・ズィス　　▶ ザッ＿ズィス
　☞ 破裂音 [t] の脱落

③ **industry**　　インダストゥリー　　▶ インダスチュリー
　☞ [str] の音が [stʃr] に変化

④ **traffic**　　トゥラフィック　　▶ チュラフィック
　☞ [tr] の音が [tʃr] に変化

⑤ **at our**　　アット・アウァ　　▶ アッダ [ラ] ウァ
　☞ 2語が連結。連結部の破裂音 [t] が弾音化

⑥ **pleased to**　　プリーズド・トゥー　　▶ プリーズ＿トゥー
　☞ 破裂音 [d] の脱落

⑦ **not only**　　ナット・オウンリー　　▶ ナッド [ロ] ウンリー
　☞ 2語が連結。連結部の破裂音 [t] が弾音化

⑧ **win an award**　　ウィン・アン・アウォード　　▶ ウィナナウォード
　☞ 3語が連結

⑨ **best booth**　　ベスト・ブース　　▶ ベス＿ブース
　☞ 破裂音 [t] の脱落

⑩ **interested**　　インタレスティッド　　▶ インチャレスティッド
　☞ [tər] の音が [tʃər] に変化

⑪ **in our**　　イン・アウァ　　▶ イナウァ
　☞ 2語が連結

⑫ **In addition**　　イン・アディシャン　　▶ イナディシャン
　☞ 2語が連結

⑬ **committed**　　カミティッド　　▶ カミディ [リ] ッド
　☞ 破裂音 [t] の弾音化

⑭ **All in all**　　オール・イン・オール　　▶ オーリノール
　☞ 3語が連結

⑮ **it was**　　イット・ワズ　　▶ イッ＿ワズ
　☞ 破裂音 [t] の脱落

⑯ **it was**　　イット・ワズ　　▶ イッ＿ワズ
　☞ 破裂音 [t] の脱落

⑰ **due to**　　デュー・トゥー　　▶ デュードゥ [ル] ー
　☞ 破裂音 [t] の弾音化

⑱ **commitment**　　カミットメント　　▶ カミッ＿メント
　☞ 破裂音 [t] の脱落

🔊 ビジネス・リスニング（5回目）

Unit 48

新しい販路
Expansion of Market/New End Users

Stage 01　穴埋めビジネス・リスニング

音声変化に注意してCDでビジネスのダイアローグを聴きながら、空欄部分を埋めてみよう。

ダイアローグ音声収録

Tom: How ① _____ _____ meetings go yesterday?

Mike: Well, Master ② _____ is ③ _____ on board. They want to send ④ _____ _____ their design engineers here next month to see if they can use our system on their new car models that launch ⑤ _____ _____. ⑥ _____ _____ close time-wise, ⑦ _____ _____ _____ they can't they are almost sure to buy from us ⑧ _____ the year after next. That's a sales value of one-point-six million a year easy.

Tom: How about Liberty ⑨ _____? They were the ⑩ _____ _____ ⑪ _____ _____ during the expo.

Mike: They are still a ⑫ _____ hesitant due to cost. I ⑬ _____ _____ it's ⑭ _____ _____ ⑮ _____ _____ sure to pay off in the long run, especially since they have been ⑯ _____ lately in safety ratings. I'm going to meet with them again ⑰ _____ _____ few weeks to see if I can get them to come around.

Tom: Where are we as far as production capacity goes? Do we need to try and speed up our schedule for completion of the plant expansion?

Mike: Production ⑱ _____ is looking into that now. I think we should be OK.

🔊 ビジネス・リスニング（1回目）

Stage 02 ビジネス・ボキャビル

ビジネスのボキャブラリーを CD で確認しよう。そのあとでもう一度、ビジネス・リスニングにチャレンジ。Stage 01 でできなかったところをもう一度聴き取って、穴埋めを完成させよう。

英日 音声収録

CD 3-41

1. definitely — 明確に；断然
2. on board — 乗り気の
3. design engineer — 設計技師
4. new car model — 新型モデル車
5. launch — 売り出される
6. close time-wise — 時間的にぎりぎりの
7. almost — ほぼ
8. sure to ... — 確実に…する
9. sales value — 売上価値
10. easy — 楽に；容易に
11. during ... — …の期間に
12. hesitant — 躊躇して
13. due to ... — …によって；…が原因で
14. investment — 投資
15. pay off — うまくいく；引き合う
16. in the long run — 結局は；最終的には
17. especially — 特に
18. struggle — もがく
19. safety rating — 安全面の評価
20. come around — 意見を変える
21. as far as ... — …に関しては
22. capacity — （生産）能力
23. expansion — 拡張；拡大

🔊 ビジネス・リスニング（2回目）

Stage 03　日本語トランスレーション

ビジネス・ダイアローグの日本語を確認してみよう！　その上で、ダイアローグを聴きながら、まだできていない部分の穴埋めに再チャレンジしよう。

Tom: 昨日の打ち合わせはどうだったの？
Mike: えー、マスター・モーターズは、完全に乗り気です。来年スタートする新型モデルにうちのシステムを使えるかチェックするために、来月設計技師を数名派遣したいそうです。時間的にはほんとうにぎりぎりですが、もし不可能でも、うちからの購入を再来年からスタートするのはほぼ確実です。年額で160万ドルを容易に超える売上に相当しますよ。
Tom: リバティー自動車はどうかな？　エキスポの期間中、最初に私に電話してきた会社だけど。
Mike: コスト面でまだ少し躊躇していますね。長期的に見れば元が取れる投資だと説得しています。特にあそこは最近安全面で評価が悪化していますので。2、3週間以内にもう一度会いにいって、意見を変えられるかどうかチェックしてきますよ。
Tom: うちの生産能力はどうなっているかな？　工場の拡張工事完了のスケジュールをスピードアップさせる必要はあるのかな？
Mike: 製造管理のほうでいま検討していますが、問題はないと思います。

🔊 ビジネス・リスニング（3回目）

Stage 04　英文トランスクリプション

ビジネス・ダイアローグの原稿を確認してみよう！　穴埋め部分の正解をチェックして、英文を理解し直そう。そのあとで、もう一度ダイアローグを聴いてみよう。

Tom: How ① did your meetings go yesterday?
Mike: Well, Master ② Motors is ③ definitely on board. They want to send ④ some of their design engineers here next month to see if they can use our system on their new car models that launch ⑤ next year. ⑥ It's really close time-wise, ⑦ but even if they can't they are almost sure to buy from us ⑧ starting the year after next. That's a sales value of one-point-six million a year easy.
Tom: How about Liberty ⑨ Automotive? They were the ⑩ first to ⑪ call me during the expo.
Mike: They are still a ⑫ little hesitant due to cost. I ⑬ told them it's ⑭ an investment ⑮ that is sure to pay off in the long run, especially since they have been ⑯ struggling lately in safety ratings. I'm going to meet with them again ⑰ in a few weeks to see if I can get them to come around.
Tom: Where are we as far as production capacity goes? Do we need to try and speed up our schedule for completion of the plant expansion?
Mike: Production ⑱ control is looking into that now. I think we should be OK.

🔊 ビジネス・リスニング（4回目）

Stage 05 音声変化をチェック

まとめとして、穴埋め部分の音声変化の特徴をスロースピードとナチュラルスピードで確認しよう。下記に示したカタカナ表記で音声変化を確認して、もう一度ビジネス・ダイアローグを聴き直してみよう。発音変化のルールは適宜復習しよう。

2種類の音声を収録　　CD 3-42

① **did your**　　ディッド・ユア　　▶ ディッジュア
　☞ [d] 音と [j] 音が同化

② **Motors**　　モウターズ　　▶ モウダ [ラ] ーズ
　☞ 破裂音 [t] の弾音化

③ **definitely**　　ディファナトリー　　▶ ディファナ＿リー
　☞ 破裂音 [t] の脱落

④ **some of**　　サム・アヴ　　▶ サマヴ
　☞ 2 語が連結。摩擦音 [v] が脱落することもある

⑤ **next year**　　ネクスト・イヤー　　▶ ネクスチャー
　☞ [t] 音と [j] 音が同化

⑥ **It's really**　　イッツ・リーリー　　▶ ＿スリーリー；＿ッツリーリー
　☞ it's の [ɪt] あるいは [ɪ] 音が脱落

⑦ **but even if**　　バット・イーヴン・イフ　　▶ バッディ [リ] ーヴニフ
　☞ 3 語が連結。but と even の連結部の破裂音 [t] の弾音化

⑧ **starting**　　スターティング　　▶ スターディ [リ] ング
　☞ 破裂音 [t] の弾音化

⑨ **Automotive**　　オートモウティヴ　　▶ オード [ロ] モウディ [リ] ヴ
　☞ 2 カ所で破裂音 [t] が弾音化

⑩ **first to**　　フゥースト・トゥー　　▶ フゥース＿トゥー
　☞ 破裂音 [t] の脱落

⑪ **call me**　　コール・ミー　　▶ コー＿ミー
　☞ [l] 音の脱落

⑫ **little**　　リトゥル　　▶ リドゥ [ル] ル
　☞ 破裂音 [t] の弾音化

⑬ **told them**　　トウルド・ゼム　　▶ トウルデム
　☞ told に弱化した them [ェム] が連結

⑭ **an investment**　　アン・インヴェストメント　　▶ アニンヴェストメント
　☞ 2 語の連結

⑮ **that is**　　ザット・イズ　　▶ ザッディ [リ] ズ
　☞ 2 語が連結。連結部で破裂音 [t] が弾音化

⑯ **struggling**　　ストゥラッグリング　　▶ スチュラッグリング
　☞ [str] の音が [stʃr] に変化

⑰ **in a**　　イン・ア　　▶ イナ
　☞ 2 語が連結

⑱ **control**　　カントゥロール　　▶ カンチュロール
　☞ [ntr] の音が [ntʃr] に変化

🔊 ビジネス・リスニング（5 回目）

Unit 49

パーティーでの祝杯
Celebration Party

Stage 01　穴埋めビジネス・リスニング

音声変化に注意してCDでビジネスのダイアローグを聴きながら、空欄部分を埋めてみよう。

ダイアローグ音声収録　CD 3-43

Tom: Wow, ① _____ _____ a great meal!

Mike: The steak here is absolutely incredible.

Tom: Yeah, the company really splurged on this ② _____. I guess everyone deserves a ③ _____ pat on the back for all the work we've been doing.

Mike: No ④ _____ _____ that. ⑤ _____ _____ see who they brought in as after-dinner ⑥ _____ tonight?

Tom: The famous magician from Vegas, right? I love his show.

Mike: I have never ⑦ _____ _____, ⑧ _____ _____ hear he's really good.

Tom: By the way, I propose a toast. Here's to a job well done. We had a ⑨ _____ _____ hurdles to ⑩ _____ _____, ⑪ _____ _____ ⑫ _____ _____ _____.

Mike: I'll drink to that! There were times when I wasn't sure everything would come together in time, ⑬ _____ for the expo.

Tom: I've ⑭ _____ _____ admit, when the prototypes ⑮ _____ failing I really thought we ⑯ _____ _____ in big ⑰ _____ ... ⑱ _____ _____ must say China Semicon really came through in the end.

Mike: That reminds me, I ⑲ _____ _____ give May a call and say thanks. In fact, I'm going to do it now before the magic show starts.

🔊 ビジネス・リスニング（1回目）

Stage 02 ビジネス・ボキャビル

ビジネスのボキャブラリーを CD で確認しよう。そのあとでもう一度、ビジネス・リスニングにチャレンジ。Stage 01 でできなかったところをもう一度聴き取って、穴埋めを完成させよう。

英日 音声収録

CD 3-44

#	英語	日本語
1	meal	食事
2	absolutely	絶対に
3	incredible	（信じられないほど）すばらしい
4	splurge on ...	…に散財する
5	deserve	当然値する
6	pat on the back	ねぎらい
7	no doubt	間違いない；疑いない
8	entertainment	余興；エンタメ
9	by the way	ところで
10	propose a toast	乾杯する
11	Here's to ...	…に乾杯
12	hurdles to get over	乗り越えるべき障害
13	There were times when ...	…なときもあった
14	come together	うまくまとまる
15	in time	時間内に；間に合って
16	especially	特に
17	admit	認める
18	come through ...	…を乗り切る；切り抜ける
19	in the end	結局；最終的に
20	remind	思い出させる

🔊 ビジネス・リスニング（2回目）

パーティーでの祝杯

Stage 03　日本語トランスレーション

ビジネス・ダイアローグの日本語を確認してみよう！　その上で、ダイアローグを聴きながら、まだできていない部分の穴埋めに再チャレンジしよう。

Tom: すごいごちそうだったね！
Mike: ここのステーキはほんとうに信じられませんよね。
Tom: うん、会社はこのパーティーにだいぶお金を使ったね。まあ、やってきた仕事に関しては、全員がちょっとはねぎらってもらっても全然おかしくないよね。
Mike: そのとおりですよ。ディナーのあとのエンターテインメントに、会社が今夜だれを呼んでいるか知ってます？
Tom: ベガスの有名な手品師だよね？　彼のショーは大好きさ。
Mike: 見たことないですが、ほんとうにすごいって聞いてます。
Tom: まあ、乾杯しようよ。大成功した仕事に。乗り越えるハードルは多かったけど、われわれはうまくやったよ。
Mike: 乾杯！　特にエキスポに関しては、すべてが時間内にまとまるのか自信がもてないときもありました。
Tom: 私も、プロトタイプが不合格になったときは、ほんとうにまずいことになるかもと思ったよ。しかし、チャイナ・セミコンは最終的にはとてもうまく切り抜けてくれた。
Mike: それで思い出しましたよ。メイに電話してお礼を言わないと。そうだ、マジックショーが始まる前に電話しておこうかな。

🔊 ビジネス・リスニング（3回目）

Stage 04　英文トランスクリプション

ビジネス・ダイアローグの原稿を確認してみよう！　穴埋め部分の正解をチェックして、英文を理解し直そう。そのあとで、もう一度ダイアローグを聴いてみよう。

Tom: Wow, ① that was a great meal!
Mike: The steak here is absolutely incredible.
Tom: Yeah, the company really splurged on this ② party. I guess everyone deserves a ③ little pat on the back for all the work we've been doing.
Mike: No ④ doubt about that. ⑤ Did you see who they brought in as after-dinner ⑥ entertainment tonight?
Tom: The famous magician from Vegas, right? I love his show.
Mike I have never ⑦ seen it, ⑧ but I hear he's really good.
Tom: By the way, I propose a toast. Here's to a job well done. We had a ⑨ lot of hurdles to ⑩ get over, ⑪ but we ⑫ did it.
Mike: I'll drink to that! There were times when I wasn't sure everything would come together in time, ⑬ especially for the expo.
Tom: I've ⑭ got to admit, when the prototypes ⑮ started failing I really thought we ⑯ might be in big ⑰ trouble ... ⑱ but I must say China Semicon really came through in the end.
Mike: That reminds me, I ⑲ need to give May a call and say thanks. In fact, I'm going to do it now before the magic show starts.

🔊 ビジネス・リスニング（4回目）

Unit 49

Stage 05 音声変化をチェック

まとめとして、穴埋め部分の音声変化の特徴をスロースピードとナチュラルスピードで確認しよう。下記に示したカタカナ表記で音声変化を確認して、もう一度ビジネス・ダイアローグを聴き直してみよう。発音変化のルールは適宜復習しよう。

2種類の音声を収録　　CD 3-45

① **that was** 　　ザット・ワズ　　▶ ザッ＿ワズ
☞ 破裂音 [t] の脱落

② **party** 　　パーティー　　▶ パーディ [リ] ー
☞ 破裂音 [t] の弾音化

③ **little** 　　リトゥル　　▶ リドゥ [ル] ル
☞ 破裂音 [t] の弾音化

④ **doubt about** 　　ダウト・アバウト　　▶ ダウダ [ラ] バウ＿
☞ 2語の連結。連結部で破裂音 [t] が弾音化。末尾の [t] も脱落することがある

⑤ **Did you** 　　ディッド・ユー　　▶ ッジュー；ディッジュー
☞ [d] 音と [j] 音が同化。did の頭の [d] 音も脱落する場合がある

⑥ **entertainment** 　　エンタテインメント　　▶ エナテインメン＿
☞ 2カ所で破裂音 [t] が脱落

⑦ **seen it** 　　シーン・イット　　▶ シーニッ＿
☞ 2語が連結。末尾の破裂音 [t] も脱落することがある

⑧ **but I** 　　バット・アイ　　▶ バッダ [ラ] イ
☞ 2語が連結。連結部で破裂音 [t] の弾音化

⑨ **lot of** 　　ラット・アヴ　　▶ ラッダ [ラ] ヴ
☞ 2語が連結。連結部で破裂音 [t] の弾音化

⑩ **get over** 　　ゲット・オウヴァー　　▶ ゲッド [ロ] ウヴァー
☞ 2語が連結。連結部で破裂音 [t] の弾音化

⑪ **but we** 　　バット・ウィ　　▶ バッ＿ウィ
☞ 破裂音 [t] の脱落

⑫ **did it** 　　ディッド・イット　　▶ ディッディ [リ] ッ＿
☞ 2語が連結。連結部で破裂音 [d] の弾音化。末尾の [t] も脱落することがある

⑬ **especially** 　　イスペシャリー　　▶ ＿スペシャリー
☞ 頭の [ɪ] の音が脱落

⑭ **got to** 　　ガット・トゥー　　▶ ガッ＿ドゥ [ル] ー
☞ got の破裂音 [t] の脱落。to の破裂音 [t] の弾音化

⑮ **started** 　　スターティッド　　▶ スターディ [リ] ッド
☞ 破裂音 [t] の弾音化

⑯ **might be** 　　マイト・ビー　　▶ マイ＿ビ
☞ 破裂音 [t] の脱落

⑰ **trouble** 　　トゥラブル　　▶ チュラブル
☞ [tr] の音が [tʃr] に変化

⑱ **but I** 　　バット・アイ　　▶ バッダ [ラ] イ
☞ 2語が連結。連結部で破裂音 [t] の弾音化

⑲ **need to** 　　ニード・トゥー　　▶ ニー＿トゥー
☞ 破裂音 [d] の脱落

🔊 ビジネス・リスニング (5回目)

Unit 50

メイへのお礼
Thank You Call to May

Stage 01 — 穴埋めビジネス・リスニング

音声変化に注意してCDでビジネスのダイアローグを聴きながら、空欄部分を埋めてみよう。

ダイアローグ音声収録

May: China Semicon, May Chang speaking.

Mike: Hey May, it's Mike with AAA Safety.

May: Hi Mike. How are things ① _____ _____.

Mike: Really well. Things are going even ② _____ than we had hoped. I ③ _____ _____ ④ _____ _____ a call and say thanks for all your help.

May: You're welcome, ⑤ _____ _____ caused a fair ⑥ _____ _____ trouble for you all too. I'm just glad we were able to ⑦ _____ _____ _____ in the end.

Mike: Those things happen, ⑧ _____ _____ how you react to problems ⑨ _____ _____ ⑩ _____. From that perspective, you guys really saved us.

May: Well, we appreciate that. As ⑪ _____ _____ sure is the same with you, customer service is the key to success in any business.

Mike: Speaking of which, we were just ⑫ _____ a new project with a new customer. I don't have all of the ⑬ _____ _____, ⑭ _____ _____ the designs are complete I'll be in touch.

May: That's great! But hey, you ⑮ _____ _____ celebrating … I can hear that you're still ⑯ _____ _____ ⑰ _____. We can save the work until the weekend is over!

🔊 ビジネス・リスニング（1回目）

Stage 02 ビジネス・ボキャビル

ビジネスのボキャブラリーを CD で確認しよう。そのあとでもう一度、ビジネス・リスニングにチャレンジ。Stage 01 でできなかったところをもう一度聴き取って、穴埋めを完成させよう。

英日 音声収録　CD 3-47

1	even better	さらによく
2	hope	期待する；望む
3	cause	生じさせる
4	a fair bit of ...	相当な…
5	work out	解決する
6	Those things happen.	よくあることだ
7	react	反応する；対処する
8	from that perspective	その観点から
9	save	救う
10	appreciate	感謝する；ありがたく思う
11	As is the same with you, ...	御社も同様でしょうが…
12	customer service	顧客サービス
13	key to success	成功への鍵
14	speaking of which	そう言えば
15	award	（仕事を）与える
16	details	詳細
17	be in touch	連絡を取る
18	celebrate	祝う
19	save	取り置く
20	over	終わって

🔊 ビジネス・リスニング（2回目）

Stage 03　日本語トランスレーション

ビジネス・ダイアローグの日本語を確認してみよう！　その上で、ダイアローグを聴きながら、まだできていない部分の穴埋めに再チャレンジしよう。

May: チャイナ・セミコンのメイ・チャンでございます。
Mike: やあ、メイ、AAA セーフティーのマイクです。
May: こんにちは、マイク。そちらはうまくいってますか？
Mike: すごくいい感じですよ。期待以上にうまくいってます。あなたの手助けに感謝の言葉を伝えたくて電話したんです。
May: どういたしまして。でも、みなさんにかなりのご迷惑をおかけしたのも確かですし。最終的になんとか解決できてよかったです。
Mike: よくあることですよ。大切なのは、問題にどのように対処するかです。そういう面では、みなさんよく弊社を助けてくれましたよ。
May: そう言っていただくとありがたいです。御社でも同じだと思いますが、どんなビジネスでも顧客サービスこそ成功への鍵だと思っておりますので（当然の対応をさせていただいただけなんです）。
Mike: そう言えば、弊社では、新しい顧客から仕事をもらったところなんです。まだ詳細のすべてはわかりませんが、デザインが完了したら連絡させてください。
May: それはすばらしい！　だけど、ほら、いまはお祝い中でしょう？…まだパーティーをしている音が聞こえていますよ。仕事は週明けまで取っておきましょう！

🔊 ビジネス・リスニング（3回目）

Stage 04　英文トランスクリプション

ビジネス・ダイアローグの原稿を確認してみよう！　穴埋め部分の正解をチェックして、英文を理解し直そう。そのあとで、もう一度ダイアローグを聴いてみよう。

May: China Semicon, May Chang speaking.
Mike: Hey May, it's Mike with AAA Safety.
May: Hi Mike. How are things ① going there.
Mike: Really well. Things are going even ② better than we had hoped. I ③ wanted to ④ give you a call and say thanks for all your help.
May: You're welcome, ⑤ but we caused a fair ⑥ bit of trouble for you all too. I'm just glad we were able to ⑦ work it out in the end.
Mike: Those things happen, ⑧ but it's how you react to problems ⑨ that is ⑩ important. From that perspective, you guys really saved us.
May: Well, we appreciate that. As ⑪ I am sure is the same with you, customer service is the key to success in any business.
Mike: Speaking of which, we were just ⑫ awarded a new project with a new customer. I don't have all of the ⑬ details yet, ⑭ but when the designs are complete I'll be in touch.
May: That's great! But hey, you ⑮ should be celebrating … I can hear that you're still ⑯ at the ⑰ party. We can save the work until the weekend is over!

🔊 ビジネス・リスニング（4回目）

Stage 05　音声変化をチェック

まとめとして、穴埋め部分の音声変化の特徴をスロースピードとナチュラルスピードで確認しよう。下記に示したカタカナ表記で音声変化を確認して、もう一度ビジネス・ダイアローグを聴き直してみよう。発音変化のルールは適宜復習しよう。

2種類の音声を収録　　　　　　　　　　　　　　　　　　　　CD 3-48

① **going there**　　　　　　ゴウイング・ゼァ　　　　▶ ゴウイネァ
☞ going 末尾の破裂音 [g] の脱落。[ゴウイン] の [n] と there の [ð] の音が同化

② **better**　　　　　　　　ベター　　　　　　　　▶ ベダ [ラ] ー
☞ 破裂音 [t] の弾音化

③ **wanted to**　　　　　　ワンティッド・トゥー　　▶ ワニッ＿トゥー
☞ wanted の破裂音 [t] と末尾の破裂音 [d] が脱落

④ **give you**　　　　　　　ギヴ・ユー　　　　　　▶ ギヴュ；ギヴャ
☞ 2語が連結。弱化して [ギヴャ] と発音されることもある

⑤ **but we**　　　　　　　　バット・ウィ　　　　　▶ バッ＿ウィ
☞ 破裂音 [t] の脱落

⑥ **bit of**　　　　　　　　ビット・アヴ　　　　　▶ ビッダ [ラ] ブ
☞ 2語が連結。連結部で破裂音 [t] が弾音化

⑦ **work it out**　　　　　　ワーク・イット・アウト　▶ ワーキッダ [ラ] ウト
☞ 3語が連結。it と out の連結部で破裂音 [t] が弾音化

⑧ **but it's**　　　　　　　バット・イッツ　　　　　▶ バディ [リ] ッツ
☞ 2語が連結。連結部で破裂音 [t] が弾音化

⑨ **that is**　　　　　　　　ザット・イズ　　　　　▶ ザッディ [リ] ズ；ザッツ
☞ 2語が連結。連結部で破裂音 [t] の弾音化。短縮形の that's の発音になることもある

⑩ **important**　　　　　　イムポータント　　　　　▶ イムポーダ [ラ] ント
☞ 破裂音 [t] が弾音化

⑪ **I am**　　　　　　　　　アイ・アム　　　　　　▶ アイム
☞ 短縮形 I'm の発音

⑫ **awarded**　　　　　　　アウォーディッド　　　　▶ アウォーディ [リ] ッド
☞ 破裂音 [d] の弾音化

⑬ **details yet**　　　　　　ディーテイルズ・イェット　▶ ディーテイルジェット
☞ [z] 音と [j] 音が同化

⑭ **but when**　　　　　　　バット・ウェン　　　　　▶ バッ＿ウェン
☞ 破裂音 [t] の脱落

⑮ **should be**　　　　　　シュッド・ビー　　　　　▶ シュッ＿ビ
☞ 破裂音 [d] の脱落

⑯ **at the**　　　　　　　　アット・ザ　　　　　　▶ アッ＿ザ
☞ 破裂音 [t] の脱落

⑰ **party**　　　　　　　　パーティー　　　　　　▶ パーディ [リ] ー
☞ 破裂音 [t] の弾音化

🔊 ビジネス・リスニング（5回目）

メイへのお礼

本で学んだことを通勤通学中に気軽にチェック!

書籍版との併用でさらに効果的に『英語の耳』をマスターしよう!

iPhone版アプリ
『英語の耳』になる!

大好評
「『英語の耳』になる!」シリーズから**アプリ**が新登場

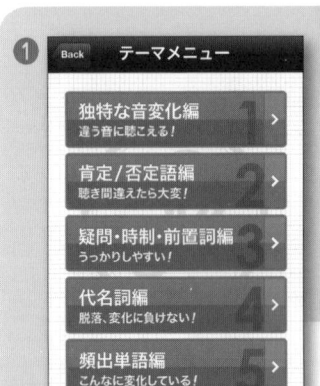

Appストアで **Available on the App Store** [🔍 英語の耳になる ⊗] で検索!

あなたの耳は何イヤー?
▶▶▶ 聴き取り○×クイズ

書籍版にはない5つのテーマで約400問を収録。
あなたの苦手なフレーズを自動で判定、問題をカスタマイズします。
テストは1回たったの1分半程度。
繰り返しクイズをするうちにいつのまにか『英語の耳』に!

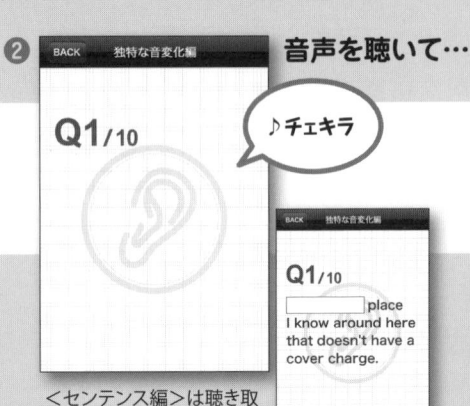

① テーマメニュー
- 独特な音変化編 — 違う音に聴こえる!
- 肯定/否定語編 — 聴き間違えたら大変!
- 疑問・時制・前置詞編 — うっかりしやすい!
- 代名詞編 — 脱落、変化に負けない!
- 頻出単語編 — こんなに変化している!

② **音声を聴いて…** ♪チェキラ

＊フレーズ編＊
フレーズの聴き取りクイズで耳慣らし。「can be＝キャビ」など、2、3語単位の音変化クイズです。

＊センテンス編＊
音変化に耳が慣れたらセンテンスでの聴き取りクイズに挑戦。聴き取りポイントの音声が、表示されるフレーズと合っているかを○×で答えます。

＜センテンス編＞は聴き取りポイントがブランクに。▶

Q1/10
_____ place
I know around here that doesn't have a cover charge.

発売中！

最新情報は：http://www.sanshusha.co.jp/

じっくりトレーニングしたい人は ▶▶▶ 耳慣らしトレーニング

クイズで使われているフレーズを含む豊富な例文を約900収録。
どういう仕組みで音が消えたり変化したりするのかについての詳しい解説付き。
音声は画面を消したロック状態でも再生可能。
連続再生モードもあるので、電車の中などでの聴き流しトレーニングに便利です。

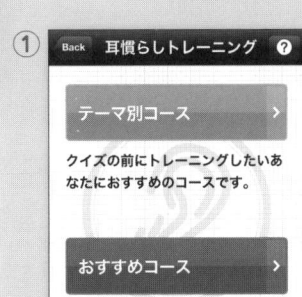

① 耳慣らしトレーニング

テーマ別コース
クイズの前にトレーニングしたいあなたにおすすめのコースです。

おすすめコース
クイズのスコアをもとに、あなたに最適なトレーニングを自動的に集めたコースです。

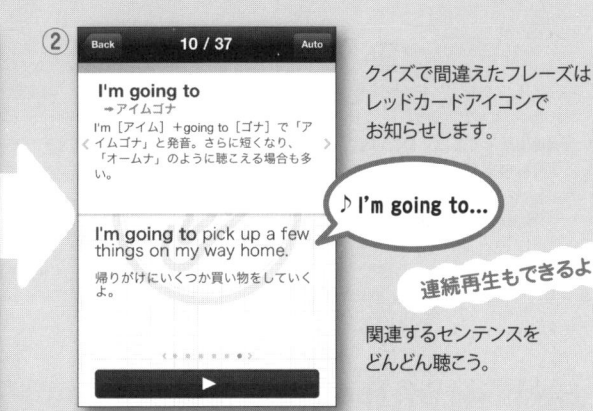

② 10 / 37 Auto

I'm going to
→アイムゴナ
I'm [アイム] +going to [ゴナ] で「アイムゴナ」と発音。さらに短くなり、「オームナ」のように聴こえる場合も多い。

I'm going to pick up a few things on my way home.
帰りがけにいくつか買い物をしていくよ。

クイズで間違えたフレーズはレッドカードアイコンでお知らせします。

♪I'm going to...

連続再生もできるよ

関連するセンテンスをどんどん聴こう。

**表示される
フレーズと
合っているかを
○×でタップ！
制限時間は5秒！**

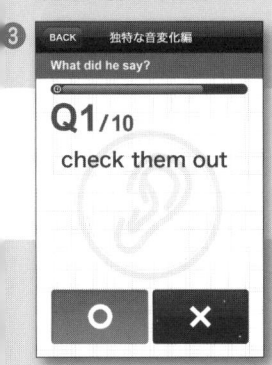

③ 独特な音変化編
What did he say?
Q1/10
check them out
○ ×

**不正解時はレッドカードが
正答を表示します。
これを繰り返すだけ！**

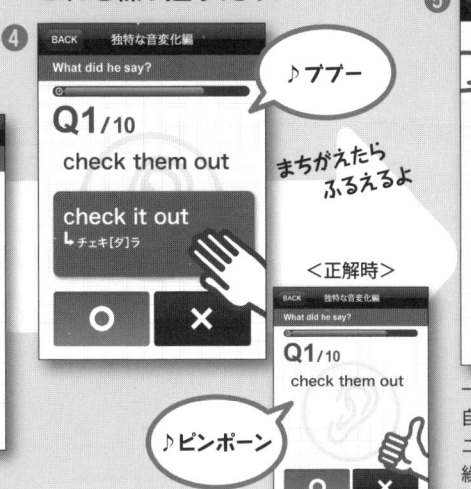

④ 独特な音変化編
What did he say?
Q1/10
check them out
check it out
└チェキ[ダ]ラ
○ ×

♪ブブー
まちがえたら
ふるえるよ

＜正解時＞
独特な音変化編
What did he say?
Q1/10
check them out
○ ×
♪ピンポーン

**最後にあなたの
『英語の耳』を6段階で判定！**

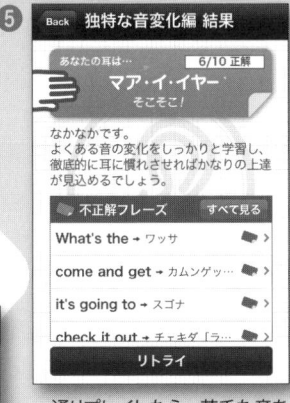

⑤ 独特な音変化編 結果
あなたの耳は… 6/10 正解
マア・イ・イヤー
そこそこ！

なかなかです。
よくある音の変化をしっかりと学習し、徹底的に耳に慣れさせればかなりの上達が見込めるでしょう。

不正解フレーズ すべて見る
What's the → ワッサ
come and get → カムンゲッ…
it's going to → スゴナ
check it out → チェキダ [ラ…

リトライ

一通りプレイしたら、苦手な音を自動解析。あなただけの苦手メニューで繰り返しプレイできます。繰り返せば繰り返すほど『英語の耳』力がアップします！

■ 著者略歴

長尾 和夫（Kazuo Nagao）

福岡県出身。南雲堂出版、アスク講談社、NOVA などで、大学英語教科書や語学系書籍・CD-ROM・Web サイトなどの編集・制作・執筆に携わる。現在、語学書籍の出版プロデュース・執筆・編集・翻訳などを行うアルファ・プラス・カフェ（www.alphapluscafe.com）を主宰。『つぶやき英語』『カンタン英会話パターン 88』（アスク出版）、『絶対「英語の耳」になる！』シリーズ（三修社）、『起きてから寝るまで英会話口慣らし練習帳（完全改訂版）』（アルク）、『英会話 見たまま練習帳』（DHC）、『英語で自分をアピールできますか？』（角川グループパブリッシング）、『ネイティブ英語がこう聞こえたら、この英語だ！』（主婦の友社）ほか、著訳書・編書は 200 点余りに及ぶ。『English Journal』（アルク）、『CNN English Express』（朝日出版社）など、雑誌媒体への寄稿も行っている。

トーマス・マーティン（Thomas Martin）

米国在住、米国オハイオ州出身。南山大学卒業。日本語・日本史専攻。株式会社 NOVA での豊富な英語指導経験を活かし、同社出版局に移籍。雑誌『NOVA Station（ノヴァ・ステーション）』をはじめ、英語・異文化交流関連出版物の編集・執筆・翻訳等に携わる。フリーライター・翻訳家として 98 年に独立。知的財産関係の翻訳や日本最大のビリヤード専門誌『CUE'S』の連載を手がけた経験もある。著書に『新方式対応 TOEIC テスト厳選トータル問題集』『小学生の英語かきとり＆ききとり自習ドリル』（すばる舎）、『つぶやき英語 ビジネス編』（アスク出版）、『覚える!!ミニマム英単語 通勤解速トレーニング』（マクミランランゲージハウス）などがある。

絶対『英語の耳』になる！ ビジネス英語リスニング 難関トレーニング50

2012 年 7 月 10 日 第 1 刷発行

著　者	長尾和夫　トーマス・マーティン
発行者	前田俊秀
発行所	株式会社三修社
	〒 150-0001　東京都渋谷区神宮前 2-2-22
	TEL 03-3405-4511　FAX 03-3405-4522
	振替 00190-9-72758
	http://www.sanshusha.co.jp/
	編集担当　北村英治
印刷・製本	壮光舎印刷株式会社

©2012 A+Café　Printed in Japan
ISBN978-4-384-04510-9 C2082

®〈日本複製権センター委託出版物〉
本書を無断で複写複製（コピー）することは、著作権法上の例外を除き、禁じられています。
本書をコピーされる場合は、事前に日本複製権センター（JRRC）の許諾を受けてください。
JRRC〈http://www.jrrc.or.jp　e-mail : info@jrrc.or.jp　電話 : 03-3401-2382〉